With Bare Hands

With Bare Hands

The true story of Alain Robert,
the real-life Spiderman

BLACKSMITH BOOKS

With Bare Hands:
The true story of Alain Robert, the real-life Spiderman

Paperback: ISBN 978-988-99799-2-8
Ebook: ISBN 978-988-19003-3-3

Published by Blacksmith Books
Unit 26, 19/F, Block B, Wah Lok Industrial Centre,
37-41 Shan Mei Street, Fo Tan, Hong Kong
Tel: (+852) 2877 7899
www.blacksmithbooks.com

Edited and adapted by John Chan

Contents

Foreword 7

Prologue 9

1   A Newly Discovered Mountain Range 21

2   Le Tour de Paris 37

3   The Hatchling. 64

4   European Trilogy. 86

5   Jailhouse Rock 103

6   Fantastico!. 124

7   Liberty Bell. 144

8   Alain and the King 188

9   Spiderman. 214

10 Fears and the Sears 236

11 Asia Rising 259

12 The Sands of Time 287

FOREWORD

The things I do not understand intrigue me. I am looking forward to reading Alain Robert's book because I hope to find answers to the questions he has relentlessly posed me over the last 20 years. I focus on hand surgery and rehabilitation, and I am drawn to Alain's case in particular.

How has he managed to fully recover and even surpass his prior abilities to climb smooth walls after his terrible fall? That fall should have left him permanently disabled!

And disabled he is… on paper. His wrists have limited movement; his elbows do not open fully any more, restricting the reach of his upper limbs; the two bones of his forearm still do not properly meet. He cannot direct his hands as he would like to, nor can he completely unfurl the muscles of his fingers, the nerves of which have been compressed for too long.

How then is he able, with such limbs, to grip onto small protrusions of only a few millimetres and then have the audacity to risk his life in solo climbs? How does he manage to exceed his natural abilities and compensate for his failing joints? Answers are probably to be found less in medical journals than in the following pages.

In the course of our meetings, Alain has provided some illumination. Without divulging anything which may affect his reflections, I have come to understand that it is his particular philosophy which may hold the key. Alain would ask me whether we have several lives. At worst, he says, we have only one, and therefore we must do our utmost to fill it with the people and the things we love. There is no time to spend horizontally on a hospital bed if we have chosen to live vertically.

On reflection I understand how he convinced me to let him attempt walking so soon after his pelvic fracture. The pain? It wasn't a problem for Alain. He accepted it as the price he had to pay and also as a boundary, a natural red line.

Every time we completed a new surgical procedure to repair prior damage he requested my approval to try out his new limbs as soon as possible on the rock face, accepting the consequences of his bravado. Alain would overtake me as I strode breathless on a rough but easy footpath on the rocks of Saou while he was already at ease clutching onto a '7a' overhang just a few days after his umpteenth round of surgery...

These are astonishing results that a surgeon, blinded by his own vanity, could boast about if they weren't the outcome of the victim's determination rather than the success of the orthopaedic setting.

But 'victim' is not a term that applies to Alain Robert, because at no point along the path of his surgical saga has he displayed a victim's behaviour. Never has he looked to shirk responsibilities, to point fingers, to obtain financial compensation or potential benefits from disability status. There was no time for such behaviour. There was no strength to squander in these diversions from physical recovery. To hell with the tribunals, lawyers, experts, certificates, or indeed insurance and disability allowances – even though he was entitled to them!

Alain Robert remains a medical enigma, one of excellent functional outcome in spite of an unimpressive anatomical result. I had given him a poor prognosis and he has proven me wrong, and for that I thank him.

I look forward to learning how he did it.

Dr Gérard Hoël, Surgeon

Prologue

It's June 1994 and the telephone bursts into life at my little home in my native southern France. It's a rather intriguing – and, as it turns out, fateful – phone call. A man from Sector, the famed sporting watches brand and one of the biggest sponsors in adventure sports, is on the line. Apparently the trendy firm wants to make a documentary about climbing entitled *No Limits*.

The guy on the end of the line introduces himself as the film director and tells me that he has seen what I can do on the rocks and would like me to feature in his documentary. In an Italian accent he outlines his vision and says he is keen to show something different from the usual mountaineering stuff we are all used to seeing; he wants to break the mould and take the audience into pastures new.

The initial image he conjures up is the copper sandstone beauty of Utah, rugged landscapes belonging in popular fiction to the realms of the Marlboro cowboys, but in reality of course to those who live on that arid land, the Navajo Indians. The second image he describes are the big city glass mountains, locations which teem with humanity to such an extent that we have utterly reshaped the environment, creating our own termite mounds of glass and steel. The director explains he wants to surprise the audience by drawing a parallel between the famous stony pillars of Utah and the gigantic office blocks of New York or some other city. In this documentary, he says, it will be necessary for me to clamber up these dreamlike sandstone obelisks and also to attack a high rise office block. He asks if I would be interested.

My curiosity is aroused and it seems to be quite a neat idea. It sounds pretty cool. Why not?

The director butters me up. He boldly declares he has all the angles covered and I need not worry about anything at all. We shall have shooting licenses and we will use a nice sturdy rope. Safety, he tells me, is naturally his highest concern. Location managers are devising a plan to obtain the rights to climb city skyscrapers as we speak. His crew is canvassing administrations and private owners to gain legal access to dramatic urban settings. If this falls through, the director will use special effects and models to recreate the city surroundings. The task for us is to come back with mesmerising, provocative and juxtaposing images forming a nice climbing story 'made in America'.

I ask a few questions and he gives encouraging answers, and it all sounds positive, verbally anyway. So I tell him I am in. He makes a final round of assurances and tells me his staff will immediately make travel arrangements for me. As briefly as it began, the call ends.

Fissure escalation – the ascent of igneous, metamorphic or sedimentary rocks – has been my job for more than ten years. It's no problem, I've mastered it. I have tackled some of Europe's toughest climbs and have become known for pushing the envelope further by dispensing with safety equipment and climbing with my bare hands. Climbing in Utah sounds like a nice day at the office for me. But it has to be said that scaling the window panes of a tall building is something else entirely. What kind of idea is that? But never mind, I decide, let's give it a try.

Actually I have never even thought of the possibility of climbing manmade monuments. It has barely ever been done and I now wonder how I am going to do it. One of France's top rock climbers, Jibé Tribout, had scaled a building for an advertisement shot in Houston, so I decide to call him to get his point of view and gain his impressions on the feasibility of the project.

Jibé picks up the phone and listens thoughtfully before relating his experiences of such a climb. According to him, the ascent of a skyscraper is more hypothetical than realistic considering the height and the nature of the surface we have to work with. Besides, he hardly climbed a floor before jumping onto a crash mat like a stuntman. Even though he climbed a very different building, his experience had not left him a very positive impression of building escalations.

I thank him for his input and mull it over for a while. No one really knows anything about such a climb – it is a step into the unknown and will remain so until I attempt it. But within a few days I am flying to Chicago and any misgivings are packed in with my luggage.

On arrival I disembark to the news that we have only ten days to scout locations. I would have liked to have gotten over my jet lag, but to make good use of the day I head downtown to get a more precise idea of what we are looking at.

Once I get to downtown Chicago and walk the streets I am shocked! The profile of the buildings is quite a contrast to the modest heights of French cities. French cities have been around a lot longer and therefore tended to spread outwards over the centuries, rather than rocketing upwards as they have in countries where economies have exploded. Sure, there are tall buildings in France, but we have nothing like this. Here high rise blocks spring from the street, shooting up so far that they give the impression of overhanging the asphalt. They're incredible!

I walk the sidewalks with my chin pointing skywards, almost overwhelmed by the scale of it all. I remember having felt the same shudder, the same sensation of immoderate, gigantic size, the first time I discovered the Verdon Canyon in southern France. The famed gorge is the second largest in the world, and one of the most spectacular on the planet. Looking up at these glass cliffs I feel that same sense of awe. It is a long process, this adjustment, this experience of being tamed by a new universe and redefining your objectivity. The prospect of scaling these walls chills me. Even with ropes it looks immensely difficult or even impossible, and of course there remains the substantial risk. What was I thinking?

Right now I cannot imagine that I seriously intended to get my hands on a license and rope my way up this building armed only with the blessing of a priest. It would make more sense to cycle up Mount Everest. In the shadow of Chicago's cityscape it occurs to me that I have probably agreed to one of the most stupid proposals I have ever been made.

But it is necessary to believe in oneself, to believe in the impossible, and not to give in to appearances. Naturally that's very easy to say. It's easy to laugh off a challenge, to dismiss it as a boyish prank, but when one is confronted directly by the challenge, suddenly there is nowhere to hide. Looking up at these monoliths I really start wondering what I have got myself into.

Then the Italian director really brings me down by giving me details about the hard tarmac below. The security services of these buildings are akin to George Orwell's *Big Brother*, with alert eyes and ears embedded in the concrete. Watching… eavesdropping… spying… They will be on the lookout for troublemakers like me.

The director reminds me that the type of people found in the security industry are by nature physically aggressive, and some of them are drawn to an occupation that gives them the perfect excuse to assault people, especially here in 'kick ass' loving America. I dart a worried glance at him, surprised to hear there could be a problem – I thought he had it all covered?

Cautiously we scout the city, visiting numerous sites each day, some higher than others. But there's no chance for me to set foot on any of them yet, as I am still waiting for official permission from any of the building managers the team has canvassed. A select few of these high rise buildings seem effectively 'climbable', on the premise of being able to use the rope every now and then to grab a little bit respite to regain my energy. It's all looking and sounding very different to what I heard on the phone in France. And now here we are, at the launch pad, and the director drops a bombshell. He suggests it would be preferable if I were to climb a building without ropes! I wonder if he is joking or not. It doesn't look like it.

Answers to our questions don't come, so we fly on to Dallas and at my suggestion then to Houston, the city where Jibé managed to get permission. The same dramatic vertical topography exists here too. Skyscrapers, thousands of shiny glazed windows. But still there is this shitty uncertainty about permits. It appears that no one will entertain such a notion, that is, if they are even taking us seriously. It is hardly surprising really, given that very little is in it for them. Why would they want someone to dangle off their nice shiny building if he is not the window cleaner?

Another day passes and the whole project is still on hold, pushing up costs and mounting the pressure on the director. Then, for sudden technical reasons, the shooting date is rescheduled to mid July. Apparently there is nothing I can do here any more, for now at least. So I head back to France, and an extra month of indecision passes by. In Valence, I try to climb some buildings to find the beginning of an answer, but it is impossible to compare a modest three-storey house with a fifty-eight floor skyscraper. It's rather like climbing a big pebble before facing the vast cliffs of Verdon. But anyway, I need to start somewhere, so I start climbing houses. As I climb a few of my friends' houses I notice that the French stone is cut, worked, sculpted, with any sheer verticality broken by ledges and mouldings. Such surfaces have absolutely nothing in common with 250 smooth metres of a North American glass wall. My bewildered friends watch on from their back gardens as I keep trying. I find a tennis ball but I get no closer to a solution to my dilemma.

A little before mid July, Sector calls me with glum news. It will be impossible to obtain licenses… but the company has already spent a lot of money on the production and locations… and it's too late to stop the project! The company informs me that they will be shooting a base jump soon in the USA, and we shall therefore take advantage of the timing to shoot images of my rock escalation in Utah. But as for my proposed city climb, nothing is confirmed. If this mess of wretched permit papers arrives along the way, so much the better. If not, we shall just have to see what happens. *Insha'Allah.*

This disarray is what I face on my return to the New World, the wide open country of dreams and dreamlike landscapes. I am set to leave France with mixed emotions, possessing both a light heart and a heavy spirit. For me, climbing a pillar in Utah is a bewitching prospect while climbing a building is a bedevilling one. But regardless of the unfolding quandary I'm going to the United States to at least attempt the climb. In a twist of fate the planned departure date is Quatorze Juillet, or the 14th of July, the French national holiday to celebrate the storming of the Bastille. I find the date quite fitting. As the French national anthem goes, *The day of glory finally came.*

The first week in the United States is difficult but magical. I make my first trip to Utah, a most beautiful corner of the world. The state is a predominantly empty region of stark plains and purple sunsets. The whole day long I enjoy this wonderland, scrambling cliff sides in the abundant light of the brilliant sun above. I clamber up the rocks and survey the surroundings. Utah offers some truly impressive scenery. And some high temperatures: it is 43 degrees Celsius in the shade or, as our American cousins prefer to say, 110 degrees Fahrenheit. The cliff absorbs and emits heat like cast iron, but I keep fighting, sweat percolating from all the pores of my body. The climbing equipment can take it but the heat is so intense that I have to protect my hands with bandages to avoid sunburn. On the side of a rock I soon understand why the Native Americans have suntanned skin as strong and durable as leather.

The sweltering film crew however obviously cannot understand why we came here to climb in the scorching heat of the summer. Hey, this wasn't my idea, people! I am not complaining – I'm in my element. But it's not a time or place you would enjoy for long if you weren't a rock climber.

Cameras roll as I climb sheer cliff faces with ropes and climbing equipment. Safe rock climbing involves belaying, pairs or groups of climbers with equipment controlling the feeding of a rope to each other, so that any slippage means your companion does not fall very far. Being by myself I have to secure my own ropes. But I can also climb free solo – alone and without ropes. Climbing with my bare hands with nothing to support me, nothing to save me should anything go wrong.

After shooting me abseiling down a cliff the director asks if I can climb this giant rock face solo. Of course he knows the answer to that question. The entire crew know that I live for free solo. I give them a little smile then up I go, doing what I am known for.

I ascend the rocks with nothing but my hands and climbing shoes, clutching at small irregularities in the rock face, inserting my feet into small cracks and grooves wherever I can find them, pushing ever upwards. As I pull myself further up the vertical cliff, the film crew shrink into the vast surroundings. There is no safety net, no rope. If I were to fall then it would all be over. Kaput. Violins. Some of the guys beneath me dwell on this and are obviously quite nervous. But I am not worried at all, as I have done this countless times before upon the French cliffs.

Not everyone can do it. It must be said that in most cases, climbers who have only climbed solo indoors in leisure centres find places like Verdon or Utah a good cure for constipation. This is also quite true for many observers. But for me it has always been exhilarating. I thrive in this environment! The rocks of Utah are cooperative and supportive, offering me plenty of grips and routes up their steep sides, plenty of options and variety. With this type of rock there's lots of resistance and very little chance of the grips crumbling away or, with the arid conditions, of me slipping. My hands and feet easily find grips and footholds and my audience below are stunned by my little party trick. The cameras zoom in with hushed excitement as I ascend higher and higher, pulling off increasingly difficult moves.

Being totally alone up here is the sweetest solitude, a blissful and tranquil escape. There is risk, of course, so it is not a relaxing type of solitude. But I find holding onto my life by my fingertips to be a sublime experience, an elating kick. Many might find the two emotions incompatible, but I would counter that it is quite easy if you place yourself in the right setting with the right attitude. All sorts of sharp emotions invade me up there. It is difficult for me to explain the mix of wonderful feelings I experience when climbing solo in the mountains.

The film crew beneath me enjoy the show but as the days pass they soon become weary and the heat begins to wilt them. It is clear they'd much rather be filming somewhere with a bar nearby, somewhere serving ice-cold beers. I peer down every now and then to see them fanning their beetroot skin and wheezing, panting, swooning. Despite the uncompromising weather we get some superb images and the week is both a real success and a memorable diversion.

Our time in Utah concludes very nicely as far as the natural shots are concerned. But as we expected, or rather as we dreaded, no licence materialises for the urban shots. A crew member announces that we are up a certain creek without a particular piece of paddling equipment. What next? Am I going to have to climb on a mock-up on a film set, surrounded by green screens and technicians? Alas, the budget dictates no opportunity for this kind of whim.

Options limited, the director asks if I would agree to take the risk of climbing alone… with the possibility of being arrested. He seems most ill-at-ease as he makes this request. He does his best to hold my gaze, like a poker player risking everything on a bluff. Big beads of sweat pearl on his forehead. His eyes try to hide his flustered thoughts but fail. *Does he hold a flush or a pair of sevens?* Naturally I want to learn more, so it's back to Chicago. If I feel okay, then I shall play my trump cards, on his behalf. But if I feel my luck is starting to turn then I will have to fold rather than lose my entire stake.

The director nods keenly and we fly to Chicago to hunt down a suitable building. He doesn't care which building it is, so long as it looks dramatic on film. I however need something that is possible to climb, something with ledges or protrusions that I can hold onto. And the search for such a structure is not easy. Skyscrapers are designed to suspend people hundreds of metres high on the inside, not on the outside. Soon I start having the same thoughts as I did when I first got here – it seems insane to attempt such a thing.

From the observation deck on the Sears Tower, then the world's tallest building, we scour the horizon and pick out a few options. We walk the streets once again. Glass, steel and concrete are all smooth and featureless, lacking the crags, pits and nodules I depend upon for grip and leverage. With this in mind I seek buildings with textured facades. Eventually one or two emerge as realistic targets. None of these are easy by any means and I am unsure how I can attempt to scale their sheer and slippery sides. But by the evening we have selected a potential candidate and have taken a closer, low-key look at the chosen high rise. The tower I select meets my climbing criteria and is a handsome building for the director. It is decided. I will attempt to climb Chicago's Citicorp Citibank Center, a building well policed by guards.

The corporate tower looms over me, all 48 floors of it. The tension rises a notch. Chicago is the city of Al Capone and organised crime and everything seems absolutely hostile. Security services will be after me, the police and fire brigade will want to get their hands on me. What will happen? I am scared by the prospect of being accosted by big angry security guys, or arrested by US cops, cops who carry guns and are not afraid to use them – not to mention the fact I might actually fall off a high rise building.

Over the course of the following days, I return there, alone, to study the structure, trying to feel the building, trying to imagine my movements, to estimate the effort necessary for such an escalation. I look around gingerly to check the coast is clear, then put on my climbing slippers. Without trying to climb the first few metres, I put my right foot on the grips to discover the touch, to tame it. I am amazed to find great interest in the slightest detail. My climbing brain starts whirling.

From the hotel across the road, I eye up my target with binoculars to find its faults, its weaknesses, the secret keys to my success. With no experience at all of such an ascent I am very uneasy about the prospect. Buildings are new territory indeed and are not my forte at all. In fact no one in the world climbs them – you'd have to be a bit crazy to even consider it. And beyond the physical problems there's the law. Every one of us knows I am going to get into trouble with the American police. I have never been in such a situation anywhere, let alone abroad, and have no idea what will happen. Is it really worth it? I feel like an early navigator, about to embark on a global quest, torn between the temptation of adventure and the fear of losing my life. I am almost literally on the dizzying edge of a cliff.

I check in to another hotel closer to the Citicorp Citibank Center. In the meantime we decide to set the shoot the following morning, to avoid the risk of Sector falling into a judicial spiral which they stand no chance of escaping. Although all these people seem to regard this procedure as normal, for me the latest line from them is a very hard blow. Sector will watch from a safe distance and get their documentary footage and I will be left to face the wolves alone. It weighs heavily on my mind throughout the day and I am full of doubt as I settle restlessly into bed. Where is the support I need?

The telephone rings at 7:00 sharp. I've been wide awake for several hours so I'm not pissed off to be called so early. Guess who? It's the desperate director telling me that there is nothing less than a full marathon organised at the foot of our office block. A marathon? This is a complete nightmare! Is it some sort of joke? How could this 'small detail' have been overlooked by these guys? Thousands of pairs of American shorts will be bouncing along below the Citicorp Citibank Center under the eyes of an impressive police presence and ranks of race stewards. An escalation? No way. All bets are off while this citywide sports event is in progress.

I flop back on my bed, flattened by this ridiculous development. My phone blares out again. I answer it and listen to the latest hastily cobbled together plan. The director still wants to go ahead with the film shoot and the cameras will roll as soon as the streets are cleared. But when that will occur is anyone's guess.

It may be only a few minutes past seven but I am already exhausted by the day's events and I decide to try to get a little sleep. But after ten minutes I concede it is useless. I have far too much adrenaline coursing through my veins and lying there motionless is even more stressful. I spring out of bed and look for something to distract me. Minutes pass slowly. I feel like a smouldering pressure cooker, and I need to expel my growing sense of stress and helplessness. Making hourly phone calls to my wife Nicole back in France is my only escape valve, my unique catharsis. Between phone calls I perform an endless series of press-ups, partly to warm up and partly to burn off agitation. I waste plenty of time.

A little before midday, it seems the coast is finally clear. We are free at last... Regrettably, the sky darkens and the first rainy drops spatter onto the panes. *Merde!* It's all off again. I can't climb in the rain since the surfaces will become slippery and dangerous, and the director won't film as he is looking for a clear and uplifting image, not a melancholy or moody one.

Distinctly wound up, I pace back and forth in my hotel room, to and from the bathroom, and peer out of the window every two minutes. Wait, wait, wait, we always have to wait... Huffing and puffing I stride around and jump into yet another round of pumps. Usually, I would take this situation in my stride, but today serenity seems to have deserted me. After several hours of this I am fed up. Hoping for a nap I lie down. As a last resort, I channel-hop from one pointless TV programme to another, an exercise which, in the United States, can allow you to waste an entire lifetime.

My telephone wails out once again. By now much of the day is gone. The afternoon is dying but the sun bathes Chicago once more. The director, who seems to have lost some hair throughout the day, explains the latest development. He has just sent the film crew down to set up their equipment and I have to commence the escalation in less than an hour. Alexis the photographer will accompany me to the building in a taxi, then drop me off and depart for the heliport to take aerial images. The director asks me how long I think it will take to complete the climb. Short of benchmarks, I estimate the time of ascent at more than one hour; an hour and a half at most. He ends by sheepishly reminding me that the city fire brigade possesses a number of 60-metre ladders, a distance which I will have to climb extremely fast to escape capture. The call abruptly ends. Nice. Thank you for your kind advice, Mr Director.

Even though I am less than ecstatic about how the day is unfolding it's certainly a relief to leave my claustrophobic hotel room. Time, which was moving torturously slowly, now accelerates to breakneck speed. The taxi takes us to the Citicorp Citibank Center and soon Alexis is gone and everything, apparently, is in place. At the foot of the tower everything seems quiet. I look up and swallow hard. I wonder how a guy is supposed to look natural when he is about to climb up the side of a building. Does he whistle and stroll down the road with his hands in his pockets? I make a clumsy, self-conscious attempt at casually walking down the street, then decide to abandon this demented charade and just bolt up the side of the office block.

The first few metres of the escalation is negotiated in total alarm and with such haste that I cut my hands on rough edges of metal protruding from the building, a feature I had not anticipated. My movements are ill-timed and erratic, there is certainly no art to this diabolical climb. It looks more like a jailbreak than a professional ascent… In angst I race upwards in broken movements, fearful that at any moment a ladder with a burly fireman will spring up next to me and whisk me away.

As I rocket further upwards I discover just how tough it is to climb a building. Steel and glass are nothing like any rock I have ever tackled at all and I have to adapt my movements accordingly. Worrying is the likelihood that my audience, usually fully behind me in my climbs, will this time be totally against me, seeing me as an outlaw, a crook, or a lunatic in dire need of a straitjacket. Furthermore, the intense reflection of the sun on the mirrored panes enhances the difficulty. I am like an ant scurrying around under a magnifying glass as the dazzling light seems to focus on me alone. But when I glance down for the first time, the ground below has already sunk away by more than a hundred metres. A true sprint! And much to my relief there is no fire engine.

With no ladders to worry about I turn my attention back to the building. On this pioneering climb, the difficulty results more from my inexperience, and from the incredible impression of imperviousness which emanates from such a building, than the movements I need to make. Up here, all alone, I am creating an imaginary hostile environment. The street drops away a little more with every movement, reminding me of the immediate violence of the penalty below should I make a mistake. This is a stressful climb, to say the least, and not much fun with all these unhappy thoughts bouncing around my head. I carry on for another 20 minutes, so focussed on my escalation that I had not bothered to look down and see a growing group of people gathered at the bottom. I find the same grips, push with the same movement and gain on the finishing line at the top. Technically it is very different to a rock formation but it is not extreme and towards the top I make better progress than I had originally expected.

And soon the top of the building, the summit of this urban rock, is within sight. I start to relax a little at the thought – it looks like I will really make it! Scanning around I can see no architectural obstacles near the rooftop as I close in on my goal. Finally I am within inches of the top. I place one hand over the lip of the summit and then the other. Cautiously I poke my head over the edge.

To my amazement a multitude of policemen, firemen and security guards await me. All this activity on my account is a bewildering sight. I pull myself over the top, not sure what to expect. Maybe it will be like one of those American cop shows? I expect at any moment a rugby tackle, guns drawn or the FBI to swoop in behind their dark glasses. Right now this is all very new to me, but I shall soon become used to this kind of reception. They all seem to be waiting for me to do something. Some reaction perhaps, some sort of cue so they know what sort of person I am and how to handle me. I break the ice with a broad smile and a greeting in shattered English and my thick French accent.

"Hi guys! Do not worry, I am professional rock climbeur. Zere is no mountain to be climbed in Chicago, so I decide to climb zees high rise! No problem! Everything is okay…"

They cock their heads and frown. Neither side is quite sure what is going on. It looks like they do not really appreciate the joke, but still I feel no hostility. And it doesn't matter. What can worry me now?

The cops grab me by the elbow and I am under arrest. Arrest? I have never been arrested. But strangely as I am led away I feel a surge of accomplishment. Handcuffs, mug shots of my face from the front and from the side, fingerprints and – for the first time in my life – a few hours detained in a prison cell. But after these last days of fear and uncertainty, being locked up feels like liberation! This is a great achievement for me, make no mistake about it, especially since a few years earlier the doctors had condemned me to remain nailed to the ground, after two successive falls in the mountains led to crippling multiple fractures.

Without realising it, the direction of my life had changed dramatically and irrevocably. This day would be the one that would help define me. Little did I know it, but the city of Chicago had just opened a door to a whole new universe… a range of mountains of glass and steel.

A NEWLY DISCOVERED MOUNTAIN RANGE

Paris. The legendary capital of arts, romance, fashion and the human spirit. Arguably the world's most cultured and chic city, graced by the presence of the Notre Dame cathedral, the Louvre museum, the Eiffel Tower, and the Champs-Elysées – the world's most beautiful avenue, it is said. Well, at least by Frenchmen. Paris means so many things to so many people. It is also synonymous with social success, a place where dreams become reality, as Hollywood would be for cinema actors or London would be for musicians. The connection with climbing? None, except that the French capital marked the real birth of my urban escalations: my *eureka* moment was stumbled upon accidentally in the bend of a traffic jam on the Parisian ring road.

Leaving my native Drôme in south-eastern France and heading into the sprawl of Paris is inevitably a disorientating affair, the capital of any country being dramatically different to the land over which it rules. At the time, my recent escapade with Sector in Chicago was very fresh in my memory. The American newspapers were filled with the exploits of a French climber the journalists called 'Spiderman'. The trip had been an eye-opening diversion but for me it still remained an isolated incident. Despite the ultimate completion of this assignment I had to admit the experience had been a bit disturbing, as no one knew what the hell they were doing and with taking on something untried I could have been killed. I had gone out there with a set of assurances from Sector, which to be fair had tried to arrange things, but we had got into a bureaucratic mess which had ultimately resulted in my arrest! It was hardly what I was led to believe would happen. And on the building itself things could have easily gotten out of hand. Okay, the arrest had eventually turned out to be harmless, although very distressing at the time, but this is not something one seeks out. Indeed the experience had deterred me from attempting such an action ever again.

I was still like everyone else in the game, a rock climber scaling mountains and cliffs. Like Jibé Tribout I considered I had engaged in an advertising stunt, a one-off movie thing. The rocky cliffs and pillars of Utah had been my forte, I was right at home there. I had spent intoxicating days climbing in the gorgeous desert wilderness as well as a terrifying hour vaulting up a high rise building. Now it was back to reality, which for me was France and the cliffs here I love so much.

For several years, my solo cliff ascents had attracted the interest of professional photographers seeking dramatic and provoking images and this had led me to develop relationships with several journalists at *Paris Match*, one of France's leading weekly magazines. But as yet I was unable to support myself purely through my passion. I continued to work part-time in a small sports store in my native Valence, with little climbing stunts for several sponsors allowing me to make ends meet.

This particular day, my car was immobilised in the droning fumes of the Paris ring road. Disc jockeys did their best to entertain the scores of thousands of bored Parisian drivers caught in an endless shuffle of metal and rubber. Tired, I cast my eye over the city skyline. For some unknown reason, two enormous towers drew my attention, fertilizing my imagination. These glass arrows dominating the cityscape became majestic spurs. Climbers would leave towns or cities like this to tackle the most distant rocky or icy summits. Then it struck me – why not try to climb these urban mountains? The most impressive natural summit, protected by vertical walls and ice slides and shielded by horrendous climatic conditions, nevertheless has its weakness, its Achilles' heel. The solution is founded upon discovering this weakness. Once you have uncovered it you may open up a logical path upwards along the most evident route to the summit. And then, when one is ready, and presuming one hasn't used up too many lives, one increases the challenge by looking for the most audacious passages. By adopting such a state of mind, simple office blocks were suddenly transformed into Himalayan summits.

It was quite a revelation. My whole life I had seen such buildings as dwellings, manifestations of a giant replicate interior. I had never stopped to ponder the exterior other than recognising it as a shell required to keep everything from falling out. Late in the afternoon, sat in gridlock a kilometre away from the gargantuan twin forms, buildings I would later learn were named the Mercuriales Towers, my eyes grow wide. And then I look around. Other forms, other buildings, endless miles of them! *Everything is here.* A whole city! The city is many things to many people, but for me, right now, it is a total revelation. It is a newly discovered mountain range.

The next day, I head to the Champs-Elysées to visit the editorial staff of *Paris Match*. My proposed project? The escalation of the Mercuriales Towers. And since it is my speciality I will go solo – without ropes. Is this just a pipe dream? I'm not sure. But maybe the journalists will be interested, so I reveal my vision.

We get chatting and they like the idea a lot, and straight away propose the Eiffel Tower instead. The Eiffel Tower, that iconic symbol of France, has already been climbed early in the 20th century by a team led by Pierre Allain. But for the magazine journalists, guided by a motto along the lines of 'the weight of words, the shock of photos', the Mercuriales seem very flat. To these guys they seem two-dimensional, perhaps in terms of visual appearance and relief but also in terms of their aura and persona. The magazine looks for the visually spectacular while I need real challenges in term of escalation.

In the course of our animated discussion, a host of potential projects takes over the desk, some more interesting than others. Soon it is clear there is no single building that can satisfy all agendas. Bit by bit, the so-called 'Tour of Paris by Façades' takes shape. We come up with a whole host of buildings across the city and decide that I will attempt to climb as many of these famous landmarks as I can. *Paris Match* undertakes to involve the media through the press agency Gamma, a company I have enjoyed a lot of cooperation with from my earliest rock-climbing days. Without really knowing what I am doing, or even considering the judicial risks ahead, I calculate I have the financial means to attempt the project. The Tour of Paris needs research and organisation but it will go ahead. I am going to climb some buildings!

Suddenly things start happening. Whilst *Paris Match* and Gamma are helping to put the Tour of Paris together my phone rings again. After our success in America, Sector have got hold of me again and tell me about their ambition to film the escalation of a high rise building in France…

Until recently, I thought skyscrapers could only be found in North America. But since I set eyes on the Mercuriales and bounced ideas off

Paris Match I am suddenly seeing new possibilities. The Mercuriales really appeal to me in spite of their comparatively weak dimensions. I learn that since my first escalation in Chicago, Sector has coincidentally been thinking of bigger challenges, thinking of skyscrapers in Paris. It is as if something new has just been born.

Like most European cities Paris is pretty flat, with proportionately little modern high rise architecture, but the business district of La Défense in the western quarter breaks with the rest of the city and is the obvious choice. Apart from Le Grande Arche, a third-millennium cuboid salute to the Arc de Triomphe, I do not know much about the buildings in the area. A visit is imperative so it is back to the ring road and I point my car west. Little by little, aerial silhouettes emerge then come into sharp focus. In La Défense I park my car and head out to explore. I turn a corner and then on the square right in front of me... Utter shock! A bold glass skyscraper of approximately 200 metres, the highest I have ever seen in France: Le Tour Elf, the Elf Aquitaine Tower. What an amazing sight! The Mercuriales suddenly take a back seat and the Elf Tower pushes its way onto centre stage.

At a good distance from the objective, the Elf Tower remains a tower of Babel, mysterious and inaccessible. Before America I would have attacked the whole thing very differently. But with my Chicago experience under my belt, I am able to consider an escalation in a whole new way. I make a conscious effort to penetrate its defences and track down its weakness. I have a bunch of ideas but right now there is no way for me to be sure of the feasibility of scaling this awesome structure. I take photos of the Elf Tower and some of the surrounding buildings for Sector and *Paris Match*. Full of beans I look at the tower again, like a child in a candy store. How will I get to the top of this jewel? There is no obvious way up it. Chicago was chosen due to the fact it was a climbable structure, but Elf has been chosen purely because I like the look of it.

Sincerely, I do not really remember what fascinated me the most that day – the absolute beauty of the buildings or being thunderstruck by this new perspective of escalation. Maybe both, because without a shadow of a doubt, climbing the Elf Tower would be a massive and irreversible step.

Sector seems openly excited and motivated by the project. So am I, even if I still do not know what I intend to do about it. Once, twice, ten times, I return there, to study the towering structure, to restudy and reconsider it, and try to locate the keystone. I muse over numerous equations which will lead me to its summit. A possible answer? There is a crack, a narrow fissure which as far as I can see runs all the way up the building. I measure its width and its depth with my fingers to determine where I can wrap bandage protection for my fingers. I observe the structure with binoculars and try to imagine the full range of scenarios. I am racked with doubt. I realise that by attempting Elf, I am playing in a field which I have not mastered. Am I falling in love? Am I going to cheat on my loyal cliffs for a new concrete and glass mistress? If Chicago was only a reckless one night stand, when I look at the Elf Tower I feel deeply agitated. I am charmed...

Once I have got my hands on the architectural blueprints and analysed them, I discover a problem. How do I get onto the roof? Are there any grips at the top that will enable me to complete the climb? Flapping and rustling the papers I find nothing and feel less than convinced about the achievability of the ascent. Being faced with two metres of building face without the slightest blemish or ridge when stuck in a nasty posture is bad enough, but at the end of a tiring climb this would be a real problem. I would be too engaged by this point to hope to come down again. Two metres! A trifling, piffling, insignificant distance but it could cost me dearly.

I cannot risk the ascent without a better look, so through friends – and thanks to a little stratagem impossible to describe here because it is rather illegal – I have the chance to gaze at my temptress through the window of a helicopter. The air over Paris is subject to severe control legislation. But it doesn't matter, and I grasp this timely snippet of fortune that comes my way. A helicopter trip will allow me to confront my doubts even if the dynamic viewpoint has the effect of multiplying my emotions. Space can only be understood from the summit. Curiously, a pair of binoculars may bring you even closer than a helicopter but you see more detail, you feel more detail when physically elevated.

I hover close to the summit of the tower not far below our spinning blades. The sense of height transcends me and helps me to sublimate my ambition. Overcoming difficulties and the unpredictable has always been a tremendous passion in my life. The proximity to my temptress affects me even more. Resistance is futile. The Elf Tower playfully reveals a little more of herself and seduces me. I must climb her. I must.

My strategy is laid out and before long the day of the climb arrives.

Opposite is the Gambetta Tower, a 37-storey block of flats deprived of a police contingent which gives Sector's cameramen the location they need to bed down comfortably and securely. Sector wants a series of dramatic shots so we have a helicopter ready complete with cameraman and photographer. The helicopter is not really supposed to be there, so it has to fly around for half an hour after the beginning of the operation, and then swoop in as if by chance.

This is it now: the research has been done, the preparation is in place and I have no more doubts. Except for one. I did not tell anybody my fears, being afraid that they may laugh at me. At the base of the Elf Tower is a fire station, and if the alarm is raised and word gets out that there is a man hanging off the side of the building, the response will be so quick that I fear I will not be able to escape the reach of their sizeable turntable ladder. I keep thinking of it over and over. The Parisian fire brigade, those honest and extremely fit professionals, will pluck me like a ripe fruit before I have managed fifty metres of escalation. Such a prospect appals me. The only possible counter to this threat? Speed.

There is always a security presence in the financial district so I keep a low profile at the foot of the tower. There is quite a bit of camouflaged media around if you look closely. A photographer here, a cameraman there... Not to be unmasked, I enter the square of La Défense dressed in overalls I borrowed from my sister, who happens to be a decorator. My footsteps make a rather perplexing crunching sound. Why? Under my slippers, adhesive strips protect the soles from the contaminating dirt of the ground, and these can be peeled off very quickly when I start.

A glance to the left, to the right... Everything is quiet. I rip off the strips, irrationally nervous that the tearing sound may spur the fire brigade into action. Restless, I begin my ascent. In my haste, my feet slip and slide pitifully and continuously and I grope and fumble as I cannot find good finger grips. I am totally vulnerable and begin to sweat. And I am not the only one: with all my floundering and skidding my pensive family is also wondering if I am in control of my movements. My wife Nicole, who is about to give birth to our third son, gets tired of the sight of this distressing spectacle. I guess it is understandable – how many heavily pregnant women would want to see their husband behaving in such a manner? After some involuntary Inspector Clouseau impersonations I eventually get away and start making progress up the building.

For Nicole, as well as for me, this is all new. This novel experience of a building escalation is entirely different from climbing a cliff. On the square of La Défense, Nicole is much more afraid than during my other solo ascents, even though she has already seen me in some rather tricky positions. Thankfully the fire brigade has not yet moved. Looking back, I realise that I must have been very inexperienced then to believe that a ladder would have appeared out of nowhere and I would have been 'rescued' by a tough fireman. After a few minutes pulsing with adrenalinee I have clumsily raced halfway towards the summit and Nicole decides to waddle into the shopping centre to sit down. I don't think she is enjoying it very much. While I maintain my assault a friend jogs to and fro to inform her of my progress.

Soon I start losing my bearings. The multitude of mirrors all around makes me dizzy and disorientates me. My vertigo kicks in and I fight to regain my wits. I feel lost in a vertical labyrinth. The escalation is certainly challenging and it is more physical than I expected. Breathless, I try to rest and cool down by propping my shoulder against the building and letting each arm hang alternately. The technique is effective and helps me regain my strength. While recuperating I also consider the poetic element of the escalation. If it weren't for the fact that the authorities were due to give me a yellow card, I would choose to climb this tower again and follow a spiral route to prolong the escalation, prolong the pleasure. Structures of course rarely allow such a whim but now I realise the potential of this building. By attacking directly and rapidly due to my excitement on the square, I have wasted this project. I have rushed it, just as when we sprint up a cliff way too quickly to the detriment of artistic style, or wolf down a fine meal. For sure, success matters but so does the beauty of the gesture itself. The helicopter crew, misled by my erroneous estimation of my completion time, has missed most of the climb but arrives just in time to film my last movements.

Scaling the Elf Tower has taken me just 21 minutes. I overcome the final two metres I had previously worried about to reach the summit. As it turns out, fortunately there were grips. The fire brigade, finally there on the roof, are accompanied by the security services. And amongst the crowd at the top is the CEO of the multinational oil company, Monsieur Loïk Le Floch-Prigent himself. He steps forward in his grey suit, immaculately dressed and groomed, and the group parts to let him through.

Le Floch-Prigent walks up to me stiffly.

"Why did you not ask for a licence?" he bellows.

"Because you would not have given it to me," I say laconically. His eyes bulge.

"That's right!" he fumes, beside himself with fury.

I shrug. Until proven otherwise, I did not damage his high rise, nor make a naughty splash on the square below. In addition, I am polite, non-violent and a professional rock climber responsible for my actions. His disdainful, contemptuous attitude begins to irritate me. He walks up and down as if we should tremble in his presence, hands behind his back and his nose to the sky. His eyes are aflame as he glares down his nose at me. I tell him with barely masked irony that there is no sign forbidding escalation at the foot of the building. A few stifled sniggers come from the direction of the firemen. That does it. For him, enough is enough. Dramatically raising his arms towards the sky, he vows to take me apart in court and then storms off as if he had just delivered the cliff-hanger line in a corny soap opera.

How curious – the air of Paris seems a bit clearer now. The reaction of the policemen and firemen is radically different to that of the CEO and fills me with confidence. There is no disproportionate deployment of cops as in Chicago. With an almost collusive smile, the chief fireman quietly tells me that during fire drills, it takes them much longer to reach the summit by the stairs than I did by the façade.

At the police station, our whole team is there. Everybody has been arrested for a routine interrogation by the cops, and I learn that within that briefest of periods Elf has already pressed charges! Le Floch-Prigent did not waste time. My case turns out to be a little more delicate than it does for the others, who are immediately freed. It appears that I must be detained a little longer. I am taken to a glum cell and flop onto a bench. Exhausted by the day's events and post-adrenaline rush, I sink into a mildly addled sleep. In my slumber I turn over and crash onto the cold floor in front of two swaying drunkards and a sour-looking prostitute. Already relaxed with me, the police guards guffaw as I am startled awake into that horrible twilight confusion and alarm when you don't know where you are. It is much worse when you awaken in such surroundings and with such an audience.

Late in the afternoon, I am freed from detention. But it is not yet time to say *au revoir* to the authorities as I have to return for a meeting in court. By the evening, the media machine has really got carried away. TF1,

France 2, France 3, all the television news channels tell of the ascent of the Elf Tower! They show my progress up the showpiece of vertical La Défense, our Parisian Manhattan. It is no exaggeration to say that these news bulletins mark a change in my life. Things will never, ever be the same again for Alain Robert.

Over the following days, my brand new celebrity status opens doors to the hippest places of the city. For the countryside guy I am, this is a bitter discovery. People who yesterday would not have even looked at me now hug me as if we had collected peaches together in Valence. I learn about segregation within our society, about special clubs where it is necessary, it is said, to go and be seen. But why? For me, drinking a beer with pals should not be about ending up in the pages of gossip magazines. I am not taken with this outlook on life or the artificial friendships it entails. Fortunately, I am not that kind of guy.

In court I am under attack by the mighty oil conglomerate. It's Elf versus me, hardly an even fight, and I am totally out of my depth. My sponsor Sector is not involved in legal proceedings, despite having asked me to take the same risks as in my Chicago ascent. In Chicago I was simply dismissed but here I am in a courtroom, assailed by a multinational. I am on my own and have no idea what is going to happen.

The trial opens with a pleasant surprise: the Public Prosecutor's Department, preoccupied with far more important cases, have looked into the whole affair and have decided that I have not broken any laws. It appears that I have done something new – no one has ever stood before a judge for having clambered up a building. The bottom line is that no law has been passed to stop rock climbers or anyone else scaling public buildings. The courts declare they have more important things to do and will not prosecute me. In a matter of minutes it is all over. Elf have lost!

I leave the courtroom in jubilation with my friends. I can't believe it. Huge smiles, big hugs and slaps on the back, it's a great moment. But soon I discover that Elf's CEO is really upset by this turn of events – so much so he has instructed a legal team to have me prosecuted at all costs. He will turn the full power of this state-owned oil giant against me for climbing his pretty tower, and he will pursue me relentlessly. Le Floch-Prigent is not going to let me go and will not rest until I am broken by the courts. His dramatic rooftop pledge still stands. Like Captain Ahab he will hunt me down and harpoon me like Moby Dick.

I am not too bothered about Elf, my life goes on. My lawyer draws legal proceedings out and sends me letters updating me on developments. But I have already boarded a plane for New York to appear in more material for the documentary I am making with Sector.

Travel is a new experience for me and I snap up the chance to see a little more of the world. Sector needs some fill-in footage so here I am in the Big Apple. It's an amazing place, vibrant, cosmopolitan and one of the true vertical cities of the world. There are so many incredible structures here: the monetary power of the twin towers of the World Trade Center, the classic façades of the Empire State Building, the architectural masterpiece of the Chrysler Building and of course the Statue of Liberty, which the French donated to the Americans in 1886. But alongside these sublime marvels of engineering, there are dozens of wonderful towers in New York. None of these fine courses are on my menu due to the legal problems we experienced in Chicago and Paris. My climb in Chicago did not lead to legal action but I was still embroiled in lots of horrible wrangling with Elf due to the impassioned vow of Le Floch-Prigent. Sector make it clear I am not supposed to do any illegal climbs this time. So we get some innocent footage together, a bunch of interviews and space fillers in US settings. The shooting is pleasant enough but it seems such a waste not to admire one of these buildings from an elevated close-up angle.

After wandering around close to my hotel I find a nice shop where they are selling some excellent snakeskin vests and jackets. I try a few on and admire myself in the mirror. Wonderful stuff, absolutely top notch… My wallet however cannot stretch to these lofty prices, so I ask the attendant if I can talk with the boss. After quite a long chat with him I manage to persuade him to sponsor me. Not for money of course, but if I climbed a building wearing one of his snakeskin vests with the name of his company printed on the back of it then I would get that nice green jacket he was otherwise selling for $5,000. The contract I signed with Sector for the *No Limits* documentary said that when I climb I must do so in their clothing. But personally I didn't fancy climbing in those ugly clothes; instead I would like to have some fun climbing in a nice snakeskin vest.

Of course when I later tell Sector's film crew what I am doing they are mad with me, especially the producer! Since they had sponsored me they felt that they should be able to control my climbing activity. I can see why they are not happy but I know that I am neither right nor wrong. I was not supposed to do another ascent for them and I wasn't doing one for them – this was my own one! It will be purely for fun, an ascent that I want to do and not one I have to do because someone else had chosen it on my behalf.

The shit hits the fan with Sector but I am comfortable with my decision. I am drawn to 101 Park Avenue, a shiny black towering building with an irregular footprint. Its angles interest me and I return several times, sometimes at night, to check it out and to quickly test a few movements. I am convinced I can climb it but still I am impressed – 200 metres straight upwards and as flat as a pancake. It is an awesome sight! Doing this alone is much better – I can choose the best buildings and prepare properly, I can set my own agenda and do not need to worry about paperwork, schedules or bullshit. I have artistic freedom of expression and do not need to worry about exterior personalities influencing fundamental parameters – these are all important things for a climber.

The owner of a restaurant in Greenwich presents me to a big bunch of journalists from the mainstream television news channels. They will all be present at the climb. For me all this attention is overwhelming. I am familiar with journalists and accustomed to the company of a photographer and even the odd film crew. But this looks like it will be quite something – a newsworthy event! Word gets out and finally the people at Sector surrender. They decide that obviously it makes sense for them to record additional footage if I am going up anyway. Sector will film me even though I will be in a lovely snakeskin vest promoting an apparel outlet rather than wearing their unappealing kit and promoting them. I guess it has been a difficult decision for them but I feel that I am better off handling this alone. Now that I am empowered, I feel excited rather than worried. Also, with the media in attendance, I feel a little more reassured – I imagine that with their presence, my chances of being jailed are slimmer.

The day of the climb arrives and I head to 101 Park Avenue in a yellow taxi. I am racked with nerves and on the verge of breaking down. Is it the size of the task ahead? For sure, this escalation is my toughest urban challenge to date, and only my third. I have no idea what lies ahead. So is this fear of the unknown? Or is it stage fright? For even now I have a microphone poking around under my nose. I see the eyes of the New York cabbie curiously watching the scene taking place in his rear view mirror. A journalist named Isabelle is interviewing me with forceful and melodramatic questions. I am really not in the mood – I desperately need some time to focus on my escalation. My fear must be showing because Isabelle, like any good journalist zeroing in on human misery and suffering, has the idea of asking me whether I am afraid. I am completely stressed at this moment and I start to cry! I am not sure whether I will still be alive in one or two hours from now, and that stupid question is just too much for me. The taxi driver has no idea what is going on as we approach a media circus with a merciless journalist prodding me with a microphone and me in tears. I realise this show is not going at all well – can you imagine if it fell apart and ended like this? What a terrible outcome!

I pull myself together and mop my face, now more determined than ever. The taxi stops and I fly out the door and run straight to the particular face I had previously planned to attack. I don't know if the taxi driver thinks I am trying to evade a fare but he must be surprised at what he sees. There is a huge bank of cameras and journalists waiting to interview me, but I am totally focussed and nothing can stop me! I plough through them and climb the first few metres of the building. A security guard, who no doubt thought these cameras were waiting for a VIP, suddenly realises what is actually happening. He is shouting like mad. But I have selected to climb the corner, and it proves to be a good choice as I have already scaled ten metres by the time he reaches where I left the pavement.

The cameras capture all the commotion as I pull away from the ground. My fear has gone and is replaced with exhilaration as I realise that I can do it. All I need to do is keep my rhythm and I will be able to reach the top. As I climb I look through the windows and see people stunned, amazed and leaping to their feet! Office workers take photos and gawp to the background din of the sirens of police cars and fire engines! It is completely surreal. I feel like a carefree bird and I really think I have found myself. No matter what the consequences, I will make it to the top!

As I pass every window all I can see is excitement and happiness. It's great… I feel like a showman with a loving audience. Maybe I am indeed a performer – perhaps I should go by the name of 'Snakeman'? Even though I am beginning to tire, I really am having buckets of fun! Climbing this hooded black tower in the centre of Manhattan is a breathtaking experience and the view is sublime.

Sometimes I look down and the people crowded around the building look like ants. I begin to take in the magnitude of what I am doing and am even starting to impress myself! Wow, I really am quite daring! I feel like my childhood heroes!

The top of the building isn't far away now and I am trying to keep a little stamina in reserve as I can feel my muscles tightening due to elevated levels of lactic acid. I hurry a little to make the top, and then a slip… and I nearly fall. Just one second of inattention and my foot slid out from beneath me – but the will to survive is strong, and fortunately my reflexes are highly tuned, and somehow I manage to grab a ledge with the very tips of my fingers to avoid catastrophe. It is a close call and reminds me that I have much to learn about the nature of the materials I am working with today. But thankfully I recover and catch my breath. Then I make one last move to surge towards the top. The wall of black gives way to blue – I make it!

As I pull myself over and plant my feet on the rooftop I see there are a lot of cops and security officials waiting for me, but I feel such immense joy that the prospect of being arrested and going to jail is not even the slightest issue. The moon could have exploded and I wouldn't have cared! I am so happy that my state of mind is nearly indescribable. I had climbed up 101 Park Avenue with my bare hands!

Why was I ecstatic about this climb rather than the two that preceded it? Maybe this monstrous tower, a building King Kong might also have climbed if he had stomped Manhattan today, implied a greater sense of achievement – or maybe it was because I didn't give a shit about sponsors or contracts or bureaucracy or limitations. Chicago had been disappointing in the sense that Sector was so frightened of getting caught, yet not concerned that I could be arrested and prosecuted. Paris had been the same story but it had turned out worse and now I had this high-profile corporate madman, Loïk Le Floch-Prigent, after me. Sector had some nice people and I was sad that they could not have supported me a little more. This solo done off my own back and on my own terms was an amazing experience and a liberation: it was what climbing was really about!

A few minutes later I have a nice pair of silver bracelets behind me and I am escorted off the roof and towards the elevators by dozens of cops. Some of them are cheerful, others are pissed off. Once the lift gets to the bottom – pandemonium! We exit the building to a voracious and enormous pack of media, pushing and shoving, filming, photographing, waving microphones and booms, crying out, desperate to get clips of my arrest! It is an incredible scene! I feel like I am in a movie, except of course everything is very real, the handcuffs and the rudeness of a few of the cops reminding me that this is no Hollywood red carpet.

We press through the media and push into the car. Flashes are going off in my face and I give a few of the guys a smile. Amid all the chaos I can just make out the crew from Sector, fighting a losing battle to get a scene for the documentary... The police car pulls away with lights spinning and sirens wailing, leaving the media whirlwind and Sector in our wake. I don't know much about what is going on or what is in store for me. This had to be more serious than Chicago, but I am quite confident I will be okay. This is the country of Uncle Sam, the country of freedom and liberty, right? Well, at least that's what I thought.

Ten minutes later I am at the police station where, to my surprise, everyone wants to see me... not the media – the cops! The reaction of the police seems positive and it looks like things aren't going to be too bad. Everybody is trying to communicate with me at once, but my English at this point is so bad that any discussion is very limited. I am led to a room and the door closes on the onlookers. I sit down at the stark desk as the cops pull out the paperwork. For the third time I am at a police station going through the same old formalities. Frontal and profile mugshots with my matriculation number, endless fingerprinting sessions and questioning as to how I ended up scaling the tower, my motivations and so forth. And of course the name of my father. It always perplexes me, this question – surely I am a big boy now? Cops jot down notes about my reasons for climbing 101 Park Avenue with either raised or furrowed eyebrows and I get the impression they don't understand me – not my crap English, but my philosophy.

I had originally felt quite optimistic about being released, but now I am being transferred to a big cell with several dozen prisoners. I'm not so convinced I will be freed so fast. It has gone 7:00pm and, as I understand it, everyone must stand before a judge before being released or being transferred to a jailhouse, so it seems I am going to spend the night here! This would actually be my first night in a prison cell, my previous two arrests being followed soon after by a daytime release.

The bars slam behind me. I am the only bare-chested prisoner – apart from the snakeskin vest I am wearing with a company logo plastered all over the back. The guys are watching TV to pass the time and we are all wearing handcuffs, maybe so we can't fight each other, maybe as some sort of protocol. Unlike the events of several hours ago when I was in the middle of a maelstrom, here I am happily anonymous. It is a large cell but there isn't a great deal of space available for me to sit, given the number of prisoners. At one end of the cell is a public phone and everyone is using it for collect calls. Unfortunately I have no numbers and do not know who to call. Shortly after I enter, they bring us plates of toast with some cheddar on it. It is a truly ugly mechanical cheese, totally rubbery and synthetic, and of course a processed variety made in the USA. It always amazes me how the Americans tolerate such heinous cheese. But I guess this is a prison cell, not five-star luxury. We are not supposed to enjoy the experience. Maybe this star-spangled cheese is part of the punishment.

With no windows I am unable to gauge time and cannot tell if it is day or night. But by now I am starting to feel tired. The sizeable discharge of adrenaline has subsided, leaving my body heavy, empty, drained. Shattered and aching I attempt to sleep on a low bench, slightly away from the other prisoners. I have to sleep curled up in a foetal position because of hefty metal rings placed every metre, apparently for chaining us down if need be. After a period of restless dozing it is plain that I can't balance here and I lay out on the dirty concrete floor instead.

An hour later the prisoners wake me in an over-excited state. Blearily I retreat, wanting to keep away from any rioting or fighting. But as I come to, I realise these are full-blooded cheers and whoops of joy. The images of my ascent are all over CNN and ABC. By channel-hopping, a fellow inmate is able to show me being broadcast on several channels across the airwaves of America! Several big lads pull me to the TV, pointing and yelling wildly. My eyes open wide as I take in the images of myself 200 metres up 101 Park Avenue – I am on TV! In huge excitement they all scoop me up and carry me in triumph around the cell. I am tossed and thrown in the air by a crowd of howling maniacs in a New York jail. Images of my arrest amongst a media and police scrum are wildly cheered as I bob like a cork in a human sea. For the inmates it is a sort of victory, a win for us over them. I will never forget such a moment… It was surreal and very, very moving.

The guys treat me as a hero in there and I barely get a wink of sleep. When the morning comes I am parted from the guys with high fives and generous cheers, and swiftly brought before a judge.

It is immediately apparent that these people do not seem overjoyed to see me. Serious faces, uptight people, proper haircuts. The court settles and all eyes are on me. The charges are read out: criminal trespass, disorderly conduct, reckless endangerment... The judge leans forward and asks the lawyers a series of questions. They respond in turn. The judge frowns and pauses and removes his glasses. It is clear he is not quite sure what to make of it all. He leans forward and looks straight at me from under his bushy eyebrows, as a headmaster would a naughty pupil. He points the temple of his spectacles at me and tells me that the case will be dismissed if I promise not to do it again. My lawyer shoots me an eager look. In my simple English I humbly promise the judge I won't. The judge gives a satisfied nod and dismisses me. And that's it! I am free to go.

Soon I leave the courthouse to the Manhattan breeze, my heart racing, my spirits soaring. The last 24 hours have been a joyous voyage of personal discovery, an enlightenment you might say. I have never felt the way I did yesterday and I want to feel it again. However, I fully intend to keep my promise to the good judge. I resolve to keep my word and never climb 101 Park Avenue again...

2

LE TOUR DE PARIS

I leave the United States buzzing from my climb and relieved with my good fortune. I got away with not so much as a fine – a real escape from New York. I return to Paris fresh and invigorated by my adventures. I had left France shortly after my court win over Elf, and thus had left my Parisian tour on the drawing board. But only a few days have lapsed since then and so I return to the *Paris Match* offices to pick up where we left off.

I exit the elevator to meet up with the journalists and am immediately greeted by big smiles. It seems they are aware of my high-profile success in America and are keen that I pursue my escalations here as soon as possible. Mesmerising potential targets once again fill the agenda. I can't wait.

Act 1: The National Library and the Mercuriales

After the Elf Tower ascent, *Paris Match* published an article on the inauguration of the final major construction project envisioned by the French president, François Mitterrand – the National Library. The building is structurally intact but not yet finished; there is much internal work to be done and quite a bit of time needed to achieve it. But I am told media interest is guaranteed with Mitterrand himself having recently inaugurated it.

I accompany *Paris Match* to visit the site. I must say I am not charmed by these four symmetrical L-shaped buildings barely reaching 90 metres. They lack dimension, there is an absence of a real summit, their lines are nondescript – all in all they have nothing in common with a beautiful high rise building. My two partners, the magazine and the press agency Gamma, were enthusiastic at the beginning but are now sceptical regarding media interest in the escalation. But does it really matter? At the end of the day a climb is a climb. The way I see it, the National Library will allow me to pursue my challenge of a 'Tour of Paris by Façades'. And I like climbing. Why deprive me of earning my living in this way? There have been thousands of climbs during my career, and of course they were not all major ones. Far from it. Generally, when tackling a cliff, the rock climber initially exploits the most beautiful routes in his area, then, if he wishes to progress, widens his radius of action to other routes that are harder or less beautiful. Climbing rocks and climbing buildings of course cannot really be directly compared. Nature is a flood of chaotic mathematics quite different from the order of manmade structures. Nature does majestic things. If a line visually has no purity, it can however reveal some surprising movements, unexpected difficulties and generate some unforgettable experiences and enjoyment. And there are some manmade structures that approach this randomness, this uncertainty. The National Library doesn't really fall into this category – but its lines lack purity so I can probably learn a lot from them.

Again, gauging the activity at the location is imperative if this is going to work out. We eye up the construction site, which is hemmed in by a high fence. Hundreds of workers go about their business, trekking backwards and forwards across the mud to the overwhelming noise of machinery. As one would expect, the access points are strictly guarded by a group of sentries, and all in all about thirty security agents protect the complex. I seek an answer but there seems no obvious way to get past all this and then scale the building without getting caught. We must think laterally and hatch a plan.

We hit a bar and over a few drinks we brainstorm different ways to achieve our mission impossible. As the evening progresses we rule out many harebrained approaches and home in on the only realistic solution – the eternal male fascination with pretty girls. Whether we like it or not, men become totally irrational and ineffective when enchanted by an attractive woman…

Isabelle, an exceptionally good-looking friend, accompanies me to the National Library the next day. She is armed with an absolutely devastating miniskirt. Standing back from the entrance of the construction site, I watch her walk away, beautiful as an angel. Only three guards defend this door, not enough to resist my secret weapon.

Behind her glasses, a coy Isabelle plays hard. She looks just like the French actress Isabelle Adjani from the movie *Fatal Summer*. As an 'ardent admirer of architecture', she would like to get a little closer to this magnificent building, if only these charming young men would agree to accompany her. She twirls her hair and bats her lashes, tilts and totters on her high heels. This is the most exciting thing to happen to these guys for months and they are going crazy. And no wonder: her miniskirt seems even higher than one of my own escalations! Compare delightful Isabelle with the depressing catwalk within – drab overalls, fluorescent jackets, safety helmets and grubby wheelbarrows. The only skin bared is the hairy upper buttocks of grunting builders, an abhorrent sight and not something that a red-blooded Frenchman gets excited about. Isabelle has caused quite a stir and the guards are tripping over themselves to escort her around. No one wants to be left behind. All of them leave the gate and, as if by magic, the way is free.

Isabelle has trailblazed a huge gaping hole for me to exploit. I approach carefully and enter the site, cross the flight of steps and nip round the base of the library. It seems effectively okay for climbing but I cannot define which technique I need to use. It is impossible to try the slightest movement in my cowboy boots. *Merde!* I need my slippers and they are in the car. There are workers around me but everyone is on autopilot and nobody pays any attention to my presence. I check out the surroundings and there's still no one in front of the entrance. So I walk out naturally, whistling, then I come back and head towards the library again. This time guards are around and they immediately recognise me. Four monsters approach. I back off a little… it looks like it is not going to be my day…

But no! Pats on the back, laughter, autographs… I am totally taken aback by their friendliness and their cooperation. These smiling hulks seem proud that I am interested in the François Mitterrand Library and I thus pursue the visit in a very official way, as a VIP. I indicate to them that I have already spent quite a while outside the surrounding wall. Accompanied by my unexpected friends for the day I walk everywhere, and see the whole site – even the roof! This is immeasurably better than a simple stake-out or even the most successful covert inspection; this is a full conducted tour, with commentary and technical details. Only a slide show is missing to complete the picture! On top of all this, one of the guards desperately wants to take photos of the ascent. For me, the more madmen there are, the better. I explain the problems inherent in this kind of escalation. Structurally there are no major problems, but there is an environmental issue which concerns me – there is an ever-present cloud of airborne dust which settles in a thin film on the structure. It will be necessary to be vigilant – but with an army of vigilantes, I quip, for sure there is no need to worry. They enjoy a good laugh, a guard remains a regular guy regardless of the uniform. After a distribution of my signed picture postcards, I return to the agency, satisfied with my day. For once, the photographers will be able to take their images as they like and from where they like, allowing for artistic freedom and, one would guess, much better pictures. Gamma's staff sit up and take notice: this could be a story after all. On Saturday, the climb; on Wednesday I'll grace the pages of *Paris Match*. Good work!

On Saturday morning I arrive genially by car at the same front entrance I had sneaked through a few days before. I wish to park inside the surrounding wall in order to unload all the equipment belonging to the photographers, who this time number quite a few. Two large guards approach and tell me to get lost. I lower my car window, explain the situation and ask to speak to my pals inside. But it seems that I no longer have friends in there, even if certain faces are familiar. The National Library, still in a state of construction, has just been equipped with a vast network of security cameras. The guided tour I was given on my previous visit, complete with tips and a full photographic record of the site, was not appreciated by the security director who threatened to fire his employees if I ever carried out my escalation project. In a country with more than five million unemployed, blackmail in the workplace is regrettably a commonplace reality.

Bewildered, I lose my usual sense of humour and do not know how to answer. If I get out of the car, they threaten to release their salivating Alsatians. I look into their eyes and realise it is useless trying to negotiate with them. I collide with walls thicker than those of the library. I reverse the car in a huff. I do not want to play any more. Not for the moment anyway…

The further I drive from the library, the madder I get. Did I really think I could rely on guards whose duty it is to prevent the kind of acts I like to commit? Really, this whole thing is my own fault. I have been way too naive!

I drive back towards the agency, in an almost deserted office district of Paris, but I cannot quite bring myself to ditch the project. At first I was not particularly motivated about climbing the National Library, but now I take it as a personal affair, as a matter of honour. My decision is made.

Same guys. Same hour. Same project. Illegal version. My car turns around and heads back.

This time I take care to park a safe distance away. In another car, Gilles, a journalist from *Paris Match*, is on the watch. His job is to indicate to me the exact moment when the guards are as far as possible from the attack point of the building. This morning's escalation gets a little more complicated – I have to leap over a fence, run 100 metres, dash up the stairs of the square, sprint again for about 50 metres and then ascend the 90-metre walls of the National Library... all this while avoiding the clutches of the motivated and alert security guards. Rugby is not my favourite sport and the climb so far remains largely hypothetical.

Gilles waves at me from the car. It's my signal! I run to the fence, which is too high to jump over: I have to climb it. But because of my weight, it bends and flexes wildly, bowing back the wrong way. Confronted with this miserable spectacle, Gilles signals me to stop. Right now the exploit looks like more a charade. Imagine a guy reddened with exertion, suspended from a drunken fence creaking over the pavement of a Paris boulevard. It's not a scene that either he or I would want photographed. Few people would be impressed with this climbing episode.

I feel silly, this situation is ridiculous. I release myself from this elastic fence and retreat. And it's just as well, for the guards are patrolling again and we must wait once more. Ten minutes later, Gilles gestures to me that the way is free again. This time, I decide to climb the phone mast against which the barrier is anchored – then, without a sound, I pulverise the 100 metres world record. I navigate the stairs and make the home straight. But the cat is out of the bag! I don't look back but I am fully aware of the surrounding commotion and yelling. When I get to the base of the attack point and begin my first movements, the guards are only a dozen metres away from me. *Sorry guys, no time to greet you. If you want to exchange pleasantries, the meeting is at the summit!* I fly away. Luckily, thanks to their earlier kindness I know this building and the structure allows me to take off without losing a second. I am out of reach, safe. On the ground, the guards – who my ego has just put out of work – roar, scream and shout. Many of them tear off to intercept me at the top.

I climb steadily and easily with no hiccups or problems. The dust is a little slippery but nothing major. It's a pleasant climb and I gain more insights into city escalations. At the summit, a large contingent of security guards wait for me, faces like thunder. I don't think they are too happy to see me here today.

"Hey guys!" I say as I throw a leg over the top, "It looks like I am faster than you!" My attempt to calm the atmosphere seems to inflame it. I hardly end my sentence when I am almost floored by a punch. I try to stay on my feet as a rain of punches and kicks come down with a real street fighter edge. Rather than fly off the handle and try to play the superhero, I do my best to avoid the worst of it. Simultaneous punches coming in from opposite directions are the only things keeping me off the deck. They really mean it! It appears that I am in for a painful finale. But within a few seconds the cavalry arrives, better late than never, and police inspectors pull me out of this tight spot.

In front of the police, the guards are suddenly urbane and professional. They bow and relent. The police act swiftly. There has been a disturbance and I do not look like a law-abiding citizen right now. For the first time in France, the police handcuff me and frog-march me away. With the security guards abandoning their posts there is a good presence of television cameras on the square below. I am a little tender and dazed but I realise it all augurs well for a media success. It has worked. *Paris Match*, a genuine barometer of fame, will print a four-page spread on this visually dramatic episode. It's quite a scoop. The escalation of the National Library will serve as springboard to better, higher, bigger and more beautiful things. After Elf Aquitaine and the National Library, I really can seize the day.

At the police station, the inspectors remove my handcuffs. They tell me the move was necessary in order to calm the guards who, according to the police, would not be losing their jobs. Any blackmail would have been purely 'extra motivation' on the part of the security director. Of course they saw the hammering I received, and they ask if I want to press charges against the security services. They explain that if I do, I will have to go to hospital for a check-up, but since there are no visible marks or injuries it would be a bit difficult to pursue. I am not that bothered about the whole thing and tell them to forget about it. Amicably we leave it at that. They get on with the paperwork and leave me in my cell.

Later, as usual, I engage in a couple of exercises to pass the time. This catches the attention of one of the inspectors and triggers some good-natured competitive banter between us. He loves to work out and wants to outdo me. The inspector dashes into a series of drives on a door frame and looks satisfied with his performance. Sure, he is fit, but he can't match the ace up my sleeve: a beautiful perfectly horizontal board. I suspend myself from the door frame and draw my legs up so they are parallel to the floor. My whole body straightens out, completely horizontal, hence the name of the exercise. I hover there in a totally unnatural pose, suddenly resembling a madman afflicted by some sort of supernatural possession. I must admit that I find this exercise really difficult – it takes a big effort. Breathlessly I drop to the floor with a grin. This manoeuvre leaves the smiling inspector some work for years to come.

I am later released without any complications, free to pursue my next objective. Thanks to the success of the National Library ascent, an escalation of the Mercuriales Towers suddenly becomes much more interesting to the media. The images we achieved were well received by the public, and copies of the magazine sold well, of course the bottom line for the editor in chief. News teams are keen to find a nice story to slot in at the end of their bulletins. Regardless of external interest, the project is very important to me, I guess as a sort of pilgrimage. Since I do not wish to upset the guards again, I decide to ask the security officials for a licence to climb in these terms:

"With or without your agreement, I am going to climb the Mercuriales. If I can thoroughly inspect the building, if I can obtain technical information on the solidity of the structure or the hazards she may have, the ascent will go smoothly."

The security director decides to slip into the discussion that a part of the structure has just been redone because of solidity problems. However, he does not deign to tell me which face it is.

"Never mind," I maintain gaily, "I shall climb one of the faces at random." Nobody can prevent me from doing it. Considering the modest load I am going to impose upon the tower, the risks I flirt with are comparably tiny. Unless this modern tower is in terrible shape it is unlikely to shed panels so easily. The news is not especially welcome but it's not the end of the world. The security director of course has his own agenda and tells me that the building is dangerous. I tell him he should demolish it then. He shrugs and the meeting ends.

A ground inspection reveals that the building's exterior panels are hung on only by hooks, as on the Grande Arche of La Défense, but the solidity of the tower is doubtless.

Go! I vault up the Mercuriales. The security director obviously did not take me seriously. Too bad. Curiously, the guards seem very open-minded – none of them give chase and they even let a photographer work on the rooftop. The window frames are only clipped on to the structure and are not very sturdy. I inspect them carefully and treat them with respect. They could unhinge quite easily, but they are still robust enough for someone as light as me, who knows how to balance his body and properly distribute his weight. The Mercuriales offer a good workout and I make it all the way with only a light sweat. Thirty-five minutes, 35 floors, rather appropriate I think.

However, during my escalation of this corporate grey monolith, there is an unforeseen occurrence. One of the Mercuriales security guards had something of a nervous breakdown. A journalist once wrote that the emotional problems connected with my ropeless escalations are not mine, but actually belong to those on the ground. People certainly react differently when they see a man outside a tower a few hundred metres in the air. Maybe a psychologist could analyse your personality by such a response. I was surprised to witness this bear-like man truly sobbing at what I was doing. He honestly bawled, he was in such a state. I was quite lost at this reaction. I have no idea whether he was crying because he was artistically moved by seeing something he felt was incredible, or because he was terrified I was going to fall. Maybe seeing a man deliberately put his life in danger is too much for some. But don't people realise that they take risks every day? How close are we to a fatal head-on collision every time we step into our cars? Think of all the vehicles we drive past on any given day. Just a slight tug on the wheel and our lives would end. Each car, each day, all that risk adds up. What if the front tyre of a bus blew out as it approached a zebra crossing? Rarely will you see a man crying at the kerbside due to the traffic. I get down safely without arrest or fuss, though I see several guards comforting and consoling him. Oh well, I hope he is okay now.

Elf, the National Library, the Mercuriales... what's next?

Act 2: TF1

Local television channel Metropole 6, or M6 as it is commonly known, had offered me the opportunity of climbing the façade of its building for a special show. Their building was particularly ugly so I had declined the invitation. In contrast, the new premises of channel TF1, a magnificent dark glass cylinder on the banks of the River Seine, had appealed to me but regrettably nobody there had implored me to take their outside staircase. In spite of its weak height, approximately 60 metres, the idea of going up TF1 particularly motivated me because the French anchor Patrick Poivre d'Arvor and the TV host Christophe Dechavanne had enthusiastically discussed a number of my escalations. TF1 had built itself a reputation of adventure and dabbled with the spectacular, and it seemed much more appropriate to climb for these guys. In addition, the challenge was actually very tough. My eyes flickered up and down images of their headquarters, searching for clues. From what I could ascertain, it would not be easy to conquer this tower. Soon Dechavanne got wind of my thoughts and I was invited on for a show – not for a conventional interview, but for a televised climb.

So I travel 600 kilometres north from my hometown to Paris and test the location with my climbing slippers, observing the lines of the building. I plan my route up and consider the movements I will employ. Everything seems to be going well: the building is climbable, the channel optimistic. And then, before we even start, the project sinks into oblivion – Dechavanne pulls the plug on it, telling me he doesn't want to set a bad example to French youth! He says that if we televise me going up their headquarters, somewhere a teenager will try to copy me and will fall to his death. There would be a young French corpse, a grieving family, and Dechavanne would feel responsible. Dechavanne believes he is saving a life somewhere, saving someone who will not even know that they owe him their life. My answer to this? Bullshit! But there is no changing his mind, he believes a teenager's life is at stake and I am left high and dry.

But it is too late now. I am here and so is the tower. A gauntlet, once thrown down, cannot be taken back. I have already done my homework. I feel very confident about the climb and I do not try to hide it. Everyone knows what my next move will be. I approach the building and the TF1 guards intercept me, nice and playful.

"Don't even think about climbing here, Alain! Naughty naughty, no?"

"We shall see tomorrow, my friends…"

These cordial relations reveal a certain confidence on both sides. An exquisite game of hide and seek is about to begin. The dimensions of the TF1 Tower are laughable when compared to the Elf Tower, and security is not as stringent, but I must still take all threats seriously even though I calculate I only need a few seconds to become inaccessible. These guys are very capable of catching me and terminating my escalation so once again it is necessary to be a little sly. For the occasion, two well built pals from the suburbs, Thierry and Bambi, will accompany me in case events transpire against us – guards against guards.

The stage is set and it's a perfect day. Our car approaches. All in all, our team includes three vehicles and a motor scooter. Thierry and Bambi arrive first on the scene, casually, acting like tourists or groupies. The second car is to drop me off while the *Paris Match* journalist parks some distance away from the front. On the scooter is my sister. Her duty? A live commentary of events via her mobile phone to my wife back in Valence. Nicole is happy at home with what is now three kids but as always she takes a keen interest in how things are going.

I glance at my fellow conspirators and watch as everyone settles into position. Without even realising it we are beginning to perfect these stealthy attacks and becoming more and more skilled at outwitting security. Even before the car grinds to a halt, I spring out 20 metres from my target. Slightly withdrawn from the stage, Thierry and Bambi each casually smoke a cigarette. Security, on the alert since dawn, is waiting for me. The chess game we have undertaken is in many ways very similar to Morpion Solitaire, the game practised by generations of pupils on school benches. The one who begins the game usually wins – if he does not make a false move. I strike first.

I run the short distance to the building and start the escalation exactly where a pair of rails provide a comfy grip. Without warning, two metres from the ground, a hand seizes me! My right foot, snatched by an invisible force, tries to wriggle free. A huge weight drags me downwards and also backwards. I clench my fingers to resist the substantial downwards pull. My flailing legs are now free of the structure completely, my hands clamped on for dear life. If I lose my grip in this posture, I must be ready for yet another broken nose. But then, and I do not know how, I manage to escape. I race up three more metres before taking a brief break on an electronic surveillance camera, my forearms aching from the strain. I am not used to a violent intrusion to my climbing like this and now the lactic acid is coursing through my muscles too close to the departure point. The struggle was so severe that I still wonder how I got away. Right now I feel invincible, muscular, unstoppable, and my confidence rockets. In fact, I later learn that I owe my liberation to the robust intervention of Bambi and Thierry who took out a guard who had been hiding round the corner just two metres from me!

From my look-out post, identical to the view from the monitors in the CCTV room, I see them sprinting away from the entire security force. TF1 has sounded the alarm. Desperately outrunning a swarm of angry security guards, my pals bolt towards the escape car belonging to the *Paris Match* journalist who, seeing the crowd of aggravated guards sweeping down on him, shouts: "Hey! I don't know these guys!"

Too late. There is panic on board, the press ship sinks by all the hatches. Right now the battle is being fought elsewhere. I am in the clear and can pursue my escalation in peace.

The ascent is testing but relatively straightforward and good fun. Due to its moderate height, the escalation takes me just 15 minutes. I clamber over the top to meet the security troop. Disappointed, and a little hurt to have been cheated, they remain courteous. After the earlier skirmish, plus the battle by the car, the reception could have been much less cordial and much more physical. None too pleased, they detain me until the cops arrive.

When the cops get there, the pissed-off guards raise a complaint for assault and forced entry. Logical, I suppose, I can't really argue with that. Two police officers arrest me and it's off to the station again. Once we arrive they sit me down for the nicest interrogation of my career. They took me back to the station via a tremendously circuitous route I could have entitled 'the complete tour of police stations of Paris and everywhere else'. I think they just wanted a nice chat with their friends and a leisurely day.

One question torments me though – who raised the complaint? Was it the channel management or was it the security? If it is the management, then this is really a joke. They are supposed to be the channel of boldness, adventure and fresh ideas – if not always the channel of the best taste. TF1 is a channel of the young, a tabloid channel which continuously sacrifices ethics for audience ratings. Would they really mount a complaint for an escalation which they could have broadcast for their adventure show *Ushuaïa* or their reality show *Everything is Possible*? TF1 trumpet my climbs and are always behind me when they report me climbing somebody else's building. Frankly I cannot believe it. Paradoxically, this media escalation remains completely unnoticed. I understand there are no images, with the photographer submerged in a mass brawl. And of course the other channels have found the story too 'sensitive' to report on, not wanting to upset fellow media bosses or invite controversy. At the police station, I learn that the cops enjoyed the stunt we pulled over the security, overcoming the reputation of immunity that TF1 had acquired. In later years, having climbed a lot of buildings built by the Bouygues group, of which TF1 is part, I knocked on the door of the parent company and the reception was decidedly cool. Where was the sense of humour of the producers of this channel's hilarious satirical shows, the *Grosses Têtes* or the *Bébête Show*? I struggled to find it after I climbed the TF1 Tower!

Two days after the escalation I bump into Gérard Carreyrou, presenter of political debates at TF1. Two curvaceous admirers jiggle towards him in search of autographs. He tells them to ask me instead, making many complimentary remarks. I discuss the climb and the arrest at the headquarters with him for some minutes. Soon it is clear what happened – the security department raised the complaint and the company for the most part knew nothing about the episode.

A fortnight after this encounter, I am invited to a very posh cocktail party for the launch of LCI, the new 24-hour information channel overseen by TF1. A week is a very long time in media and politics and in no time everything has changed. *Paris Match* dedicated six pages to the story, with a beautiful double-page photo perfectly highlighting the TF1 Tower and its logo. Parisian celebrities and socialites are there and I help myself to petits fours and champagne. I have chosen to dress from head to toe in leather for this chic party. I know nobody there, except through my TV screen. Before long Corinne Bouygues, the advertising manager, greets me.

"When I saw you climbing by my office window, I was so surprised that I called Mougeotte (vice chairman of the NDLT channel) to find out whether it was for an organised show or not!"

There are many bigwigs milling around with their sparkling glasses. The Minister of Justice, Jacques Toubon, seems to know a lot about me and obviously knows a thing or two about the courts. This is someone who can teach me a lot about the judicial risks of my little excursions. Between sips of Champagne, he confides that my escalations are neither legal, nor really illegal. I'm involved in full legal vagueness. It is all down to interpretation, but that is in itself not really enough for a jailable conviction. I ask whether things might change now there is awareness about such behaviour; behaviour that the authorities obviously take exception to. He scoffs at the idea then adds, smiling, "Come on! Parliament is not going to discuss an Alain Robert law!"

For sure, there are more important things for Parliament to worry about. The power of the law will only be brought to bear if the state feels threatened. But television... we cannot imagine the power TV stations can have. Just like the Roman emperors, who decided life or death for the gladiators, television can decide your existence. It is quite amazing how your life is transformed when you become recognised in public. Sure, it can be flattering, but one negative comment by a journalist in the papers or on TV and it is amazing how the daggers can come out, how pliable public opinion is. Some individuals I know in the public eye feel it is absolutely necessary to fortify their homes like Fort Knox in an effort to stem the acute focus of attention. This attention encompasses the whole spectrum of human emotions. The most important thing is to remain the same, to remember who you really are and not to betray yourself or try to impress.

For example, for *Nulle Part Ailleurs*, a very popular primetime show on NDLT, I found it quite natural to arrive at the studio through the window. I didn't want to walk onto the stage and bow like an actor or celebrity, it would be unnatural for me. I am a climber, that's all. Unfortunately, for a different show on Canal +, the studios were situated in the basement and required a more conventional entrance. Another time I made an appearance on a popular late night show. Here I experienced the dark side of entertainment, where the aim is often to embarrass or humiliate fellow guests. There are plenty of egos out there, all competing for attention and adulation. The trick lies in being able to remain yourself when provoked, but also to push forward in front of them and if possible, make the other guests shut up. It's not always easy, of course, but a good sense of humour goes a long way. Even if I do not like this stupid game, I think I can handle it when someone attacks me. Not with Machiavellianism but with sincerity. Okay, okay, some could lay the accusation that with my clothes I also try to draw attention. Sorry guys, but I like my non-conformist look, my snakeskin jackets, my Indian jewels and my long hair. What's the problem? I dress this way every day. I like it.

Television has been good fun though too. It's nice to have a whole TV crew pointing at you, with everyone showing sincere interest in what you say! Let's just say this disproportionate interest in our words or opinions is hardly normal and is very flattering. Among all the TV shows I have participated in, my favourite remains the broadcast with Michel Drucker. Drucker is one of France's most influential journalists, but truly, I very much appreciate the guy. He is simple, human and relaxed. The show we did was fun and our exchange of questions and answers appeared in the 'best-of' rerun.

A week or two later, television is again at the forefront of my mind. In fact it is at the forefront of my forearm. At the behest of the TV guys, in this case Canal +, I aim to overcome the Crystal Tower in Grenelle. I am to escalate this 27-storey building on the banks of the Seine with a clip-on microphone and a small video camera attached to my wrist, so the audience can get up close and personal with the escalation. Curiously, the channel management are not afraid of the illegal character of the ascent. Rafts of cameras are fitted with wide-angle panoramic lenses to amplify the impression of space. Thankfully they do not need a running commentary – I only have to add a small personal touch with live dialogue every now and then. I am very uncomfortable carrying the camera, as it is most distracting and interferes greatly with my movements. Also I am not in the habit of talking during my escalations. Canal + however get what they want – nice dramatic pictures from many angles, from the river, from the air and also an angle never filmed before: from the wrist of a solo climber.

The images might have been much more spectacular if, once I reached the summit, I had not narrowly avoided a fall. After successfully navigating the vertical bulk of the structure, I was faced with a short but slippery 45-degree section leading to the pyramidal summit, a few metres above. But on this oblique surface, I could not find a single grip. The only feature was a joint protruding by a mere two millimetres which I had to alternately push against with my hands and feet for leverage. Tricky but just about manageable… until one of my slippers gave way. A fall directly filmed by a wrist-borne camera and transmitted right across France! Sky, window pane, flailing arm, sky, window pane, sky... silence… shock in the studio… dramatic pause upon the windswept top of a skyscraper… Fortunately the fall terminated on a horizontal area between the pyramid and the precipitous edge.

"I am okay! Hey! We must have blown the audience away with that one!

I bet they loved it!" Not really sensible though. Thanks to this escalation I have learnt not to sacrifice too much to the screen. Pictures are great but they can come at a very high price if I let the directors and producers dictate my climbs. I really ought to have learnt this by now.

Act 3: The Eiffel Tower

The escalation of the Eiffel Tower has long been a classic among French, and indeed international, rock climbers. Illegality does not stop those who, by night, often after two or three glasses of wine too many, want to horse around on the iconic Parisian landmark. Notre-Dame Cathedral is also appreciated by revellers in spite of its evident fragility, perhaps drawing attention mostly due to its famous bell tower and the literary antics of Quasimodo. Beyond the anecdotal, the escalation of the Eiffel Tower is nevertheless rarely accomplished. Generally, rock climbers start their ascent at the first floor and finish at the second. A nice after-dinner stroll you might say.

My ascent was not exceptional, even if it was a matter of climbing the whole 300 metres of scrap metal which, according to urban myth, have been sold over and over again in a good dozen scams to gullible businessmen. I had no project, no agenda. I wanted to mark the New Year by climbing this mythical building, just for the pleasure of it. I did not want to simply eat a dozen oysters before kissing everyone, as I did every other year. I wanted a little solitude at this special moment.

In the daytime, the Eiffel Tower does not catch a climber's eye, nor inspire him. The enormous mess of steel girders makes it look like an immense ladder, without any real technical difficulty. But by night, the tower wraps itself in mystery, shadows and magic. It becomes a wondrous labyrinth, a staircase to the stars.

On December 31st 1996, snow had invaded the capital and smothered everything. A Siberian cold transformed the city into an icy wilderness. Paris was hidden, reclaimed. One wouldn't have been surprised to see the wolves of Serge Reggiani's song. This night was also chosen for an anti-terrorism and crowd control exercise which had spread 5000 supplementary policemen in strategic places, the Eiffel Tower of course being one of them. GIGN, France's elite counter-terrorism and hostage rescue unit, was regularly engaged in climbing training around France. A few days before the New Year a GIGN specialist had bizarrely told the tower's managers and a few friends that he had heard of my desire to spend New Year's Eve on the Eiffel Tower. How on Earth did he know that? The project was supposed to remain secret because it was a personal ascent and no media had been informed. Very few trusted friends knew. I am no longer paranoid enough to believe that my phone was being tapped but this anecdote remains enigmatic to say the least.

This evening my friend Stef, a doctor and amateur photographer, wished to accompany me. Stef felt like something a bit different this year too. A little before they locked the elevators, he had gone to the second floor to settle down discreetly in the stairwell to await my passage. My years of experience in the high mountains allowed me to choose the most suitable equipment. The temperature was an aggressive minus 15 degrees Celsius with a wind chill effect which made it very cold up there on the exposed frigid metal. It was impossible to use rock climbing boots as they had no dexterity. Slippers too would not be up to the job. They would be too thin and would freeze and crack on the spot, possibly sticking and ripping while also exposing my feet to sub-zero metal. A pair of sporting shoes, a decent pair of warm trousers, a polar fur-lined jacket, a second Gore-Tex overcoat and a pair of fleece gloves made up my equipment.

It is 11:15pm sharp, time to start. I decide to avoid the foot of the tower fitted with a pocket-sized police station and attack by the east pillar instead, but the wind has encrusted iced snow on this oblique part, making the escalation particularly delicate, perhaps even impossible. I attempt to ascend but after just two metres, I descend again in a woeful slide. It's just bad luck… But after several fruitless attempts, my climber's instincts resurface: if the east pillar is plastered in ice then the west one must be dry, assuming the wind has been constant. It seems logical. Some more warm tea and here I am, ready to go.

As expected, the west pillar is more forgiving and I quickly leave the launch pad. It is now a matter of briskness because security can easily apprehend me at the first floor, or indeed at the second one. Once I am past the second floor I should be okay as the third is at the summit and there is little chance that anyone can interfere with me once I make the spire. At first the savage metal robs the heat from my hands and I have to add a pair of mittens, a second protective layer for my frozen fingers. But soon I fall into my stride and I warm up, ditching the cumbersome things.

The legs of the tower begin to converge at the first floor, a critical stage I must pass swiftly if I am to evade capture. In spite of the icy contact with the metal, I remove my gloves as I need the grip. My hands feel fine, as I am generating a lot of heat with my efforts, and under my polar jacket it is like a steam room. The arches curl over and overhang here and I eventually find myself upside down. But the structure is generous and supportive and I surpass it with few problems.

Having passed the first floor, the security guys detect me. A few yells ring out and it looks like the negotiation to reach the second level is going to be tough. They want me to descend immediately to the first floor – but I tell them I haven't finished yet. In the nearby staircase they shadow my progress and put me under prodigious pressure. One guy wants to kill me, the other one resents me because, as he says, he is risking his life because of me just after his wife has delivered a child. Is the night so cold that he has to tremble like that?

At the second floor, as expected, they lash out, swing, grope and grab at me! The pressure rises a notch. They want nothing other than to fight with me, my safety is not an issue for them. I have no choice but to stop the adventure as they seem capable of making me fall.

"Okay, okay, okay guys, I surrender..."

To get closer, I cross the struts horizontally and join a beam leading to the stairs and the guards. My head sinks slightly with disappointment. I quit. The atmosphere relaxes, the pressure loosens, their shoulders drop a little. Détente. I edge closer along the beam towards my satisfied captors. And then I fly away.

"Bye bye, see you on the third floor! Happy new year!"

They seem even more upset now. I continue my climb and take in the view. It must be around midnight now: the big reconciliation hour, peace, forgiveness and goodwill to all men. But not for the tower guards who are raving lunatics, utterly hysterical. The air is crisp and sounds travel for miles. Their roaring must be heard from the Basilique du Sacre Coeur to La Défense. Goodwill to all men? For sure, our watches do not indicate the same hour.

A little higher and my sleight of hand does no favours for my professional doctor and amateurish photographer friend tucked into the stairwell. Stumbling upon him in an excitable state, the guards assail him with gusto. Later, Stef will tell me that their breath was loaded with festive alcohol, which could explain their quasi-surrealist nervousness.

I peer between my feet. I can hear much of the commotion from here. It sounds like Stef's new year celebrations are not so enjoyable this year. But for my part, life is beautiful. The structure narrows and the escalation changes, becoming more aerial and exposed, and more silent. The setting is wonderful, the view over the snow-clad capital is hypnotising. I climb up rung by rung absorbing the magic of midnight Paris.

Below the final overhang, a few metres before the summit, I hesitate and wonder which method I shall use. This is the difficult part. And just to spice it up a little, the police are waiting for me. At the midnight hour at the icy pinnacle of the Eiffel Tower, a discussion occurs between climber and cops.

"Okay, I am coming out, but promise me I will not be struck by the guards!"

"No problem, we are in charge here."

The security lads, demoralised, promise me they will catch me some time. But tomorrow is another day. I climb up the last wire netting then jump over onto the top balcony. Firemen rub me down with blankets.

"Thank you very much, but I am actually very hot. But you guys must be frozen!"

At the small police station in one of the four feet of the tower, the guards want to press charges, but my dishevelled and limping doctor friend can testify to the fact they are completely drunk and were acting very dangerously. In addition, he could also press charges for assault and battery... It all balances out so no charges are pressed and the cops, who aren't in the mood for busting anyone tonight, send us on our way.

The ascent of the Eiffel Tower in these wintry conditions on New Year's Eve, by myself with neither crowd nor media, barely disturbed by a couple of intoxicated bully boys, remains a great recollection. Ideally I would have preferred a glass of Champagne at the summit with Stef, and perhaps to nibble on a piece of sausage. It is good for the soul to sit on the top of a mountain at sunset, or as the moonlight gently illuminates your face. Everyone should be able to savour these magic moments. The authorities did not let me enjoy my new year this time. Too bad.

The Eiffel Tower may be the most famous historical monument but it is not the only one worth escalating in Paris. Notre-Dame Cathedral and the Sacré Coeur have already received a number of guests. But strangely, two beautiful buildings of weak dimensions had not attracted anyone yet: the Obelisk at the Place de la Concorde and the column in the Place Vendôme. Beyond the technical aspect of both escalations (they are much more complex than they appear), their great locations in the city and their captivating histories confer them a particular charm. I couldn't resist either of them and spontaneously climbed these two pillars without any plan at all. Why did I do this? It was love at first sight. While others feel compelled to photograph such a handsome feature, I feel compelled to climb it. But since both actions are so modest it is only a short-term love affair, a tryst.

The 3,500-year-old Luxor Obelisk set in the Place de la Concorde is only 23 metres high but it is not at all easy to get your hands on. To protect it from vandalism it is placed on top of a seven-metre pedestal and these first seven metres are completely smooth, flat and impossible to climb. However I once noted there was a small cable running up one side of the pedestal: a wire which was needed to provide electricity to a set of lights which would illuminate the Obelisk at night. From atop this pedestal the Egyptian jewel would be accessible. Curious, I tugged on this cable, testing its strength. A judder and a tempest of dust advised me to proceed no further. The wire was clearly unsafe and, sadly, giving up seemed more reasonable. Too bad, because once the pedestal was crossed, the following 20 metres of immortal red-granite hieroglyphs would certainly have led me to the summit, in the heart of the most beautiful square in the world. But with no safe way onto the pedestal this would not feature in my tour of façades that year.

I return there one Sunday afternoon in 1998. In Paris and with nothing to lose I venture to the Place de la Concorde for a second look at the Obelisk. The temptation is still there – and so is that temperamental and unreliable cable. I remember my abandoned attempt a few years beforehand. Back then I decided that if I grabbed it incorrectly it could easily snap off, perhaps taking some of the lights with it – landing me back on the pavement and in deep shit. Maybe I had been a little too cautious?

I step over and can't resist having a little tug at it. It seems to be okay. I know it is a bit of a gamble but I decide to give it a try. Gingerly I ascend one of the seven metres. It is a bit scary but I manage to take a few steps up before jumping free to the ground. I take another look at everything then try to climb two metres – and surprisingly it still holds okay. I drop to the ground again, this time emboldened. A third check of the cable and the lights, which I really don't want to fall on top of me, then I go up again and this time reach three metres. From this point there is a slight overhang but from where I am I decide that I should be able to overcome it.

So later that night I go back, check the coast is clear, and grapple with the cable again. I pull myself up on the cable gently so as not rip the light fittings off, and after a quick few strides I overcome the overhang. Upon the pedestal, my tentative fingers at last come into contact with the timeless Obelisk. Of course I dare not damage this magnificent pillar and inspect it meticulously before deciding whether to go ahead. The engravings feel strong and secure, being carved in granite, and I consider it extremely unlikely that they would crumble or give way. Such an occurrence would lead to a potential tragedy for me but more so for this ancient work of art.

Satisfied that climbing it is feasible I insert my fingertips into the Obelisk and lift myself upwards. My fingers and feet find useful notches and grooves, and within a couple of easy minutes I reach the summit. Floodlit by the lights I had earlier feared would crash onto my head, I stand atop this historic landmark like Admiral Nelson upon Nelson's Column in Trafalgar Square, and gaze around the Place de la Concorde. As my eyes sweep the scene below I see that I did have an audience after all. One solitary figure had been watching me: a beggar. The Obelisk has no doubt seen much over the millennia – armies, pharaohs and emperors – but I doubt it has ever seen any scene quite like this.

The column in the Place Vendôme is 44 metres high and a monument to the great victory achieved by Napoleon's army at Austerlitz. It has a slight green copper tint to it, as it is cast from the bronze of 133 cannons captured from the enemy. This proud column, vaguely resembling a metallic lighthouse, also gave me a headache.

One day, passing unwittingly by the Place Vendôme, I had hopped out of my car. It was deep winter, with a frosty gentle wind, and night had fallen particularly early this day. Out of pure curiosity I had approached to observe the reliefs and was intrigued and inspired by what I saw. Without a second thought I return to the car, put on my slippers and attack.

There is a randomness to the column quite separate to what one would expect in other man-made features. Every move is different, involving a search for the best grips in the same way one would vary one's position when tackling cliffs. But this assault is in near darkness, with only the diffused glow from streetlamps to guide me. My fingers freeze against the icy metal. On a building, once you have worked out your preferred climbing method, the difficulty lies more in duration required to defeat it since the structure is uniform and the pattern of movements is replicated all the way up. Here, every step engenders particular hesitation and error because I am incapable of seeing and knowing which grip is really the best. But worst of all, I had not done my homework and had just taken off up this column, oblivious to the design of its pinnacle.

Unbeknown to me there was a little peaked roof topping the pillar. I discover this feature only when I get there, not the best time or place to consider such an obstacle. The final overhang is devoid of grips. It is frustrating to learn of this when you have climbed all the way up to the top of a column, but in such circumstances the wisest choice is to come down again. After some consideration this is what I do. Falling from 40 metres or 400 metres leads almost certainly to the same result: death. Or perhaps there is a small chance of incapacity, another kind of death. My wrists and knees, already damaged in my youth, would not support a significant fall. I am not a stuntman and the doctors have firmly told me that I am banned from falling. Solitary escalation requires a good understanding of danger, even if this column seems visually small. Without preliminary location research, the urban climber relies on instinct and fate. Knowing when to stop is above all knowing how to survive.

Act 4: The Montparnasse Tower

The Montparnasse Tower remains for me the project I had the most difficulty in accomplishing. Sometimes, even if we feel ready for a challenge, we discover much to our disenchantment that we just aren't. We can be outdone by events beyond our control, times when our motivation alone is not quite enough. And there are simply days when nothing goes as it should and one should be wise enough to walk away. But paradoxically it is also sometimes necessary to take a stand, despite everything that is thrown at you, because this resplendent 210-metre office skyscraper – puzzlingly regarded as the oldest modern high rise in Paris, and once the tallest in Western Europe – just had to be mine. However the victory was not at all simple.

My first attempt took place after I had abseiled down a façade of the Champs-Elysées for charity. The high-profile humanitarian event was to mark the opening of empty flats in the city to the homeless and was attended by Geneviève de Gaulle and Bernadette Chirac. Afterwards I met up with the patron of the operation, Bernadette Chirac, wife of future president Jacques Chirac who was then mayor of Paris. I told her that if this simple cobweb descent could bring such success then a more outlandish action would have a greater impact. How about Montparnasse? Her response was warm and her eyes twinkled at the proposal. In spite of the illegal nature of the escalation, she supported me by promising to contact the press, and immediately so. There's no time like the present!

I made the short journey through the capital in my little car. Objective: Montparnasse. The sky was typically Parisian, melancholy and brooding, but I did not care at all – the opportunity to take on Montparnasse with the blessing of the mayor's wife was there to be grasped. When I arrived, television teams were already on the scene. Cameramen, microphones, it was all happening. I remember being amazed at the efficiency of the mayor's wife. Surrounded by the watching press, I studied the building and prepared myself for the climb. And just as I started the escalation, it started raining, slowly at first, and then more vigorously. Within minutes it was a torrential downpour and the escalation became rather hazardous. I had had enough of this crappy weather and came to a halt. That's all folks... But there was virtually no one there to disappoint as almost everyone had left the scene. Like everyone else, I ran for cover and called it a day. So much for publicity and raising awareness for good causes.

I left it for a while and got on with other climbs, but the tower still stood there patiently for me. Montparnasse wasn't going away. Eventually I got another chance. The second escalation attempt was again attached to a humanitarian operation in support of the homeless. Unfortunately for me, these awareness campaigns tend to happen in the depth of winter to highlight their hour of need...

I approached the Montparnasse Tower again, wondering about fate. No rain this time but a horrible arctic wind and the perfect temperature for penguins. It looked bad. The rain on my first attempt was crippling to my progress and forced a U-turn; the cold this time was bearable but still uncomfortable. Technically the escalation was not extreme and the cold did not necessarily put me in danger. However, when our hands freeze, funny things happen. When we squeeze grips which we cannot feel any more, being sure of the grips' solidity requires a good dose of optimism.

Never mind, the grips were still easy. Few of the people around me thought it could be done. There was lots of head shaking and pointing upwards and gloomy doubt. It was everybody waiting for me to give up that finally decided it for me and spurred me to start the fight. I attacked the Montparnasse Tower for the second time. The sub-zero wind blasted me and I quickly lost all sensation in my hands and feet. In addition to the relentless biting wind and the contact with ice cold metal, my tight slippers and the bandages compressing my hands and fingers further restricted blood circulation. As I continued being assailed by the savage wind I was not sure how tight my grip was, so I tried to massage and resuscitate my hands. It was imperative to keep them functioning. I even tried banging them against the aluminium beams to warm them up.

At each floor, firemen followed in close contact. They were very concerned and wanted to bring me back with a gondola designed for window cleaners. With this wind though, anyone in the gondola would be more likely to be washing the windows of the building next door. Besides, it looked almost impossible for them to attempt anything of the kind: the gondola would have to make an entire horizontal tour of the tower to reach me and then go back. In these conditions that looked far harder than the actual escalation.

I continued on towards the summit through gales under the grey sky. This was certainly very challenging. At every level, behind the glazing, the tower employees showed me flashcards indicating which floor I had reached. Because of my pride, I had deliberately put myself in a predicament, a real battle lasting an hour and a half! But the smiles and messages motivated me and encouraged me not to forget that even if I was having a tough time of it, I would have the privilege that night of sleeping in a warm, cosy bed, contrary to the homeless people across the city.

In such conditions it takes a lot of effort to keep warm and mobile and I began to shiver, losing voluntary control of my muscles. Finally, and with great difficulty and relief, I made the summit. The first thing the firemen did was to offer me an orange juice and the second was to physically support me, such was the effect that fatigue and cold had on my arms and legs. Later, I had the fortune to meet them for a drink and a bit of horseplay at their station, thanks to a report covering the ascent in their internal review. Both sides enjoyed and learnt from the exchange.

But before all this I was at the police station, the epilogue of all my urban ascents. I must say that this time I was pleased to be there. Out of the wind and cold I could feel blood returning to my limbs, what an agonising relief! The sweet recollection of defrosting wounds… Torn by pain, I answered the classic questions laid out to me by the inspector, who is today a friend. Alain Moulin is the second most senior policeman in La Défense and has had the privilege of arresting me some twenty times so far. A fine and likeable man, he has even given me advice about climbing in his district. Personally I think this is a good way to start such intense relationships. An outside observer might have looked at me sitting there tense and twisted, my face contorted with pain, and assumed I was being subjected to police brutality. But maybe there was another type of pain in my twisted face too. The ascent of Montparnasse, even though achieved, remained for me unfinished. I could not help thinking that a 90-minute climb to the top of Montparnasse amounted to a yacht in the Sydney to Hobart race clocking up a finishing time of a fortnight. Yes, the challenge had been achieved, but without style or panache. I had lumbered, struggled, toiled, and though I had survived and made it to the top, I had to be virtually carried off it. This was not a real victory! It was thus written that I must take revenge.

The following year on a similar date, I leap out of a car with a cameraman running behind me gonzo style. I run through clumps of curious commuters towards the Montparnasse Tower. Before anyone knows it I am up the side of the building to applause from several onlookers below, plus the odd angry yell from the security contingent. This time I conquer Montparnasse in a healthy 35 minutes, bathed by a beautiful winter sun. Unlike my prior two climbs here, on this occasion there is no charity event or excuse and I am once again sent for a meeting with the judge.

For the record, the judge ordered me to pay 5000 francs for expenses incurred by the building management to check the structure for health and safety purposes, plus an identical sum for legal expenses incurred by the owners. We tried hard to mediate this figure and to reach a mutually acceptable agreement. Sadly many years have passed since then and we still haven't settled the matter.

Act 5: GAN Tower

Is my climbing jinx a purely Parisian thing? Not really. Nevertheless, another high rise building I took on here caused me severe problems. I attempted this climb in association with the newspaper *Le Réverbère*.

When I reflect it seems particularly weird that two cursed Parisian climbs occurred when highlighting the plight of the homeless, almost as if the tragedy of their fate touches all of us that cross their paths. A bitter feeling overwhelms me when I think of these disturbing coincidences. I climbed a dozen buildings in Paris without any problems, and then... these two failures, two serious alerts where things deteriorated quite rapidly.

I exit the subway at La Défense to find a comely form sprouting from the ground ahead. Before me is the majestic GAN Tower, 178 metres tall with a footprint the shape of a Greek cross. A multitude of turquoise windows, enamelling and opened and closed blinds give it an almost reptilian texture from a distance. From close up my keen eye spots a splendid crack a dozen or so centimetres wide running all the way up to the top. The GAN is a quite perfect building and despite the stream of commuters passing by, I don't waste a minute in trying out some climbing movements.

Classic foot jammings are made more complex by the lack of indispensable horizontal ledges one needs to rest upon. When there are no horizontal struts, the feet must be wedged in a gap and pushed outwards for leverage and grip, and the same goes for the hands. In this type of escalation the body needs to remain tense and rigid – there is no possible relaxation or looseness. This is obviously more taxing on the muscles, hence managing the speed of execution becomes an important factor.

I take a good look at the GAN Tower. I have to consider how long I can play this game and also calculate the timing required to complete the climb safely. If the latter is less than the former then the building is achievable. I walk round to the point of attack, the crack, which originates near a few newspaper vendors on the pavement. With a daily newspaper involved in this climb it goes without saying I have an impressive press entourage. There will be no security issues and the reporters await my commencement.

Within a few seconds I begin my assault. But after only a few metres it is clear that this is not working well. Another step and my foot jam gives way, a hand breaks loose and I find myself in an unpleasant and pathetic situation known as the 'barn door'. The name of this uncontrolled movement is a good analogy as your body is detached from the cliff on one side and you open out like a barn door, flapping as if your supporting foot and hand were hinges. It might look good on an ice rink but figure skating is not my favourite sport. My flailing arm draws imaginary patterns as I seek to swing back towards the building. It isn't working and only wild movements from my arms and legs can salvage the situation. I turn into a human windscreen wiper in an effort to avoid a rapid meeting with a concrete mattress. This isn't looking good for anybody and it is not the sort of thing people like to see if I am nearing the top. I press on but this unhappy scenario repeats itself twice more in the first 25 metres, the exertion becoming extreme. Increasing adversity tells me it is impossible to continue. Fifty more metres of this and I would have been an unconscious heap on the tarmac, and then the media would really have a story. Too bad for the journalists, but I need to abandon ship.

Sat at the base of the tower, crimson and feverish with overheated exertion, I loosen the laces of my slippers. The event has gone out with a whimper. My anger is rising, invading me slowly until I feel suffocated. I am vague, blank, pitiful. Around me, compassionate people are saying stupid shit like "You made the right decision" and "It's good to know when to quit." This hubbub of sympathy really floors me. I know they are right. Of course it is necessary to know when to give up, and indeed I know I have made the right decision. But frankly, at this moment, I just want to wake up in my bed and for this nightmare to vanish. It is a horrible, horrible anticlimax.

Three months later I am back at the GAN Tower, raring to go. After successful experimentation and test moves at the bottom, I recommence the escalation, full of confidence thanks to a recent and beautiful cliff success. I hardly get a metre higher than my previous attempt when it starts happening all over again, the worst kind of déjà vu.

On the square of La Défense below, my friends really dread seeing me in this precarious situation. I must be a victim of some sort of curse. Were the ancestors of a security officer or the architect into voodoo or some kind of black magic? Maybe somewhere in this world there is a miniature effigy of me scaling a broom handle pierced by thousands of needles? Both attempts got off to a good start but once the escalation got going the whole thing started to unravel. I try different solutions but the outcome is the same – exhausting barn doors and defeat. I have to descend again, repelled once more by this stubborn block.

A month later, I am back again, ready to climb this handsome yet adamantly elusive building. Throughout my life I have learnt that perseverance pays off in the end. But to get past this obstinate tower will take a lot of tenacity. To abandon a project considered too difficult is, in itself, a test. But to give up repeatedly during the same ascent is a much more formidable fight. In such cases the questioning and searching is consuming. Subconsciously, new forces lay siege to your spirit and try to shove it out through the revolving doors, or hurl it out of the tenth floor window. Thoughts become darker, less Cartesian, and emotions oscillate in the shady waters of luck and fate. I decide to adopt a different technique. Physically, my preparation had been intense and I am even leaner and trimmer than usual, having lost two kilos from an already light frame. I am resolved to overcome the GAN and cannot let this one get away! I have to find a solution, I just have to. During the previous two attempts, my feet had struggled when I had jammed them into the slender gap. Pushing them outwards was draining and I could not find the anchor I needed to push securely upwards. As usual I had bandaged my hands to protect them but today, for the first time, I had also protected my slippers, binding them to give them more stiffness and strength. Big solutions sometimes arise from the simplest details.

Broader and fuller, my feet stick better in the all-important groove and the ascent takes a radically different form. Quickly and decisively, I reach the summit.

3

THE HATCHLING

Well, I must be dead!
A violent white light illuminates me, bathing the surrounding space. Soft yet harsh, smooth and enveloping. It is exactly what one would expect from eternity. I am regaining my senses, growing lucid. There is indeed a life after life… With all the risks I have been taking in my escalations and in many other parts of my life, my continuous gambling with death, I am frankly not particularly amazed to be here. I had always worked towards perfecting my solitary escalations, climbing up rock faces without ropes or safety mechanisms. I preferred to spurn the pollution of the safety net and experience the climb in its naked form. In this dangerous game I had striven to be the best. I had many escapades and had become a world record holder in a tough, extreme, but exquisitely benevolent sport. It brought me sublime moments, beyond time, beyond compare.

And now my posthumous life has begun! I think about the idea. Spiritually alive, I can appreciate my mortal end. If only I had known…

Being killed in a car accident would have left me with many regrets. God, none of us really ever have the death we truly deserve or yearn for. Barely any of us leave this world with honour, after a glorious battle – merely with the deflation of an end to an unspectacular everyday life, humdrum, flat and without zest. And we can only really be measured by the people who miss us. Me? I leave a wife, Nicole; three children, Julien, Hugo and Lucas; and some dear friends…

Fucking light!

Now it blinds me, irritates me, tortures me… This is purgatory perhaps… I also deserve this. For almost 35 years I have been pushing it. My death will be a personal tragedy for my parents – people without history, smooth and settled, too respectful of the established rules to leave any room for dreams. I was by contrast a turbulent child, a reckless person, ceaselessly tormented and driven by the spirit of adventure. A mother's heartbreaker, able at the tender age of 12 to climb seven floors of the building in which we lived. What made me do it? Well, it was always there and it had to emerge.

There are drives within us, predeterminations against which we cannot fight. Is there a gene which compels some of us to escalate vertical rock faces? Who knows what is hidden in our endless coils of DNA. But it was not evident in my parents, that's for sure.

Back then I didn't hesitate before climbing our housing block. I had baptised it the Cold Wing after one of the mythical summits of the massif in the mountainous National Park of Ecrin. Looking back, I believe that impish act was my fate. As a 12-year-old boy I had returned from school and patted my pockets to discover I had lost my keys and was locked out. But I knew that the window of our loggia seven floors up was never locked. There was an obvious solution to this dilemma. Let's climb up there! So up I climbed, floor by floor, until I was home. When my parents got in they were annoyed with me – the concierge had witnessed my break-in and reported me to them. I was in the doghouse for a while, my mother angry with me, not so much for climbing the building, but more for annoying the concierge who was less than amused by my mischief. I felt that my father, with whom I did not often speak much, looked at me in a different way from that day.

What had sparked this life-changing decision? Back in my childhood, climbing literature was hard to come by. I had discovered climbing through epic stories of famous climbers risking their lives to conquer great heights, tales which made my eyes redden each evening by the light of my bedside lamp. The heroism of these alpinists generated in me this imperious need to conquer, to overcome rationality until the irrational led me towards my dream of escalation. As a nine-year-old my inspiration was fired by a movie I had watched about an airplane which crashed near the summit of one of Europe's highest mountains. A pair of brothers, both top climbers, had decided to scale the huge and vertical mountain to see if there were any survivors. They intrepidly scaled the rock faces and battled the elements. It had everything I loved – they were courageous heroes and they were overcoming the odds and rescuing people in dire circumstances! From then on, I wanted to be a climber. Like all kids I wanted to be brave in the manner of Zorro or Robin Hood and climbing seemed to offer me that.

The blinding light loses its brightness. There's a shape. A soul. A person. Somebody bends over me. A voice.

"He's awake!"

Awake? It all sounds very earthly. This is the afterlife? Don't tell me it's the same old story about following rules, respecting schedules and speed limits... I really can't believe it. Are there rules in heaven? When I was alive, I fought a lonely battle against the politically correct – not being an individualist but simply a defender of our freedom to assume our own choices, to undertake without limitations the paths that we decide to follow. After passing over to the other side I will not allow someone to dictate the hour at which I have to get up! Heaven is a huge let-down. The voice, female, probes me for a reaction.

"Are you okay?"

The world around me gently emerges. I feel I am in an enclosure. A room? Light streaks through the room in glowing slices through a blind's narrow strips. On the right, a door. Above me, lengths of tubes, flasks and... a cobweb? It looks pretty weird for paradise... then it sinks in. It is not my time yet. Am I really alive? It sure looks like it. Apparently, I have to postpone my death... This is good news! But I am immediately scared. In what physical condition will I have to spend the rest of my life? The nurse bends more, touches my cheek, then says to me, smiling:

"We shall take care of the nose later! The surgeon has already spent more than five hours on your case."

How long have I been out of it? Hours? Days? I know that in the morning I had set off to Grenoble, something like that, but then there's a blank. With my nasty habit of not buckling my safety belt I must have smashed through the windscreen and broken my protruding proboscis yet again. I don't really care about that. I peer down and look over my broken body. I am much more afraid for my wrists, which were already little more than a fused bunch of crumbs. New fractures would surely reduce them to incapacity. Given the size of the plaster cast which entombs one of my arms, I am terrified. The nurse reassures me: my wrist is indeed broken but luckily it snapped cleanly and without the osseous explosion I had feared. The fracture, apparently, is precise, as if it had been cut by laser; and once I have recovered I shall not have any remaining after-effects. So much the better, I already have enough of those.

I search my memory, hunting for any recollections that could explain how I ended up here. I strain but find no thread of the accident.

"Is the car destroyed?" I ask the nurse as she leaves the room. I guess the impact must have been terrible. A truck... or a tree? Yes, for sure, a tree. She half-turns and responds as she leaves the room.

"What car are you talking about?"

What does she mean? No car accident? If not – then what happened? I try to remember something, anything, but there is nothing except confusion and an overwhelming, stifling fear. I want to fall asleep again, to sink straight into the oblivion of unconsciousness.

Later on, the surgeon strides in, flicking through his charts. Although my mind is hazy I recognise him immediately. Dr Gérard Hoël is the man I can thank for putting me back together several times. We know each other well and I dare to ask him the truth. The uncertainty has been unbearable. I like to know where I have been when I wake up and I also like controlling the movements of my body. Having my memory kidnapped and getting it back in this condition drives me insane.

The good doctor smiles. The truth? There was no car accident. They found me at the bottom of a cliff, unconscious, poly-traumatised. The truth hurts more than my injuries. In 20 years of climbing, thousands of solo adventures including masterpieces among the northern faces of the Alps, I never had the slightest accident. Yes, I have fallen before from ropes, but never when climbing solo, climbing unaided with my bare hands. To discover that I had fallen solo is greatly disturbing. And to find myself so injured is also very worrying. Not that I am not used to it by now. I have had numerous nose-breaking minor falls and some hospitalising medium ones. This is 1993, the third time I have been badly hurt, the third time my bones have been severely broken, cracked, smashed.

Have you ever heard the sound of a falling body? It is unbelievable, a paroxysmal violence. It is absolutely incredible that a human being can overcome such trauma. I must admit that I have never heard any of my own falls. I only remember an endlessly long plunge – and then darkness. In those few seconds, memories rush into your mind, especially the good old ones, the ones you hang onto in life, the ones that condition you subconsciously to survive. But you need luck too: a lucky fall means life, an unlucky one means death or worse.

My wife Nicole, sat by the bed, recites the inventory of my fractures as if she were the French poet Jacques Prevert (the great Monsieur Prevert, not Pervert) while I stare at the ceiling. Nicole has seen me in this state before. In fact we first met when I was hobbling around in plaster from another bad fall. This time, my right kneecap, my nose and my left wrist are broken and the bone located under the cheek is totally ruined. It has been suggested to me plenty of times to undergo plastic surgery to salvage my long-suffering nose. Sponsors had even offered to pay for the operation. But after four successive nasal fractures, I knew a fifth one would occur, then maybe a few more. My nose, so often a crumple zone for my brain, is a lost cause. Moreover, with my wrists long since wrecked, I cannot absorb any more than a minor fall with my arms. That goes without saying. My face proves it.

Two guys enter the room. I have no idea who they are and guess they have wandered in by mistake. But it seems like they know me and they appear rather satisfied to discover that I am still alive. Embarrassed at my blank expression they stutter a few incomprehensible words before Nicole interjects at this awkward moment and explains. It is a rather silly tale.

Earlier that fateful morning, these two lads had contacted me for a climbing session. Teaching represents only a small part of my activities but I like sharing my passion with those who feel that same drive and attraction to verticality. We had gone to Cornas, in the vicinity of Valence, a beautiful compact limestone blade lined with nicely spaced modern hooks, but a temporary ban had prevented us from scaling it. Due to the ban that day it was impossible to appreciate the place where I had pursued my first extreme moves. Never mind, I thought, there are plenty of pebbles around Valence. So I searched for another cliff suitable for beginners. I knew a good one, though it had not been a particularly lucky cliff for me. It had gone pretty much unused since the advent of modern climbing and seemed to fit our modest needs perfectly. Its ways and passages were easy and offered little of interest to me as an experienced climber, so this was the first time I had returned for about 11 years. But it was there on this beginner's cliff, on September 29th 1982, that I had my second accident. For a long time, I held a grudge against my fears. But time has passed inexorably and I was no longer afraid of crossing this paved limestone which had given me a hard time years ago...

My decision to climb feels natural and logical. I glance upward to where the anchors of my abseil gave way 11 years before. The cliff rises 20 metres from the ground, just six or seven storeys high, a piffling insignificance in comparison with the Verdon canyon – but it would be unwise to dismiss such a height out of hand. Ask my nose!

Height is indeed a relative thing, but beyond a certain point Newton's laws of gravity have little meaning. Death is the only constant. This holds true anywhere and at any time, apart from perhaps the odd miracle. During the Second World War an American pilot encountered the most incredible fortune when he walked away totally unscathed after a fall of more than 5000 metres. But another pilot was killed by slipping and landing on a patch of ice. Between these two extremes there is room for some logic: beyond ten metres, generally a fall proves fatal. Just ten metres! The human body can be a fragile thing. Remember to treat height with respect, because falling – whether it be down the stairs or out a window, or off a ladder whilst tending to the roof – is the second highest cause of accidental death after motor accidents.

The cliff is visible now. For a few minutes, while I am approaching the perfect place for this first lesson, images I had managed to evacuate from my memory surface again. I get flickers and flashes of that second accident, the one which should have killed me and almost ended my career. I remain silent, incapable of starting a semblance of a conversation with my students. For sure, they must have been upset by this silence, this distance, this stoic behaviour which most people would reasonably assume was either rudeness or meditation. Right now I keep my thoughts to myself and bury my demons. I cannot worry about pleasantries and I certainly do not think it is a good idea to tell them the truth. Quietly we arrive at the foot of the cliff. The guys take in the cliff in good spirits. I keep it positive though sober.

"Some consider climbing to be a dreadful activity," I explain, "Dangerous and complex. But climbing is a complete sport. Maybe the most complete one. The whole body works – fingers, arms, back muscles, abdominal muscles, calves, thighs. Flexibility plays an essential role by helping the body to stay stuck against the cliff and by exploiting the features of the rock. The mind is crucial, as the prospect of falling is part of a rock climber's everyday life. You can be in fantastic shape physically but you will fail as a climber if your mind is not focussed and resilient."

The students nod enthusiastically. I tell them that the main thing about climbing is to learn how to lighten your weight by using your legs as much as possible.

"Arm muscles will never have the power of the calves or thighs! The beginner concentrates on hand grips and quickly becomes exhausted by the effort. Never pull on the arms, but push on the legs."

Next I jump from theory to practice, and gaily demonstrate by climbing the first few metres of a nice and easy ascent, hands clasped behind my back. It's a happy visual demonstration of the truthfulness of my expert comments. The students listen attentively. But I decide to keep going, climbing a near-vertical cliff with my hands behind me as if I was climbing the stairs in relaxed contemplation. Why did I go further? I still wonder why. Might it have been my attraction to risk, as this has always guided my life? Was I just showing off? Was I trying to mock the cliff that had almost killed me ten years before?

I cheerfully ascend to eight metres with my hands behind me, giving tips and explaining to them that this is the way it should be done.

"Because of the muscle structure," I state with authority, "pushing with your feet allows you to save energy, but the use of the hands is of course indispensable for balance…"

And then I fall, before the horrified eyes of my pupils.

My third accident had occurred in exactly the same place as my second one – the same fucking place! And once again I find myself broken and comatose in a hospital bed. Once more I awake groggily to a world I have little right to see. And for the second time, Dr Hoël bleakly predicts that for me, climbing belongs henceforth to the past.

I cannot help but muse at this déjà vu. Apparently the initial news the nurse gave me was referring to the fact I could keep my forearm. I nearly lost my hand ten years ago and was told then that further damage could result in me losing it. But the surgeon tells me that although its function is further reduced I will be able to use it again for basic everyday purposes. My other fractures should be fine apart from my knee. My knee, which already had a metal plate in it, is also badly broken and will cause me problems. He pulls out my X-rays and points with his pen to the permanent and very obvious damage done. The injuries I carried from my previous two accidents have been exposed by this fall and the prognosis is grim. He tells me that with these injuries I will not be able to exert the strength or the mobility I will need to climb again. He reminds me though that I am lucky to have emerged from my second coma.

I ask him if there is any chance that I might overcome these disabilities.

He shakes his head and frowns sympathetically. More modest movements are possible, he tells me, and he is pleased with the results of the surgery considering what he had to work with when I was brought in. This man knows his stuff, but deep inside, I know that I will get up and I will climb again. It would have been easy to believe Dr Hoël, as it takes weeks to get out of hospital. But for me, getting back to the mountains is a matter of survival. I was condemned to being pinned to the ground once before and I managed to get back to my beautiful cliffs.

In retrospect, I realise that my stays at the hospital have always been the turning point of a new start. When faced with an end to my dreams I drew upon the deepest depths of my soul and summoned the motivation to go further, to dare to take on new and seemingly impossible challenges. Every time I have limped out of hospital I have been a little more handicapped but also a little more determined. In France we have a card which registers your disability and attributes a figure to reflect this. My rating is a so-called 66 percent incapacity. I have disabilities, and limited movement due to my permanent injuries, plus feelings of dizziness from time to time. Technically I am disabled but I do not receive a disability pension from the state. For some reason officials have difficulty in understanding that the handicapped person I am and the Spiderman they see on TV is the same guy… I suppose I can understand that. And actually, I prefer this pension to be left for those who are unable to move even out of a chair. I am fortunate in that I can continue to seize the day and have fun, to continue to surmount this 66 percent misfortune.

Various friends come and visit me and horse around in the ward. Some assume I will quit climbing this time, given the prognosis, but also as a consequence of the emotional trauma of such a close shave. People often ask me why I continue, whether I have a death wish. I don't, I just love climbing. It's what I do and what I live for. It's my life.

It was always in my blood, even as a child. For a long time my favourite cliffs were made of leaves. My playground? Three sturdy trees which flanked our neighbours' houses. My friends and I climbed and clambered their craggy branches every day. We would go as high and as far as the branches would allow, sometimes sagging or bending to breaking point. We had even set up a Tyrolean traverse – that is, a pair of horizontal ropes between two high fixed points – thanks to the surplus in speleological equipment belonging to my friend's potholing father. Happiness then was just two steps away from my home. My neighbours' trees became little by little our Noah's Ark, our den, our home sweet home. Together, we shared the same taste for anticipated risk, the same need to believe in the alternative, the same fascination for the inaccessible, for overtaking one another, for competing. Without these three trees, I'm sure I would never have discovered escalation. What would I have become – a stuntman, a bowls player, a homeless drifter, a civil servant? Who knows? Chance meetings with people and even with inanimate objects sometimes lead you in radically different directions. But the important thing is to believe that we can influence fate, that we can achieve goals by recognising and grabbing these opportunities as they pass. What these things turn out to be or what path they take us on is rarely clear. Luck, adversity, uncertainty – the spice of life flows past all the time. I have grabbed at them and my scars are due to my errors. As much as we try, we cannot cherry-pick the best, the magic moments of exploit and success, while avoiding wounds, heartaches and failures. Positive and negative, all things unite to make us what we are.

My friends and I knew by heart every branch, we had achieved again and again the same exploits, and our universe inexorably narrowed. Fortunately, thanks to relatives I became a boy scout. And scouting was a wonderful gift. In many ways it was the most important thing that ever happened to me and it supplied the perfect excuse to escape parental authority during the weekend. Generosity, dedication, maturity. Scouting, as a catechism, has all the necessary structure and discipline to reassure families. Too bad for my parents... it was precisely among the scouts that I caught the virus of escalation.

It was also here I met Pierre Jamet, the chief of the boy scouts. My contagion drew me and Pierre – my friend, my brother – into numerous batty childhood adventures during which, I have to admit, we took enormous and rather naughty risks. We climbed alone and often without equipment. We would jump on our bicycles and ride toward vertical masses of fallen rocks near our homes. We would often go up solo. Two kids climbing rocks as if they were trees, kids whose descent technique relied purely on motivation and raw instinct. Pierre and I attacked virgin cliffs, driven by the heroic stories of famed climbers, those deserving predecessors who had often made the ultimate sacrifice for our beloved activity. Everything we could climb, every wall or rocky 20-metre cliff, we named in reference to a mythical summit. Little by little, the neighbourhood of Valence became an Alpine-Himalayan conglomerate that geography teachers would have approved of. We invented a new mountain, invisible to the uninitiated eye but nevertheless genuinely redoubtable. The local muddy cliffs were part of our dreams and every Wednesday, every weekend, we used to don our big leather shoes and oversized kneekers, and head out to tackle our summits.

Sometimes, we also went canyoning, lowering ourselves down waterfalls on our experimental ropes. This is a popular adventure activity today but back then it hadn't even been invented. We imagined we had to traverse torrents of water and stay, whatever happened, in the river. Like many kids we developed our own world where we imposed on ourselves a tough and punishing ethic, rough, daring and foolhardy. Even in the frigid winter, even when the temperature dropped to minus ten or fifteen, we would battle the closest torrent from home. We would wrap ourselves in three woollen pullovers and set off with sandwiches encapsulated ten successive times in plastic bags and trek towards the snow-covered banks of the gully. The torrent was so transparent that one could easily tell the bitterness of the temperature. Icy water streamed down our necks as we climbed a precariously slippery waterfall. Our hands turned into dead wooden clumps, swollen like those of corpses. Often we messed up, slipping in with a freezing splash. We had chosen to be there so we were happy to wade for hours in hypothermic rivers. Once immersed in water, the pullovers would swell and be transformed into makeshift armour weighing a dozen kilos. The first pullover, closest to the body, maintained a little bit of heat while the second provided a cushion against the third one which, most of the time, began to freeze, cracking with each single movement. Wetsuits had existed for many years but we trained to experience the biting cold of the big northern cliffs described by the heroes in our books. We went a little over the top in our enthusiasm. We were young and wild, so ambitious that nothing could faze us, nothing could quench our thirst for adventure. Life was filled with exploration and adrenaline.

As we improved, Pierre and I would climb cliff sides with growing confidence and daring. After school, at weekends, or after school there were some crazy adventures upon the rocks. I remember one time we climbed up and were startled by a fantastic sight. I pulled myself up by gripping a hollow in the rock and — *holy shit!* I nearly fell. I was eye-to-eye with a huge and powerful bird, a flesh-tearing predator with a wingspan of two metres flapping at me in fury. It was petrifying! One minute climbing in delicate silence, and the next being attacked by a colossal bird of prey! She left the nest and I clung onto the cliff and gathered my breath, waiting for my drumming heart to stop trying to sprint out of my chest. Pierre and I laughed nervously and pulled ourselves up again. We tentatively peeped over into the hollow and had a look – it was a nest. And not only that, there was a giant 'baby' bird in this nest. Of course Pierre and I had disturbed the mother and she was simply defending her young. I took a close look. The baby had a hooked beak and fluffy immature feathers and was about the size of an obese domestic cat. It glared at me fearlessly with staring shiny eyes. The fledgling flapped about a bit as Pierre and I wrestled it into my backpack. I continued my climb up the sheer rock to the top of the cliff with this wild thing's head poking out the top of my bag, blinking, observing. When we got to the top, full of excitement, we took a photo with it, delighted with our trophy. In the photo you might be able to see its strong thick talons almost as big as my hands. Years later a surprised ornithologist would tell us it was an eagle owl, a rare and powerful bird and the largest owl in Europe. Apparently the eagle owl is only marginally smaller than a golden eagle and can even kill juvenile deer. Pierre and I admired our prize then climbed down and put it back in its nest. As wide-eyed kids, we were amazed. We would muster up the courage to return to the bird in hushed awe to follow its development. Of course we would be very careful to avoid its mother. We would visit the bird for two months until, one day, of course it had grown up and left the nest. In many ways this was a metaphor for ourselves. We too were growing and had to spread our wings, to branch out. We pushed our luck harder, took new audacious routes. Our skills developed further as we took considerable risks upon our local rocks.

Pierre, who was two years older than me, wanted to try something new. We had charted and conquered our phantasmagorical universe of Valence and needed to chart new lands. We were growing up so it was getting pretty hard to believe in our own Everests despite noble efforts. It was high time for us to burn our idols and to attack the big cliffs. This re-evaluation of our world marked the transition between childhood dreams and adult reality, with its many victories and also its disappointments.

Thanks to an article we found in France's first specialist climbing journal, *Mountains Magazine*, we began to apply the official principles of free escalation on a beautiful rock feature in the neighbouring department of Ardeche. The Chateau de Crussol is a ruined 13th-century castle sitting on top of limestone Crussol hill. Picturesque and imposing, the crumbled remains of this fairy-tale chateau are a dramatic blend of history and geology and an inspiring setting and challenge.

Armed with our 'topo' we resolved to attack and conquer this fort. At that time, these small composites of information detailing the precise route one should follow had no technical or rational aspects. Beyond the laconic quotations of every length and dimension of a crag, the lyric or even cryptic description of the route enhanced the charm of the adventure but made progress difficult and unpredictable. *'Go up to 20 metres by a smooth dihedral in order to escape on the left before the wall overhangs and then join a shield of exposed paving stones, where it is necessary to go back up quickly under the first very aerial overhang. And be careful, from this place, from that place, there is no way to escape...'*

At times understanding these topos was like deciphering hieroglyphs or a treasure map. In the evening, at the refuge or comfortably sat on the bed, the topo reading was religiously performed. Mentally we struggled to make images of these foreboding but magic words.

Before the ascent, we lived a kind of wavering moment, a few minutes of indecision, hesitation, where we tried subconsciously to delay the fight for which we had prepared for weeks. Before leaving, we drank a drop of cold coffee. The air was fresh this day, the sombre sky gave the setting a gloomy and sulking hue. We entered the cathedral of climbing in meditation, as humble believers. Nothing, not even the squawk of a soaring bird overhead, broke this quasi-religious atmosphere. We spoke little. The hour was serious, grave. The more we advanced towards the face, the more it seemed as if we were about to get lost in an anonymous sky. I studied again the mysterious topo for the ascent, trying to match its sorcery with the vast wall ahead of us.

At the foot of Chateau de Crussol our simple climbing material was taken out of rucksacks and lay at our feet, still sluggish and dormant but staring at us in anticipation. It was too late to turn back now. The literature had not pulled any punches and we anticipated the toughest climb of our lives. This was to be our first 'professional' solo climb, the first time we would enter the realm of the pros. Pierre and I had climbed our own cliffs, cliffs that were not assigned grades by the climbing community. So we invented our own ratings. Due to the lack of comparable grades, we assigned our toughest passages scores of between three and four, six being reserved for the ascents achieved by the supermen of Alpine literature. With our discovery of these mammoth and professional climbs of Vercors, then rated ED (*Extremement Difficile* or Extremely Difficult), the top end of the scale at the time, we felt tiny in front of these vertical walls of white-grey limestone. Our muddy routes of Valence seemed so petty, so non-existent, that the first contact with reality was like a frictional rope burn in the crotch. It was clear that heroism and imagination were not going to be enough. It was now necessary to play in a bigger schoolyard, one where you could not cry 'Stop!' when things went wrong. Once engaged here, you were on your own.

In silent contemplation we made our ascent. We attacked it solo, with only our hands and feet, though we carried a rope for insurance should we need it. The rope would not be a complete solution should we get into a sticky situation as there were no hooks in the cliff. Any escape by rope would require us to adapt. But once we had completed the lower lengths, we saw the truth. If this climb deserved the Extremely Difficult or ED rating assigned by the Alpine climbing community, then the most extreme of ours in Valence were without question 'Abominably Difficult'! Due to our lack of references, as we had climbed on our own, far from the vertical community of the time, we had developed a parallel system of quotations – but ours, it turned out, were sharply more austere. A rating that they would have assigned 5 by the French system would be 3 in our own. As our cliffs weren't on the climbing circuit we had no idea what level of difficulty they really were. Official French climbing grades start at 1 (very easy) and build up to somewhere around 9 (superhumanly difficult) with a, b or c designations and plus or minus signs adding further differentiation. I say 'somewhere around 9' as some of these climbs are actually impossible until proven otherwise. The toughest so far realised today is something around 9a+, and of course that was achieved with ropes. Few people can take on a climb of 7 or more, and that's with full equipment. The system is designed for equipped climbers and even fairly easy climbs without ropes can suddenly become very challenging. The parallel Alpine rating for the climb at the chateau was ED.

Halfway up the summit, having surmounted the major difficulties, we clambered onto a wide ledge to rest. Pierre had scaled this length ahead of me. I quickly joined him. Then, without a word, we exchanged glances and smiled. We had won the opening set. Our dream had become reality. We completed the climb with some strain but, in reality, little difficulty and then made our way carefully back to the bottom. Once our feet were back on terra firma we cavorted like the kids we still were. We had completed an ED! Not only that, but we suddenly realised that we were actually very accomplished climbers and hadn't known it!

After our first success, the entire Vercors Plateau from Archiane to Presles became our playground. Nothing would worry us, not even the sight of a 300-metre solo at Presles assigned ED. A bunch of hikers passing below us could not believe their eyes. Extreme rock climbing was reserved for serious people, experts, not for snotty kids! To shock the old farts we would smile and arrogantly dispense with the rope. Pierre and I would show off before horrified and agape faces. We would get extra kicks from winding up the older generation. Authority was something we had little respect for and climbing was a fine outlet for our teenage rebellion.

Time marched on. Pierre and I enjoyed some magnificent times in our numerous hair-raising adventures. Our climbing progressed, evolved, matured, and our bodies grew taller and stronger. And then one day, out of the blue, Pierre made a totally unexpected announcement. He had decided to join the police force! Pierre? Of all the people. I really couldn't believe it. And I was wounded by this move for it was true treason. Pierre explained he wanted to be a mountain cop, not a normal one, but still it was the antithesis of what we had stood for. I was baffled by this. At school Pierre was a very smart guy but he did not have the ability to shut up. How could he possibly become a cop and put up with superiors? Could he endure stiff regulations and being told what to do by some power-crazed Hitler? Apparently so. After all we had lived through together, I was lonesome, abandoned and brimming with recollections. We had always been together, spurring each other on in our adventures, challenging and competing with each other. Suddenly there was no one to climb with. No one to laugh with and to team up with against adversity. At the age of 17, I thought it was a bit early to live on memories. History could not stop here – surely this should not signal the end?

Pierre and I had the occasion to see each other again, but a misty embarrassment had settled between us, for once a play is over it can ruin the story to ask for another act. But we had lived too many intense and sweet moments to fall out, so the separation was harmless, smiling, amicable. We both knew that it was useless to maintain a flat and desperately commonplace relationship. It had been a love story where we would replace embraces with risk taking, sexual ecstasy with equally orgasmic spurts of adrenaline. The parallel may seem excessive, but the trust and closeness you find when you entwine limbs with your lover also exists when brothers put their lives in the hands of one another. A good relationship does not suffer mediocrity. And on reflection I could not begrudge my best friend his decision to follow a true profession. But still I did not feel the need to pursue anything else. Everything I wanted to do was just as clear. Magazines were full of beautiful successes on the cliffs of Provence, wonderful places crying out to be explored and enjoyed. So I carried on by myself.

Being fortunate enough to live in southern France I discovered Buoux and the incredible Verdon, the Mecca of rock climbing! The Verdon Canyon is rightly known as the most beautiful in Europe. The canyon itself is the second largest in the world, 20 kilometres long and 300 metres deep. Verdon is absolutely stunning and its infinity of escalations gave me a timely boost. Due to an absence of fellow fighters, climbing solo became the only means to continue my passion. If, luckily, I came across another solitary rock climber, we would team up to work difficult passages. Otherwise I roamed solo up the easier routes of the cliff. A short time later, I attacked the top-level ways trailblazed by the pioneers of the era, mainly the imaginative routes of a young and emerging Patrick Edlinger. I got to hang out with other young climbers, teenagers or lads in their early twenties, many of whom are famous names today. I would join Edlinger, Patrick Behrault, Eric Escoffier, Jean Christoff Lafaille, Christophe Profit and numerous other climbers in tackling great cliffs. These guys all went on to do great things. Sadly a lot of them are no longer here. Some fell, some never came back. But I admire them for the way they lived – no compromise. So many people in this world are just surviving, but these guys lived full lives even if those lives were cut short.

I was changing and so were the times. The 1980s saw an explosion in adventure sports, with an emphasis on fun rather than heroic exploration or sticking flagpoles in the ground, since Man had more or less charted the extremes of the world. Escalation caught on as a sporting activity with real growth at both professional and grass roots level. The first escalation competitions had already begun, awarding medals and trophies to the exciting new sportsmen who were reinventing free-style rock climbing, climbing rock faces in the open air free of any outside or material constraints before judges and audiences. It was quite ironic that I should follow this emerging sport whilst entombed in casts and bandages in my hospital bed with bones broken literally from head to toe.

Brushed aside from the podium because of my successive accidents in 1982, I did however have the occasion to participate – without proving unworthy in some top international matches – but my history was bound to lie elsewhere. The competitions, though fun, felt artificial to me. The rules and regulations imposed to give a framework for judges and timekeepers, and the influx of prize money for me and many other climbers, diluted and distorted the sport. Of course some climbers thrived on it, and climbing as a competitive sport is well established today, and has undoubtedly helped the sport grow. It must be said though that few observers, apart from seasoned climbers, can appreciate the technicalities on which the competitions are based. Although I flirted with competitive climbing for a while in the mid-eighties I felt the setup to be sometimes stifling and largely subjective. For me, climbing was not about racing or competing – it was about freedom and self-expression. It sounds idealist, perhaps, but I guess I am just from another generation of climbers. As climbing became more popular they added more rules and regulations and it became more like a sport than a pursuit. It was no longer about adventure. I did not want to compete against others, but against the cliff. Against myself. Alone. And with my life in my hands.

Regardless of any preferences, my accidents put competitive climbing or indeed any climbing off the menu for quite a while. For me, my falls were moments transformed into slices of life, providing a real catalyst of energy for future climbs. The first time I had a really bad accident was due to a lack of experience. I was near Aix-en-Province on 18th January 1982 and I descended a cliff from a ledge by rapidly sliding down my rope. Instead of securing my rope through a carabiner I laced it through a nylon webbing anchor. An indestructible 19-year-old, I was having too much fun and speeding the way a boy racer does with his new set of wheels. The nylon rope was secure and strong enough to hold my weight, 50 kilograms at that time, but unfortunately it split with the excessive friction and heat of my rapid and carefree descent, and my descent to the bottom accelerated somewhat. With a snapped rope I free-fell a full 15 metres. How did that day end? With a fracture of the right radius, fractures to many bones in the right carpus, a fracture across the bridge of my nose, a shattered right calcaneum resulting in an osseous infection which could easily have led to amputation of my foot. I was unconscious for about 30 minutes and my friends rushed me to hospital. I was in a bit of a mess and stayed in hospital for a while, undergoing three operations. Fortunately I landed on flat earth rather than rock but, still, it hurts a lot when you hit the ground that hard. I was not pleased with the outcome but it could have been much worse. Looking back it was a rather daft descent with a predictable outcome. Oh well, I was young then…

I staggered out of hospital partially entombed in two big fat plaster casts – one on my right hand and one on my right leg. My twisted nose would have been in a cast had such a thing existed. It was in this ridiculous state that I met my wife. One of the things I remember about this fateful meeting is that she had a dog and it was barking like mad when it saw my casts.

It took me a while to shake off my plaster casts and four months to get back to climbing again. I loved climbing so much and it never occurred to me to quit, though naturally I learnt a little more respect for the cliffs from my fall. I was just getting back into the swing of things, and nearly as good as I was beforehand, and then – *fuck!* Accident number two – and this time it was much, much more serious.

Only six months passed between my first and second accidents. On 29th September I was up a cliff again in Cornas, near Valence, climbing free solo and enjoying the pure mountain air. A few climbers approached the cliff I was climbing accompanied by some instructors I knew. The instructors shouted up to me and asked if I could fix their rope at the top of the cliff as it would take them some time, time better spent on their climbing lessons. I descended and they gave me their material and I went up again free solo to the top of the cliff to secure it for them. The steel expansion bolt at the top was not placed very close to the cliff edge so I needed to hook it to a carabiner, through another rope, and then another carabiner. Since it was easier than climbing down free solo, I made my way down on the rope towards the climbers, taking care not to descend too fast. The knot in the rope they had given me was poor, but crucially I hadn't noticed and neither had anyone else. Unbeknown to me the instructors had given it to the boys when they explained how to tie knots. The lads had done one of them incorrectly and I hadn't seen the error, assuming that what I had been given was safe and secure. At the time it seemed to be correct, and my rope felt solid and well anchored into the cliff. Well, it wasn't!

This fall was especially bad because I fell headfirst. I dived like a stricken Superman towards hard rock, my hands splayed out below me trying to minimise the impact with the rocks – rather foolishly. Wrists and head hit solid rock first, my wrists were utterly smashed and my head absorbed much of the rest.

Barely out of hospital, I was rushed back there again, being tended to by the same doctors and nurses. I spent five days in the blank, dark void of a deep coma. I had a badly fractured skull, and had closely avoided the amputation of one of my hands; both of my wrists and forearms were reduced to crumbs, my pelvis was smashed, an elbow and a knee were virtually destroyed, the bones of my face sustained numerous fractures; and I suffered a totally crushed nose, which was the third impact point of my rapid touchdown. In addition, the right ulnar nerve, which commands two fingers and the thumb, was ruined too.

When I regained consciousness and lucidity one of the first things I asked the nurse was whether I would climb again. They didn't want to tell me. Eventually I got to talk to Dr Hoël, the surgeon who had saved my left hand. For him it was obvious: he had never seen such a wrist injury that had not led to either a major or total loss of function. In many cases the patient would have lost the hand completely. The right hand was also very badly injured and would never be the same again. I would be disabled to some degree for the rest of my life. Some functions could return, but it was possible that my hands would be largely ornamental fixtures. Most of my other injuries would heal though my elbow and knee joints would not be able to support vigorous sporting activities in future.

I stared at my snapped and shattered bones on the X-rays, metal pins and rods holding everything together. The damage was obvious. I digested the news soberly. To be honest I could not feel too disheartened, terrible as this news was. Even though they were telling me that I would not climb again I was very grateful that I had survived. *I was alive.* I could not be upset about anything after being given this second chance at life. What worried me more was being unable to do simple everyday things.

Being confronted with a life of disability was frightening. The prospect would spin around my cracked head as I lay there completely useless and helpless. I couldn't use my hands and of course I couldn't walk. My voice was reduced to a hoarse, high-pitched whisper since in my coma I had been given a tracheotomy. The pipe had been removed but my feeble wheeze could barely be heard. It was horrible and unbelievably frustrating. I would have a problem in my fucking room and there was nothing I could do and nobody could hear me to assist. Imagine it. You cannot walk. You cannot use your hands. And you cannot even talk – just make pathetic whining noises and get pissed off.

While Patrick Edlinger was creating a stir on television, hanging by just one arm from the overhang of a cliff some 50 metres above the ground, I was lying prone in a bed in Grenoble Hospital stoned out of my mind on medication. I spent two months in hospital. I had six operations on my hands, elbow and knee. Pins and bolts were rearranged as they battled to restore the use of my limbs. When you are lying there for weeks on end you lose a lot of weight, a lot of muscle, and your balance goes out of the window. I recovered slowly but steadily and finally the day came when I could totter out the front doors.

Thin and corpse-like I got home and weakly stepped up to the doorway. I extended a geriatric hand but could not even turn the key inside the lock. My wrists, especially my left one, were completely stiff. They would not straighten and my left hand would droop limply. I couldn't move it or do anything with it at all. As time passed it did get a little better but not that much. I tried to lift a small pan of water and I couldn't – not a big pan, just a small one, the sort of thing my young kids could manage. I was totally bemused by my pathetic body. Holding a mug of coffee would require an intake of breath and my wife would have to go next door to get the jars opened. I was as frail as an old lady and it was difficult to adjust, especially mentally. What would I do with the rest of my life? I survived, but for what? How could I earn a living to support my family? These were deep and troubling questions.

But soon after I got home I realised that I still wanted to climb. Even if my ascent from now on would be a boulder for ten-year-olds, as placid as a flight of stairs, then why not? Despite my disabilities I still had a passion for climbing and I was determined I would climb something. Anything. So I looked for something to climb, something easy.

I wandered around my neighbourhood and not far from my house I found a brick wall. It was modest in height, only two-and-a-half metres tall and it snaked two to three hundred metres along the boulevard. I rubbed my hands along it, feeling its texture, its soul. I felt an affinity with this wall, and decided there and then that this would be my challenge. My plan was not to climb it but to cross it horizontally, some 50 centimetres above the pavement.

At the beginning I could only cross two or three bricks before falling off, such was the weakness in my wrists. The problem was that when I let go with my right wrist to reach across, my left was so weak that it was impossible to hold on. Time and time again I would fall to the pavement, but it was good – I felt a little bit of progress each time, even if the progress could be measured in mere centimetres or less. And every day I had a new target.

It took me two months to get across just a metre or so. Two gruelling months, but I managed it. I would carry on trying to cross more sections of this wall. Bit by bit I made my second metre, then my third. And finally, one day I managed to traverse the whole wall – all two or three hundred metres of it. It had taken me two years of immense effort and dedication but at last I had done it. And when I reached the end of that marvellous wall, my strength for climbing was more than restored. My self-imposed rehabilitation had in fact led me on a journey to a point where I actually felt stronger than I did before. I bore the scars of my brush with death and my wrists were still gnarled and irregular like tree branches, but my strength, balance and coordination were restored.

In actual fact, crossing the entire stretch of that wall would be very challenging even for the fittest able-bodied climbers. On reflection, it seems easy to assert that my misfortune and the resulting adversity forced me to reach deep into my heart and find the motivation and direction for my life. But over those two or three years of successive accidents, hospitalisations and recuperations there were moments of physical and emotional pain, and there was only the present tense: a torturous world of doubts.

And so, with the wall behind me and after a gap of two years due to injury, I took to my cliffs once more. My appalling accident, as with the one which preceded it, occurred during the descent and not during the actual escalation itself, as many people often think. Both times my rope, literally my lifeline, gave way. Is it because I have been betrayed twice by ropes that I have chosen to escalate with nothing but my fingertips? Is it because paradoxically I feel safer relying on myself, rather than on so-called safety devices that have twice failed me in such a spectacular fashion? I have not the faintest idea, though when I think about it this may supply a plausible explanation.

I had fought long and hard to get back on the rocks and I greatly wanted to avoid plummeting to the ground again on the end of a frayed rope. I was ready to dive right in and make up for lost time, more than two lost years when I ought to have been approaching my prime. At the tail end of 1984, I achieved my long-held target, *L'Abominable Homme des Doigts*, a fearsome route up an unforgiving rock face. From my starting point halfway up the cliff in a little cave I pushed up this very challenging route free solo. The difficulty in climbing it is almost as tough as translating it effectively into English. The name of this very, very tough climb is something like The Abominable Finger Man (told you). *L'Abominable Homme des Doigts* was a 7b+, the highest level for free solo at this time. I felt very pleased to have reached what was at that point the pinnacle of free solo climbing. I continued to push it as far as I could as a free solo climber, finding new challenges.

The following year, I opened up a new and tougher 7c variant, *L'Abomifreux* (The Abominable Ugly) on the same cliff. It was indeed an abominably difficult ascent and really tested me, especially since I had to improvise and experiment as a pioneer of the route.

Four years after that, on this same rock face, I achieved an even more extreme solo version yet, *L'Abominafreux* (The Even More Abominably Ugly). This climb was an 8a.

As a conclusion, in 1992, I combined the three routes. I did them all solo again, but this time I would start as I had in prior climbs at the cave halfway up the rock face, climb up one route, descend to the cave, and instead of setting foot in it I would link it with the next climb. Thus *L'Abominable Homme des Doigts*, *L'Abomifreux* and *L'Abominafreux* were all combined without rest into one incredible climb. It was my own free solo trilogy. An 8a ascent, a 7c descent, then a 7b+ ascent! This new combination was designated an 8b. It was certainly the first 8b ever achieved without a rope, and as far as I know, even today many years later it remains one of the most extreme solo climbs ever completed anywhere.

I had succeeded in taking a beautiful revenge on fate. I had not only climbed again but I was climbing an 8b free solo! And it was with the same belief and training that I recovered and climbed once again, despite my third big fall in 1993. The following year I would start climbing buildings.

4

European Trilogy

All great works come in threes, all epic myths or timeless sagas. Climbers also like to unite their ultimate challenges into bold trilogies, Christophe Profit's success in 1987 being a fine example. Christophe defeated the Grandes Jorasses, the Matterhorn and the Eiger, the three superstars of the Alps. Christophe was not the first to climb what has become known as 'The Trilogy', but he was the first man to enchain them, that is, complete these mighty mountains in a single outing without returning to base camp. He climbed these three arduous peaks in a total time of just 42 hours. To enchain these three inaccessible faces back-to-back, in winter, alone and very fast... that was the archetypal dream of the 1980s climber.

After my aerial tour of Paris, I decided I had to realise my personal trilogy, set my own targets. After Christophe Profit's feat, climbing lost its way somewhat for several years; it floundered in an identity crisis, lacking new direction, new challenges. Effectively, having realised the inconceivable, climbed every cliff there is to climb in just about every conceivable way, there is little left to dream of. However I was to fly off on an unexpected tangent and my climbing evolved in a brave new world.

With my discovery of this new aspect of climbing in France and America I found myself alone in a totally new and uncharted domain, so I for one had plenty to dream about. Buildings were so flat and so vertical, the challenges and terrain so utterly divergent. It added a totally new dimension to climbing and there was so much to learn about. I had to learn about precise geometry, about engineering, architecture and construction, and apply my lessons from the natural world to the modern cityscape. Indeed I was forced to learn about aspects that for many had no place in the sport: security, policing and the judiciary. It was quite a revelation for a seasoned rock climber and great fun to tread an untrodden path. Luckily even now, years later, I still do not feel my scope for dreaming has narrowed, such is the infinity of high rise escalations.

I deliberated on what I should do and decided to branch out of France and take on my native Europe. My trilogy was decided. Frankfurt, Milan and Barcelona; three great cities with wonderful possibilities, and each conveniently reached by car in a reasonable timeframe from France.

After my Parisian tour *Paris Match* wants a piece from me again. The editor hears my idea and is taken by it, and so he elects to send a photographer with me for my trip around Western Europe. Not one to pay for free holidays, the editor of the magazine sets a deadline – we must achieve the story in no more than a dozen days. We also have a tight budget. Twenty thousand francs must cover everything: travel, accommodation, food and – a little optimistically – fines. We will have to watch our pennies and hope that any arrests or fines do not devour large chunks of our time or budget.

But it sounds like another good challenge and superbly entertaining. The team is reduced to an efficient core: Alexis the photographer, my brother Thierry as cameraman, and Bambi for the security details. Thierry and Bambi enjoyed their roles in Paris. Since the experience at the TF1 Tower, the reassuring presence of a strapping lad like Bambi allows me to approach the escalation with a little more serenity.

Late in the afternoon, our full car departs from Paris and moves off slowly towards Germany, its pretzels, its Black Forest and its grey sky. As the physical part of the trip is my business, the other three take turns at the steering wheel of my nice Golf. It makes sense to split the chauffeur role. With more than 4000 kilometres of highway to be traversed, mainly by night to save francs, it would have been easy to nod off and leave the road.

The city fades behind us and the flat interior of France opens up. I love travelling. I had few chances to travel when I was young and the sight of a border delights me. That finite division between cultures, languages, peoples, that stamp in your scrapbook of life experiences. But since we set out from Paris, I have not stopped humming an entire catalogue of my favourite songs, much to the despair of my friends. My singing and humming is actually pretty good, but the three other lads squashed into a noisy car are not so enamoured with it. The atmosphere swings wildly around after three hours on the road. But it doesn't matter much, I am happy, happy to be on my first large-scale project, my first big expedition.

Within a few hours the German landscape sails by and we are heading into new territory.

We cross the city limits and drive into Frankfurt by night. I am very gratified with what I see. Sparkling in the night air, modern Frankfurt looks like a paradise of skyscrapers. It is sad to think that this is in large part due to the Allied raids of the Second World War, the destruction, the reconstruction and so on. We head to our hotel but first, we travel down several avenues to make a quick visit to my goal. Germany's banking centre represents a concentration of towers more imposing and significant than La Défense. For me it is exactly like downtown America. Clambering around on the back seat of the car, I am bouncing as a kid in front of an enormous Christmas tree. On my spruce, no festoons nor trail of tinsel, but a steady stream of glittering floors. This is a veritable forest of buildings, each measuring in the region of 200 metres in height, possibility after possibility.

Around the corner from a crossroads a familiar facade entices me – the Dresdner Bank. A rock climber, harnessed in with plenty of safety equipment, had suspended himself from the first few metres of this building for an advertisement, the image being published worldwide in various magazines a dozen years ago. Regardless of the advert, I would have been drawn to this admirable and particularly photogenic silver tower with its edges smoothed off. The lack of sharpness lends it a placid juvenile charm. I know it sounds a little weird but I want to go up to it and hug it. So, a while back, a rock climber had pretended to climb it? I decide that I shall do the job properly tomorrow.

The next morning, we have a little problem. No more car. It is gone, whisked away and sent directly to the pound. A handful of Deutschmarks and a good two hours later, the car is recovered. But precious time has been lost, one of our twelve days. Our plans and preparation are scuppered since I need an early start, making it impossible to hope to achieve the climb today. No matter, I shall use the day to peruse the location and try out some movements, because in actual fact, I have not confirmed the feasibility of climbing this famous bank. On closer inspection the likelihood of the completion of my ascent can be speculated at, but an optimist would tend to regard it as achievable. The structure is similar to that of the Elf

Tower but with more inherent complexity. We surreptitiously survey the activity around the building. The security services here do not worry me that much, as by now I have decided to leave much of the worrying to my trusty assistants. Having said that, a bank remains a bank. Security can't be that lax. Will I outwit the guards of one of the top banks in the country? Will tomorrow see me breaking in and stealing this platinum ingot?

Alexis and my brother Thierry are both ready, incognito, cameras casually concealed. They can whip these out at a moment's notice and get the images we have to nail for *Paris Match*. Bulky professional cameras are easily noticed as out of the ordinary by any security guard worth his salt, so we have to follow particularly precise timing. Bambi's part in our mission is to drive me to the foot of the tower where I will have just seconds to attack the building and get out of reach. In the mundane traffic, he takes the wrong turn and embarks on a tourist circuit of Frankfurt's grey streets. This is a time of crucial mental preparation so this setback irritates me a lot, especially as I am now on unfamiliar ground. We are both pissed off and yell at each other. It is done with a grin and isn't really serious, just a few fireworks to let us both blow off a little steam. But still, we are both aware that with losing the car yesterday we cannot afford to lose another day today.

At the bank the others watch the minutes tick past with growing agitation. What is going on? And for me the disruption of my concentration starts an unwelcome internal domino effect; the stress rises and doubt gets the upper hand.

Finally, we spot the Dresdner Bank beyond an endless trail of red lights approximately two kilometres away. After a good quarter of an hour shuffling along, I bound out of the car, hunting down my two pals. They have left their hideout to mingle with the crowd and casually sit on a bench situated in a public garden near the building. Behind a group of anonymous faces, they wave at me. I get twitchy and frown; my partners will need to rehearse a little when it comes to discretion. It is time for them to return to the preselected place for photo shots, and to unpack the equipment, but I can't hang about and they are going to miss the first part of the ascent. Too bad, but I have no other choice than to attack at once. I fear that security has probably already spotted me, and I have to commit immediately or abandon the climb. If we lose this ascent then the whole project is threatened.

I spring over to the Achilles heel at the foot of this bar of silver and launch myself up its side. Quickly I am out of danger and can focus on the climb rather than the security guards. Years later, when I look back, I realise that this fear of being recognised and grabbed at the prelude of a climb is a little paranoid, but leaks do happen. And of course being a guard is usually mind-numbingly boring, so if there is even a hint of anything to do, any excitement, they do tend to jolt themselves awake ready to pounce. This possibility is at the forefront of my mind on all escalations. On occasions, to my bewilderment, the authorities have indeed known I was coming and intercepted me at the starting pistol. In Houston, for example, I was arrested even though I had yet to commit a crime. Houston. After all that planning and travel, to be collared before I can even get one foot on the building is a bitter pill to swallow.

But climbing the Dresdner is proceeding okay. It soon becomes clear that this escalation is difficult and has to be achieved as quickly as possible. The bank is a sapping obstacle and speed is my only way to reach the summit. For the first time I glance below to check out the authorities. Yes, as expected, there's a lot of activity down there, lots of uniforms running back and forth. The German fire brigade have reacted in a way I would have expected in America. They have resorted to drastic measures and have even taken out – and I have never seen this before – an immense inflatable mattress as used by stuntmen. The mattress can save people from falls of up to 50 metres. But from where I am, it would be necessary to use three of them!

I am surprised by this little show below and turn my gaze upwards with a smile. As I push onwards the façades around me fall away and dwindle in number with my progress. Little by little, Frankfurt sinks below my feet. And it's a long way down! When climbing a building, the feeling of height is multiplied tenfold by the optical effects of your surroundings. The size of a human being or a car below can be reminiscent of being in a plane. But the effect of height is particularly enhanced by the vertical and flat nature of a building. Buildings are almost universally a collection of right angles and parallel lines. When in contact with a building, say looking out of a window or escalating it, these lines tighten and narrow to a distant point and give a dramatic sense of perspective. Such an impression is much more obvious than when climbing a cliff face. And of course there is no balcony, banister or terrace to hold your eye, and this can explain the sensation of dizziness one gets when reaching significant elevations. A stable visual reference works with the internal ear to enable balance. The dizziness and vertigo up here is very real and I need to steady myself on several occasions.

The structure is making physical demands on me as well as causing me disorientation, but I find my rhythm and make it to the summit of the bank where a multitude of smart uniforms welcome me professionally and politely. I experience a mixture of German rigour and courtesy. And a baffling surprise – some of them even show me copies of my picture postcards! They are mine alright, I can recognise the pictures of myself on solo rock climbs even from here. I am incredulous. I have just climbed in Germany for the first time, only to discover that news of my Parisian escalation has spread across this part of Europe. Am I becoming internationally famous? Right now I don't really want to know about it, and half-heartedly sign autographs owing to the flood of lactic acid in my leaden forearms.

After a while I am led away to the exit. On the flight of steps outside, inquisitive onlookers applaud 'the French serial climber' warmly. It's so heartening to see. Amongst a small motorcade of emergency vehicles, my police car awaits on the other side of the public garden. On the street, I pass innocently in front of Alexis and my brother. A simple smile and nod is enough to inform me that the photos went marvellously well. Reassured, I enter the rear of the police car and the interior becomes a virtual discotheque of revolving lights. And a second surprise – Bambi has also been stuffed in the back! With an embarrassed smile and an inappropriate booming voice, he explains that he was picked up while distributing my promotional picture postcards just outside the bank's entrance! Okay, I understand things a little better now. When the convoy moves off, the last of the observers savour the final spectacle – two idiots in handcuffs, heading for the police station in fits of laughter.

Sat in his cell adjacent to mine, Bambi asks me what may happen. Born in a poor Parisian suburb, this guy has never been arrested but has heard many rumours and tales, a lot of them urban myths of course. I tell him of my arrests to date and hazard a guess at the hours ahead. The interrogation is courteous but as soon as the cops learn about the two others, a patrol is sent to pay them a special visit at the hotel. I can imagine Alexis and Thierry's faces when the cops knock on the door!

The inspector, who speaks French perfectly, explains to me that they have to follow these procedures and then, lighting a cigarette, tells me about a stream of possible escalations in Frankfurt. My European tour project makes him smile and apparently there is no problem for him if I want to do another one.

"A little advice though, just wait a little before trying to climb here again!"

Given the measures implemented for my arrest, I could have expected a much worse reception. We are soon released and happily there is no legal action and no fine and we are sent on our way without hassle or drama. The journey can continue! It's gone very well so far and we can tackle the second summit of my trilogy. Italy is waiting for us.

Almost as soon as we exit the German police station, we set sail for Milan in my little Golf. We drive down through Germany and travel via hilly Switzerland by night. The car undulates through this scenic land, though sadly there is little to see by starlight. We are all haggard and bloodshot after the exertions of the day and night. Eventually we arrive in Milan, a city absolutely berserk about football. Even though it is not that far from the Alps, virtually no one knows anything about climbing here, so I am not quite sure how an escalation will be received. But before all that, it is necessary to locate a bed and sleep. We are all shattered and have a big day ahead of us tomorrow.

At midday, we finally manage to drag ourselves away from the soft pillows and duvets, refreshed and refuelled. Milan is clearly not a tall city, and nothing had jumped out at me on the way towards the hotel last night. We will have to hunt down my dream building, so we set about wandering this noisy metropolis. Three hours later we have seen a lot of unspectacular structures down the main avenues, and countless narrow alleys draped in the bunting of drying linen. Our purse seems to be shrinking quickly and only two buildings appear worthy of the visit: the Pirelli Tower, 120 metres of ageing and commonplace architecture, or the Banca di Milano, 110 metres of, well, pretty much the same. The contrast with lofty Frankfurt is striking. Our research is thorough and our conclusion inescapable – there are few high rise structures in Milan and nothing outstanding in terms of height to climb. It's a dilemma we toss to and fro over alfresco coffees.

Soon it occurs to us that although lacking in the skyscraper department, there is however a wealth of historic or religious buildings. Why not climb a beautiful church rather than an ordinary taller building? We decide to head out a second time for another two hours of scouting.

Duomo di Milano is a spectacular find. It is a glorious marble cathedral surmounted by a gigantic dome, built between the 14th and 16th centuries. The highly ornate exterior, interior and powerful spiritual presence draws thousands of tourists and devotees every day. The four of us approach the cathedral from the square and stand before its lively Napoleonic façade, topped off with countless decorative spires. From below, the structure seems complex yet accessible, but it remains to be seen how the summit looks. Behaving like nice tourists, we begin a cultural tour with a slightly different interest in the architectural exploits of the cathedral's builders. I imagine myself as Quasimodo up there. My unkind friends say I resemble him. With a bit of luck, tomorrow we may see the hunchback of Duomo di Milano.

Alexis is far happier with the photographic opportunities here and decides to enter. We quietly follow and stroll around this hushed and holy site. In the nave, hundreds of little wax candles flicker silently, continuously renewed by the pious believers of Catholic Italy. Alexis suggests lighting one as an act of faith. It sounds like a nice idea! I pick one, light it, carefully place it in the middle of the others and then, with my most beautiful wrinkled smile, I say a little prayer for my objective. A glow penetrating my eyelids alerts me to a miniature fire and my wide eyes reveal a disaster – my wax candle has keeled over with a flamboyant splutter and broken into a tiny blaze! The wrecked candle has split down its length and is self-destructing in a molten mess. Is this a divine sign, a bad omen, a warning of things to come? Is this disapproval from on high? Would I not be entitled to my small slice of paradise? I exchange glances with my aghast friends – the symbolism is not lost on them either. There are a few stifled guffaws which we desperately try to prevent from echoing around the cavernous interior. Pools of molten wax are all that is left of my candle, lumpy and irregular like the contours of my nose. We creep out but the comical self-immolation of the melodramatic candle stays with us for the rest of the day.

Saturday morning begins like a dream. The weather is magnificent, surprisingly agreeable for climbing cathedrals. It feels almost like a cool, brisk springtime, although it is actually close to Christmas. After a frugal breakfast, our team heads out in high spirits. The Duomo di Milano's white marble flight of steps, already transformed into a swarming ant hill of humanity, proudly reflects light onto the surrounding buildings as if to demonstrate its difference, its nobility. Away from the crowd, I innocently get geared up then quietly edge closer to the pillar by which I will make the escalation.

The ascent is complicated and will follow various miniature structures and pillars until I make the summit, only 50 metres off the ground. While there is no security to worry about, there are hundreds of people milling around. I plant my hands on the pillar, exploring it, establishing my relationship with it. The first contact with marble is always a strange sensation for a rock climber – the stone is cold, extremely smooth but paradoxically warm, princely. I give my bag of magnesia chalk a final check and then begin the escalation. I pull myself heavenwards with my hands and push with my feet against the pillars, hunting for the right balance. This is a bit of a test for me. Despite the clear sky and sunlight it is quite cold this morning and my body has not yet warmed up. One feels a little on edge when one's body isn't quite ready. I stutter, falter. It isn't a textbook start and I remind myself a shuffling approach is not on the programme today. I decide to commit. I raise another leg, then manoeuvre towards the top of the pillar, eyeing up a series of easier and smaller columns. I work to apply perfect adhesion to the marble pillar, gripping it like a gecko with my chalked fingers and slippered feet. Deliberately and without haste, I finally curl my right hand towards the top of the pillar for a firm grip...

My buttocks flat on the ground, I open my eyes. What happened? My hand, a blast of electricity, the pavement, all within a split second? All around, people pass by without even looking at me. At the foot of God they are used to this kind of extravagance. After all, everybody has the right to kneel, bow or prostrate themselves at such a place.

I sit there astonished and alarmed. Since my hospitalisations, I am really afraid of falls. But luckily, I fell vertically downwards without a shunt, spin or twist. My posterior took the impact of a three-metre fall. My weakened wrists were spared and as far as I am concerned the rest of me doesn't really matter. Regaining my senses and ignoring the throbbing sensation in my underpants, I look for an explanation for this improbable fall. I definitely took an electric shock. Was the irreverent rock climber struck by a divine bolt of lightning? Have I blasphemed and been sent back to earth by an act of God?

Strange thoughts race through my head as I dust myself down, my hand still tingling. I find Alexis and use his telephoto lens to re-examine the Duomo di Milano. Incredible! A very discreet network of exposed and potent electric wires covers any possible space which could serve as a place of repose for pigeons. I just took a severe blow of juice! My heart is still pounding. Yesterday's wax candle was indeed a bad premonition! The candle knew what was to happen! Offended, we return to the hotel, not sure whether we should be angry, afraid or if we should laugh at this unfathomable episode. Exit Duomo di Milano – there is no way I can climb it. It is necessary to immediately find another objective.

Days pass. Several of them. We find nothing and we have to be in Paris on Wednesday to submit the article to the editor. Reluctantly, I decide I must return to the Banca di Milano. The tower rises directly above the pedestal of a busy shopping centre so I obviously cannot practice any movements in advance. I study it carefully through my binoculars, keeping a keen eye out for any unexpected surprises. Everything seems fine, the escalation looks feasible although from here it is impossible to know the full story. For now I content myself with the knowledge I have. Time is pressing so the objective is set.

It is Sunday and more than a week has passed since I was electrocuted by the pigeon-proof pillars of Duomo di Milano. More than half of our time has been swallowed up and we have ticked off only one building. My brother has negotiated access to the roof of the opposite building (something doable in Italy!) in order to obtain the best angle for photography. Unlike other urban centres around the world, where humanity tends to persist more steadily throughout the day, Italian cities and towns empty and fill with people like the tides. It is now an almost deserted city and time to ascertain the best ways to get off the ground and onto the roof of the shopping centre to cross towards the Banca di Milano.

I sniff around and spot something. A metal bar designed to support verandas remains inadvertently protruding, left down by a casual shop assistant. This fortunate oversight forms my entry point and will allow me to pull myself up. I look around, conscious as ever at the beginning of my escalations not to draw attention to myself. A few figures stroll around within a block or so. It is so quiet I can hear a discarded newspaper on

a bench over the road rustle in the breeze. The coast seems clear. I jump
and catch the bar which, with an infernal noise, breaks with my weight.
This horrendous snapping, crashing, thumping and tearing metallic noise
doubtless alarms the whole district. Dramatically, the veranda starts to
unfold on one side. I cannot dwell now, no more hesitation! Action! I
attack once more and pass the half-unfurled and lopsided veranda then
quickly make the roof, and within seconds I cross the shops towards the
tower.

At the real departure point of the escalation, a nasty surprise: the
structure turns out to be a very dirty, slippery metal, obviously never cleaned
properly by the building management and seldom cleansed by a good
thunderstorm. The bank is coated in the greasy soot of years of Milanese
traffic. What had appeared through binoculars to be a stroll in the park
is immediately transformed into an errant and unforeseen war. I ascend
with trepidation. My feet slide repeatedly, and my mental red alert panels
ignite and flash. Physically, the effort bears no comparison with my most
beautiful climbs – this game is particularly unpredictable and capricious.
At no time do I feel safe, the movements I employ being tortuous, complex
and messy. Halfway up, I am amazed to be still following this ill-considered
adventure. The more a high building impresses visually, the more difficult
it is supposed to be, according to logic or predisposition. Here however,
on this average building, without style, without class, without height, the
level of difficulty is immeasurably disproportionate. It just goes to show
that unspectacular buildings, like people, can easily be underestimated. I
slip and wobble once again. What a tricky concrete pile!

After 30 minutes of intense effort, I overcome this wriggling eel of a
bank to reach the summit and clamber over the railing onto the roof,
happy to escape this booby-trapped tower unhurt. I am pleased to have
made it yet I feel as if a crucial and decorative element of the play was
missing. There was little beauty in evidence today, either architecturally
or in terms of my own choreography. I look over the handrail towards the
ground. The Banca di Milano was a treacherous escalation, and there can
be no descent. On the rail, I loosen the slippers which are torturing my
feet. Where are the cops? In fact nobody is waiting for me on the rooftop.
No one around to put me in handcuffs or lecture me. No one to wonder
if I should be taken to the local mental institution rather than the police
station. There is nothing up here at all but cooing pigeons bobbing their

heads in sync with their jerky steps. The surroundings are still and silence hangs in the air above the city. Never mind, I tell myself sitting on the rail, I am sure they are on their way. The panoramic sight of the city contrasts with dew-laden Milanese cobwebs under yellowish clouds in a delectable play of light. Such a perfect day. Absolutely brilliant.

Later, my pondering starts to transform into more searching questions. I have been up here 20 minutes and there is not the slightest revolving light in sight! This is weird. Not that I am absolutely anxious to be arrested, to enrich my collection of police inspectors' visiting cards – but how am I going to get back down before Monday morning? I have to admit it, I had never imagined that this might happen. I peer around the streets below but still nothing. Well, I have a T-shirt, which could act as a light windbreak… No, it is impossible to spend the night here. The leniency of the day will give way to the briskness of the evening and the December night will be less kind still. After another half an hour of reflection, perplexed and a little worried, I repeatedly cross the rail, making a pretence of attempting to descend the façade and abandoning it. I hope that my friends will understand the signal. Ten minutes later, I can hear far off the blaring of a siren. Hurrah! The cavalry!

Four racing fire engines and police cars stop outside the bank. Later I was to learn that my brother raised the alarm, even though he is incapable of speaking a single word of Italian. It is a miracle that they found the correct address. As in Frankfurt, they fuss around inflating an enormous mattress, then a guy tries to contact me by bellowing into a megaphone. I cannot catch a word of what he is saying and remain stonily indifferent to his efforts. Sat on the rail, I watch them moving below like insects without really understanding what they are doing. I just want to take the elevator down and get arrested and then head off to Barcelona. Come on! I don't mind taking the stairs either, I just want to get off this roof. Climbers may be very keen to make the summit but they are just as keen to get off it. What is going on?

A few minutes later the metal access door cautiously creaks and then half-opens. A head hesitantly inches out. Two firemen approach gingerly and speak to me slowly and compassionately in Italian. For sure, it looks like they think I was about to commit suicide. Maybe they thought I was one of these golden boys or hot shots that blew everything on a risky flutter on the stock exchange. As I stand to address them they take a fearful step backwards with their hands outstretched in placating gestures. They seem to be begging me, reasoning with me, showing me how much they care. I try to tell them I don't want to die. With my passport and my postcards in hand, I try to transform my French into makeshift Italian, haphazardly adding an 'i' at the end of every word. It is a bizarre situation. I feel as if I am in a slapstick comedy.

Eventually, these two parallel worlds unite in a more coherent one, and I finally pay my long-awaited visit to the police station. On Sundays, it seems, Italy stops. Milan is empty, abandoned, a ghost city. Apparently, the cops do not want to waste their time with me either. They don't want a troublesome Frenchman interrupting their easy Sunday – they are too busy chatting to each other, reclining in their chairs with their feet up on the table. I am quickly released and the policeman who arrested me at the bank even takes me back to the hotel! It is very kind of him.

Covered in soot and grime, and resembling a maintenance worker, I am back in my room. I am safe after a slippery escalation, and avoiding prison cells and fines is great news for both our schedule and budget. The four of us are glad to be at the end of the second act of our journey even if, once again, I have to hunt my car down at the pound...

We waste little time and in the early hours my recovered car leaves Italy for the Iberian peninsula. Long hours pass as we cross southern France and drive over the Pyrenees. More tarmac blurs by until finally the outskirts of the Spanish city come into view.

For the visitor it is immediately clear that Barcelona is the victim of her own prosperous economy. Unchecked urban sprawl means the infrastructure is overwhelmed by dense traffic and we lose a couple of hours even once we make the city itself. Having swallowed almost a thousand kilometres of road at sometimes hair-raising speeds it is irritating to be stuck in traffic within a few miles of our goal. We impatiently stick our heads out the window to be greeted with honking horns, gridlock and fumes.

Getting around takes forever and we follow our routine of getting lost in the meanders of the city in search of beautiful architecture. By now we are getting tired and the conversation becomes less cordial. I have visited the heart of Barcelona before and it offers us a few interesting choices. A magnificent church near the city centre, Sagrada Familia, gets me excited but the unfortunate experience in Milan and the reputed fragility of the building discourage me a little.

In the suburbs of the city, quite close to the sea, stand two towers, each about 150 metres high. Before collapsing in our hotel we muster enough strength to forge up the coast and get a closer look at these two high rises. The towers are quite attractive and very different to each other in all but height. The traditional glass building, Torre Mapfre, is about a dozen metres from the metallic framed one, Hotel Arts, a juxtaposition which establishes an interesting spectacle. Apparently they are part of the Olympic village built for the 1992 Games. I weigh them up and select the one which possesses the more original architecture: the Hotel Arts. The 600-room luxury hotel is a unique glass box encased in a metal cage, looking almost like the engineers had forgotten to remove the scaffolding after it was completed.

The next day Gilles Loth, a journalist for *Paris Match*, lands to conduct the interview. He shakes my hand and we stretch out on the beach before enormous waves breaking on the pier. If the temperature had been a little warmer, I would have enjoyed being cleansed by the sea spray, but still it's not bad at all for December. I recount our hectic week to Gilles in the shadow of my next challenge; the successes, trials and tribulations plus my assessment of tomorrow's escalation. After a while Gilles departs with a full notebook and heads back to Paris to prepare the article. I look skywards and decide there is still ample time to check out my target. Light is fading and I take advantage of the dimness to try some movements, even though I risk a premature audience or the attention of the hotel security team. I climb up and down a few metres of the hotel a couple of times, seeking to understand it. The building seems relatively easy to climb but it is clear that I will need to put the first 25 metres quickly behind me as guards could easily grab me through the windows in this zone. Beyond this early exposure, however, the escalation looks highly achievable.

During the night, an ominous rumbling of thunder wakes me. Outside, the sky is split by flashes of lighting. Rain pounds my window pane as a violent thunderstorm envelops Barcelona. Brilliant... Rain on metal, there is nothing better to frighten a climber. In Formula 1 racing, the drivers have a choice of tyres, switching to wets for the rain so they don't fly off the track. I am however condemned to remain on slicks. My slippers rely on friction to be effective and are only designed for dry conditions. Put simply, when it rains you should not climb. But I must make this escalation as the magazine deadline imposes a return to Paris tomorrow. We can make it if the police are understanding and I don't get intercepted. To reduce the risk of losing a day at the police station, the ascent is scheduled for the early morning, only a few hours from now. Worried, I sit by the window and end the night by counting raindrops. One, two, three, twenty million...

Bambi wakes me up, slumped in my chair, my head pressed against the radiator in front of the window. Great parallel grooves are etched into my face. As I derail my cheek and lips I blearily recall my last conscious moments. Counting raindrops and sheep tends to have the same effect. But good news: the sky appears to have lost its cloud cover and regained its morning colours, as if nothing had taken place. I observe environmental cues. Outside, a breeze gives a cypress tree a shiver. Conditions look right for swift evaporation, and I am confident the building will quickly dry. We grant two more hours for the sun to carry out its work and the climb is fixed for ten o'clock.

At ten sharp, I leap out of the car and sprint towards the skyscraper, then springboard away from the pavement. I make it past the first five metres without incident. As I ascend I notice that zones of humidity remain, making the escalation possibly very problematic. I rapidly cross from the glass panes onto the metal structure to scatter the security team which has just turned up in force below. They yell their anger and despair from the square, to the great surprise of their fellow Spaniards passing by.

I could move diagonally and take advantage of the numerous struts of the lattice exoskeleton of the Hotel Arts, but to save time I climb straight up. The beams cross over each other a little clear of the tower. This nice grippable structure makes climbing relatively simple, although it is still essential to remind myself to respect the building. To the left, a beam forms a giant 'Z' and invites me to modify my route. I accept the invitation and push upwards. Then – my feet slip! Without any time to react, I fall and leave the structure... I tumble over a beam two metres below me. I flail out wildly and grab onto a support, and the fall ends there. My legs swing beneath me a good third of the way up the building. I clutch the pillar and wrap my legs around it, then take stock of the situation. My slippers had not stuck to the surface! The genius architect who had the idea to place this vertical beam right here saved my life. Awash in enthusiasm and excitement, I had not noticed this hidden wet zone. Cautiously I recover, chastising my lack of awareness. But today is my lucky day. With much more focus I ascend towards the top, wary of areas of damp which could bring the escalation to an end.

At the summit the police are waiting, none too amused, a dozen metres from me. They are on the roof and I am at the top of the cage. If I do not move, they will not approach. I hesitate. Do I take the risk of descending the building and hope to slip through the net? Or do I surrender right now and pray that my dinner date at the police station is as brief as in Frankfurt and Milan?

With the lattice free of the building, the beam I am holding onto is five or six metres from the rooftop, and connected to the awaiting cops only by a ten-centimetre-wide beam. To the right of the slender beam, a 150-metre drop. And to the left, just as much. I could and maybe should crawl across, but for the thrill of it, plus due to my pride – I have an audience up here and down there – I think it's nice to finish with a little flourish. I bring myself to my feet on the top strut, then walk the tightrope of the narrow beam above a sheer drop towards my jittery captors. I hop off and greet them with a smile.

"Hola! Nice to see you guys. Well, I took the long way up because I get claustrophobic in elevators…" It looks like the policemen don't see the funny side. Their faces betray their collective thought that I am psychotic. They move in to arrest me, and as they slap the handcuffs on, they stare at me as if I was utterly insane.

There's a trip to the police station of course, but at the end of the day, everything is back to normal. Except for my car. Guess what? We have to go to the pound. Yet again. Is there some sort of telepathic link between me and my vehicle? When I get seized by the authorities and locked up, it does too. I go to rescue it as night falls. Barcelona is already shrouded in darkness by the time we start our long drive back to Paris. The three of us hit the road tired but in good spirits. In eleven days, despite several tricky issues, I climbed three towers in three different countries and we captured some nice images. It takes us all night and into the morning but we get to Paris with our mission accomplished.

I recuperate in a soft bed then head down to the offices. *Paris Match* plans to run a six-page article on my escalations, a real once-in-a-lifetime experience for a rock climber. I am very excited. The mainstream media does not usually report vertical odysseys, except perhaps during the July 'silly season'. Due to a general lack of domestic current events (politicians take a break in the summer) the media tend to fill airtime and page space with things like mountain accidents, forgetting that, statistically, swimming kills nearly ten times as many people as the mountains.

The magazine's deadlines are tight and I stay in the offices right through the night until the morning, assisting the graphic designer in selecting the best photos, juggling them around until we get it right. The article starts with a picture taken in the Milanese cathedral. The subject – me looking offended in front of my collapsed wax candle. Next follows a series of contrasting and provocative photos covering the cathedral, Dresdner Bank, Banco di Milano and Hotel Arts. The article is ready.

But then, tragedy. The famous television host Léon Zitrone dies, followed by a great film-maker, Louis Malle. Big tragedies, big news, big stories and my article is shunted out of the publishing schedule. And then the following week the former French President, François Mitterrand, passes away too. And so does any hope of publishing my European tour.

A week or so later, Canal+ TV buys some of our images for their famous show *Nulle Part Ailleurs*. They feel it is a good story for the holiday season as it has something of a fairy tale about it. The audience reacts well and the experience is shared over the airwaves, so the project is not a total loss. Although we never got the article published in *Paris Match* as planned, this fortnight remains an unforgettable memory, like the frolics of the summer holidays when you were a carefree teenager.

That Christmas, a fire is lit within me. I have no doubt at all that more escalations will follow. I shall climb again, farther, higher, with more style, more daring. My passion has never been stronger. It is a beautiful world filled with beautiful challenges. It cannot wait any longer.

5

JAILHOUSE ROCK

A young woman wails and whines. Apparently she is delirious, suffering from narcotic withdrawal symptoms, offending everyone who has the audacity to meet her glance. Sometimes, she even starts to sing. Terribly out of tune. It is incredible how a female voice can echo in such a gloomy corridor.

She shares this anteroom of the Court of Justice of San Francisco with about 50 other prisoners, chained in groups of ten, each awaiting their judgement. They are almost without exception all sturdy black men, 'outsiders' as they are sadly named on the French side of the Atlantic. Nobody speaks, and the warders have a mocking manner today which does little to steady the unhinged woman. In her orange-coloured suit, a synonym for madness and incarceration, this howling wench is the only one expressing her bitterness, her misery. The rest of us, up for sentences of less than five years, maintain the sanity to keep quiet and not to stand out. But it is fair to say that amongst this motley crew, a skinny Caucasian from France stands out quite a bit. With my hands chained behind my back I observe this unpleasantly familiar spectacle. This is the dark side of our modern societies, of our so-called liberal and civilised democracies.

I have freely exchanged my new shoes for a rotting and disintegrating pair belonging to a companion in this confinement, a Mexican cocaine dealer. Chico has worn these shoes for at least as long as he has been in jail – three long years. His shoes do not exude the fragrant aroma of the historic French town of Grasse back home, famed as the world's perfume capital, but I don't really care. Grasse can be smelt many miles downwind, and so can these decomposing shoes, but it doesn't matter because I won't be here that long. And it is not easy to see or smell my feet anyway. Because of my tiny size, the store men of the Sailor County Jail could not find a suit to fit me. It seems they have no uniforms for people of my stature – the guys in here are of a completely different demographic. I look ludicrous in this overly baggy and loose prison suit, my hands and feet hidden from daylight by unintentional bell-bottoms. If it weren't for the violent orange I would look like a Jedi knight, unlike all these tall black guys who fill the uniforms pretty well!

I peruse the scene and take in my surroundings. I am not from this world. I am an ET who wants to return home. The meaning of prison to me though is very different than it is for these guys. For me it's a brief interlude which punctuates each of my ascents. Freedom awaits me this evening, I just know it. These men however must linger in this purgatory for years at a time.

A pair of grim guards approach and seize me. It looks like it's my turn before the law. I am no longer a nameless face of the dungeons, I am to come under the scrutiny of the court and face justice. I am led up some stairs and through a set of doors to another world. Wooden panels, people in suits, supreme formality make a potent contrast to the stark surroundings of my cell. Golden sunlight pours through the courtroom windows. On his throne the magistrate briefly asks some technical questions, then the prosecutor turns to his colleagues. He seems annoyed, as if he had lost his keys. There is more muttering and rustling of papers before the magistrate addresses me.

"The law offers you the right of appeal through an interpreter but we did not foresee this requirement. You will be brought back in front of the court later."

It's deflating news. Wouldn't it be better to just guillotine me right now? I imagined that I would now be heading outside to reassure my family of my release and safety, but instead I am again thrown into a van in handcuffs. Back to square one, prison and uncertainty. And what's worse, this is the second time this has happened to me here. At this point of my life I do not speak English particularly well, at least not well enough to deal with such matters. The first time I stood before the San Francisco court, it was with neither lawyer nor interpreter. No one had told me that I had the right to a defence lawyer (or maybe they did, but it was lost in translation) and I thought I could just defend myself. Why not? I just wanted to get out of here. I casually informed the American magistrate in atrocious English that I could defend myself. He seemed most irritated by this absurd Frenchman and disagreed, sending me down until they could find an interpreter. And here we are again…

I think again of my arrival in San Francisco, of my visit to this fabulous city, and my search for graceful structures to climb. I had taken in the tourist and architectural sights, including a visit to the famous prison of Alcatraz in San Francisco Bay, within a stone's throw of the golden door which marks the entrance to the city. After eyeing up multiple locations, I was torn between the iconic Golden Gate Bridge and the magnificent Transamerica Pyramid, a truly unique tapering skyscraper dominating the business district. My preparation was logical and rather well thought out. I had omitted just one small detail: the electronic surveillance, particularly fashionable in the land of the free…

Spring, California. The amber sun is slowly sinking in the blue sky, transforming the world's most famous suspension bridge into a massive ruby jewel. An icy breeze from the Pacific blows across the bay. Neither I nor the photographer need to be told to take advantage of this magic moment. Quietly, I pull out my slippers and clean them diligently. The soles must be spotless, immaculate. For rock climbers, preparing our slippers is a real rite, a moment of meditation used to acquire the concentration and serenity demanded by the performance. You will never see a climber hastily equipping himself before a competition, or a marksman ripping out his rifle ten seconds before the kill. For me climbing solo, without ropes, is a serious undertaking. My life depends upon my physical preparation, my technique, and my state of mind. All I need are my slippers and the bag into which I plunge my hands to coat them with magnesia powder.

I peer around the bridge, seeking my route to the distant top. My choice is logical. I must climb up a cable and join one of the two heavy suspension cables swooping off the bridge towers.

The bridge hangs from what appears to be four cables running about eight inches from one another. But actually this is a pair of parallel cables looping over the main suspension cable and returning to the bridge. I will take the cable closest to the bridge tower. This makes my task markedly harder than taking a central cable, which would take me to where the main suspension cables hang the lowest. The cable I choose rises 227 metres directly upwards towards the apex of the Golden Gate Bridge. It is stark and lonely, and worst of all terribly vertical, offering no possibility of rest.

As I stare at it, the idea seems like a kind of joke. But I must focus – doubt or humour have no place, and I must remain lucid and not underestimate the difficulty.

The photographer estimates the time of escalation to be about 15 minutes. I know differently. The dimensions of the cable, approximately ten centimetres in diameter, will cause problems. My hands cannot enclose it as they could when climbing a rope, for example. I will have to squeeze the cable to support my entire body weight, which will mean a big expenditure of energy. Climbing like this for ten metres is no problem, but for 227… I am chancing it a bit. I know I must not hang around up there. Nor here. Okay then, let's climb this bridge!

I remove my jacket and energetically rub my hands with the magnesia. I breathe freely, dunk my hands in a little more powder, and then seize the cable for the first time. It is stiff, very stiff. The paint makes it slippery and perturbs me a little. But I immediately take off. At first, a series of button-like rivets allow me to speed up the cable. Then, the bolts run out and the vertical cable becomes smooth – this is where it gets serious. The wind pierces my clothes, icy and powerful. I decide to climb the cable like a rope, by taking it in both hands to pull up my arms, then bringing up my feet and hoping to use them in a similar motion. Almost immediately I realise this technique is too physical and asks for too much energy. I muse at my naïvety, my misconception that this huge bridge would constitute an appetiser before the main course of the Transamerica Pyramid. I remind myself once again that in climbing, optimism is not always your best friend. But I carry on. This technique is the only safe way to make the main suspension cable and I cannot waste time or energy on hesitation.

Although physically demanding, in a short time I have already covered a lot of ground. I am in a trance. I imagine I am on a cliff as I close my fingers around the sides of the cable while delicately placing my feet upon the cold steel. The ceaseless movement of cars below indicates no one has noticed me yet. It is the golden end of the afternoon and half of the city is returning home to Oakland, whilst the other half drives in the opposite direction. Few of San Francisco's inhabitants pay any attention to the magic of the bridge at this time of day. But do Parisians smile every morning at the sunrise over the Eiffel Tower? I am aware of the beauty around me though I cannot afford the luxury of dwelling upon it. I keep pulling myself up, higher and higher into thin air.

Ten more minutes pass. I look upwards. The cables seem to disappear in the dense blue of the sky. Wow! What a sight. I keep squeezing with my fingers and pulling my entire body with my arms. But by now I am crawling up this thick cable pitifully slowly, and using huge reserves of energy. Paralysis starts to creep into my arms just before the middle of the ascent. I know such a development can cause everything to unravel very quickly and that I cannot continue like this. On a rope, we use our feet to grasp, and that allows us to use our thighs to grip and climb. A painted cable of steel makes this impossible. I have no grip, and my legs are as much use to me for locomotion as legs are to a fly. In fact, I start to feel like a tiny fly struggling in the middle of this huge cobweb… The wind strengthens more and more, whistling through the structure of the bridge. A return ticket? Forget it! It is already too late to stop the ascent. Fatigued and increasingly disconcerted, I take a look at where I am. I am in the middle of nowhere. Worse still, I know my physical limits. *Merde* – this is not good at all. This really is a bit of a problem…

I start to panic as I now know I will not make the summit, let alone have the strength to secure myself at the top or descend from it. Sometimes, when comfortably sat in the leather of an armchair watching the television news, I wonder why the victims of a fire, for example, did not fight harder when their lives depended on it. The answer is simple. When the muscles cannot take any more, the will to survive just cannot help. I know this better than anybody, but I also know that my training allows me to be effective in spite of a massive concentration of lactic acid in my muscles. I left the ground more than 20 strenuous minutes ago. It is as plain as the nose on my mangled face that the difficulty of the challenge is far greater than my estimations, but I try to remain composed. I must act fast if I am to get out of this situation.

I decide to use another technique, less physical but more unpredictable. The crux of a solo ascent lies in the management of the unknown, in the capacity of the climber to remain quiet, lucid and capable of making the best choices. By switching to a method known by climbers as a 'Dülfer' movement (after its creator Hans Dülfer), I reduce the time of escalation but also my safety margin. This technique is meant to be used to climb corners and carries a significant risk of slippage. But my forearms are burning and will soon fail – I have no choice.

My attention turns to my feet. I place them on the two parallel cables, in the narrow grooves between the strands. I take the other cables in each hand. My arms work perpendicularly against the cables while my feet push against the other two, and I resume my progress. I use different muscles in my arms, giving a chance for the lactic acid in my forearms to move elsewhere. With the slippery paint and buffeting wind, the game becomes even harder. My limbs are working within a very small square. If my foot slips, the tension created by the opposition of the lower and upper limbs will collapse... and me with them. It's a serious – and, in all honesty, desperate – measure. I am now utterly exposed to the hazards of moisture. A speck of rain would end everything. But the sky is clear, the blue on one side giving way to gold on the other.

A helicopter approaches, then hovers above the bridge near this tiny figure of a human being scaling a cable. The beating of its blades mixes with the rush of the wind, as if the pilot wanted to remain discreet and not disturb me. Below, three highway lanes have been closed by the police. They have arrived in force and a muffled symphony of distant sirens rides on the wind. The firemen are also there, and so it seems are a bunch of journalists in TV vans. It's quite unnecessary, all this fuss. Hey! Why not call the CIA and the FBI? Swat teams? Perhaps you should scramble a squadron of F-16 fighters to launch a barrage of missiles, or maybe launch a warhead from a nuclear submarine in the bay? This American melodrama does not impress me any more, after my visits to New York and Chicago. I am simply confused as to why every time I escalate a structure it terrifies the local authorities so much. And how did they know about it? Unknown to me, one of the bridge's 15 surveillance cameras betrayed me. I had honestly thought I could climb the Golden Gate discreetly on my own, get a few snaps, then perhaps get arrested rather quietly. It is clear that I have underestimated this escalation on more than one front.

I am well behind my anticipated schedule and, as if to remind me, the light is gently fading. I keep fighting my way to the top of these endless cables. It's tough going. Powerful squalls shake the bridge, giving me the unpleasant sensation that an invisible giant is shaking my cable in an attempt to dislodge me. Great!

Apart from the odd seagull that shoots by, I am very isolated up here. My arms and legs are trembling as the exertion starts to take its toll. But the main suspension cable is now within range. I can see where my vertical cable joins the main cable, just before its meeting point with one of the bridge towers. It is approaching sunset and just below the apex of the tower I can distinguish the two boys in beige sent to arrest me. But my current problem remains climbing, nothing more than climbing. The rest is purely administrative formality, paperwork, shit.

The last section is upon me, but it will be the toughest yet. A dozen metres from the top I see a bracket between the two cables which gives me something to hold onto, but cancelling out that advantage, I see that the cable I am climbing is pressed against the main suspension cable as it wraps around the main one and heads down again. This only gives me half the cable to hold onto! I am obliged to press my fingertips like crab claws around the front of the cable, as I am unable to place a hand behind it, or use the full length of my fingers and palm. Already exhausted, the challenge is immense. It is the ultimate fight and I am using my last reserves.

Revolving lights swirl more than 200 metres beneath me, and the cable below is lost in the gently faded light. The traffic jam unnecessarily created by the police is simply gigantic, endless. With my right hand I put everything I have into hauling myself up by the tips of my fingers and throwing a leg over the main cable. I tremble and splutter but make it. I pause upon the bracket, millimetres from safety but millimetres from the edge. One last effort to get around this pipeline-like obstacle…

I pull myself over and find myself on top of the main cable and in view of the summit, shattered but delighted. I never thought I would have to go through so much to reach this point. I haul myself to my feet and regain my breath, allowing my muscles to recuperate. The suspension cable has two thin wires running either side at hand height, obviously for maintenance workers, which would enable the cops to approach me if they were game – but they are staying put. They wait for me a little higher, on a balcony used for inspections and maintenance. I follow the cable a few metres above them and mount the uppermost part of the bridge tower to reach the true apex of the Golden Gate. I climb to the little lookout post equipped with a red aircraft warning beacon, and raise my hands in triumph to give the guys in the helicopter some nice footage. The view over the bay is stunning. Serenely I take out a camera with a wide-angle lens and immortalise this magic moment. Such a sunset deserves it.

The two cops get impatient behind their railings. I tuck my camera away in the bottom of a pocket, hoping to be able to give it discreetly to the photographer below. Then I head towards the cops along the top of the main cable. The closer I get, the more impressive they appear. In fact, they are enormous. I smile and launch a shy "Hi!" just to show I am not hostile, that it was all simply a little joke. Before handcuffing me they ask if I planned to commit suicide. To me the question is a little strange. I answer in my fractured English.

"Come on, guys, I have just arrived at the summit after 45 minutes of intense effort, without the chance to take a rest! Better ask d'Abbeville why he didn't take the plane across the Atlantic, or why Marie-Jo Pérec didn't ride a motorbike to break the 400 metres world record!"

They seem to think my answer is equally weird. Maybe they have never heard these French names. I would later learn that the beautiful Golden Gate has the sad distinction of seeing the highest number of suicides in the country.

I am cuffed, and the cops push me towards the pillar in the bridge tower which houses the lift. When the lift reaches the bottom I realise we are not actually at ground level. I need to climb a dozen metres down a ladder. But the cops refuse to uncuff me. This pointless stance makes no sense – how am I supposed to get down a ladder like this? But the cops simply don't care about my situation, and for me the American dream dies this day. What are they thinking about at this moment? Are they dreaming of the number of hamburgers they are going to eat this evening? I hate them, these thoughtless imbeciles who are happy to leave me to struggle down this ladder alone in this way.

I am beginning to have some regrets about my climb. No, I don't regret climbing the bridge for a minute – it was fantastic! What I am beginning to regret is that I climbed up the Sausalito side of the bridge. There are two bridge towers, one falling under the jurisdiction of San Francisco and the other falling under Sausalito. The photographer thought the images would be better if I had climbed up the Sausalito side, and so that is what I did. Unfortunately in Sausalito the cops seem to have less to do, making them tougher on me. Little details like this can make all the difference when it comes to being busted. The San Francisco cops have more important things to worry about than their colleagues on the other side of the bay. But still, the Sausalito cops are happy to make me wait. It is crazy how long you can wait in a police station. Sometimes it feels like the only right you have is to sit and wait in silence.

Fortunately I am allowed to make a phone call. I decide to call my wife in France, to assure her and my three children that all is well, but then I am told I cannot make calls outside the United States. I have the right to make this fucking phone call but these cops just don't care. And then I am hungry. I burned up quite a few calories this afternoon, more than these languid cops do in a week. After more than two hours of interrogation they still do not feel like giving me something to eat. I am getting mad, sat on my chair, about to faint. A huge woman is interrogating me in a rude and patronising way. She seems to revel in being obnoxious, as if this was her patriotic duty. It's a terrible thing when people like her are put in this position. One often wonders if they choose the most hideous people for these roles when they interview potential police officers, so that we might be insulted into submission. This dreadful woman has an issue with my nationality and is disdainful of foreigners. She keeps telling me how proud she is to be an American. What does this have to do with me climbing the Golden Gate Bridge? This is not an interrogation or an interview – I have had plenty of those around the world from police officers doing their jobs properly, even if they weren't especially good fun to be around. This is just a massive fat bitch in a chair being a massive fat bitch in a chair, offending me with her small-mindedness, her racism and her blubber. I have had two hours of this bullshit. After several more scathing comments designed to insult me while playing up her own nationality I launch a verbal salvo.

"The real Americans are the Native Americans, the Indians!"

She does not seem to appreciate this statement at all. I have given her the excuse to do her best to piss me off, and she takes advantage of it to keep me until she begins to feel tired, which turns out to be around midnight. When she is no longer amused by this boring game, she goes home to her hamburgers, her spare ribs and her waffles. Home to her jumbo hot dogs, her soda pop, her French fries (sorry, her *Freedom* fries!), her nachos, her pizzas, her Cheetos and her fucking twinkies. Home to her great big fridge, bigger no doubt than some of the buildings I have climbed. Me? I am sent down for a complete body search and a miserable police cell. And I'm still hungry.

After the second adjournment of my lawsuit, I find myself emptied out of the police van and returned to prison. It looks like I will be here more than just a night. The initial interest sparked by the French Spiderman, which usually sees my case resolved quickly, has evaporated and I am now lost in the system. I am an ordinary prisoner like everyone else, and as they say here, that 'sucks'.

I am back in Sausalito jail which is brand new and actually, as a facility, probably the nicest jail I have ever stayed in. My cell isn't bad at all. In this increasingly familiar room, Chico the Mexican coke dealer seems particularly surprised by my return. His first glance turns to his decaying shoes that I am wearing. His reaction makes me smile yet also worries me. Do we regress to being animals so quickly when we are held in captivity? My climbing shoes look good on him and his old ones would only look good in a landfill. And they really ought to be buried as they emit the foulest fumes. The bacteria count must be off the scale, they truly are a pomander of putrescence. When he understands that I don't care about getting my shoes back, he begins to tell me about himself as if the value of my gift required a kind of commitment. Chico is 25 years old. He believed in the American dream. But he has no regrets, because in Mexico he would have had virtually nothing and he accepts his fate as par for the course. His voice is calm, almost warm. His girlfriend is also 'doing a cruise' in prison, not far from here. The expression makes me smile. Him too, although he knows that this cruise will send him back to Mexico. But for Chico it doesn't matter, he already has his plans mapped out: he and his girlfriend will have a child and return to the USA. I ask him what he will do. Apparently, since they will cross the border without papers, he will most likely have to sell drugs again. His eyes drift to the concrete ceiling as he talks of the house they will share together and his hopes for his unborn child.

Recreation hour ends this discussion of dreams. Hundreds of prisoners invade the yard like a plague of rodents. Some shout, others play fighting games. Some start doing press-ups, muscles swelling, sweat pearling on shaved craniums. This is the first time I have been here for recreation and I observe the scene. Like everyone else here I need to let off steam so I start a series of press-ups too. I do a hundred in a row. The black dudes look at me, surprised. What do they think I am? With my busted nose and my hands covered with nicks and scratches, do I look like a street fighter? Or with my long hair and leathered face, maybe I look like a crack dealer from a seedy ghetto? I guess we always need to catalogue people. I have experienced this since my first solo, when I was categorised and treated as a madman. It's all too easy. Everyone sees a madman in someone they don't understand. But by taking a different approach to life I have met extraordinary people in the prisons of the world. And there is a certain solidarity between outcasts. A sort of respect which does not express itself in a handshake or a pat on the back, just a little spark in the glance of an eye.

My series of pumps ends and they approach. They are amazed that a lad as thin and small as me just totally smashed the prison pump record! They say that if I had been as big as them, then I would have been something they refer to as an 'ass kicker'. Other hip-hop profanities follow and I add these colourful metaphors to my expanding English vocabulary. They call me 'Little Schwarzenegger' and seem particularly pleased with this comparison. When they laugh, their abdominal muscles move like waves in a sea of fury. The most enormous of these big men asks me why I am here.

"I climbed the Golden Gate."

Puzzled faces. It looks like they have never heard of it. There's a murmuring of consultation and then they seem to conclude that I wanted to blow it up, which appears to be more logical.

I show them a new game, doing press-ups on one arm. I manage about 40. My record? Eighty. They grin and nod and take to the floor. They grit their teeth, wince, strain, growl and give all they have. But for them, no way. It seems rather pointless to explain to them that for this type of exercise, it is important to have a good weight-to-power ratio. They carry much more weight than me and have to work twice, three times as hard. But also I have my lactic acid training. To these guys, if you are solid, big and heavy, then you must be the strongest – so my demonstrations have them flummoxed.

To finish I make a perfect board on the portico, right in the middle of the yard. I levitate before them. It's funny but when I undertake this exercise I always believe I should create an absolutely perfect board. My body should be as straight as, well, a board. It is not really a big deal for training purposes, but for me, it is a stylistic composition. To keep the body absolutely horizontal whilst hanging by the arms has something of a surrealist, incomprehensible nature about it. I guess it is similar to escalation, another fight against the laws of gravity. My fellow prisoners really love it and as a result of all this showing off, I become a sort of mascot for the group.

Bureaucracy and crap has led to me spending six days in a penitentiary. Apparently in San Francisco it takes six days to find a French translator! In this time I have become the clown of the prison yard, the jester. The pumping competitions in jail are a cheerful game but by the end of a week, you get a little tired of it. These guys train in their cells to fight, to defend themselves, but happily for me a fight was never going to happen. 'Little Schwarzy' was held in respect in San Francisco! But today I face a fight. I find myself before the judge, fighting for my liberty, and this time I do have an interpreter. Third time lucky I hope... I am also accompanied by my agent Julie Cohen who bails me. I am free for a few days before I must return and stand again.

From wearing a pair of ludicrous pyjamas which made me look like one of Snow White's dwarves, I return to court in my cowboy boots and snakeskin. I feel much better about my clothing, though I think the judiciary here prefer my pyjama look. I was originally charged with a felony and at first I did not know what a felony actually was. I thought a few days in jail would do the trick. But after a bit of manoeuvring, my lawyer asks me to plead guilty to lesser misdemeanour charges. I shrug and agree. I remember my childhood, the times when I got in trouble with authority for riding my bicycle where I shouldn't have, or when I got into fights. I won't do it again Miss, Sir, Mister Policeman, I promise! As a result of my humble remorse, the court thinks that my six days inside are sufficient punishment and fines me an additional $200 towards costs. No problem – I can go back to France, and instead of my prison press-ups I can restart my normal training, on my favourite cliffs of Verdon or Lubéron.

It has been a revealing six days and, as usual, quite a bit of fun. Every time I am thrown in jail in any country of the world – rich, poor, democratic or dictatorial – my physical training has led to me being pointed out and even respected. This is quite useful in there when you are one metre sixty-five high and not aggressive. To be honest I have been in prison yards where I could easily have climbed out. But what's the point? The prison side of what I do is very much part of the escalation experience for me. I am a climber, not a fugitive. Many of the guys in prison find themselves there for expressing their frustrations in illegal ways. This is what I do too, I guess. I vent my frustrations by climbing. My street fight, my vandalism, my hold-up is urban escalation. For the judges, what I do throws up legal confusion, for it is not something they have ever seen before. But ultimately for them my climbs are a disruption to law and order, the status quo, and for this I must be punished.

It sounds strange, but in prison I have always had the impression that my fellow prisoners would have enjoyed taking up the sport as a physical and therapeutic outlet. Escalation helps adapt and calm a frenzied state of mind. Reaching the summit by mastering the risks, dominating the elements, forcing oneself to respect a simplicity and discipline in life, these things would appeal to many of the guys I am locked up with. We are all misfits. But climbing lets you channel your aggression or independence into something positive, allowing you to be different but respectable. From Paris to New York, from Hong Kong to Moscow, from Tokyo to Melbourne, every time I am thrown behind bars I become a sort of symbol for the other prisoners. The reaction has always been positive. Sometimes a certain celebrity is associated with my crimes: Houdini or Schwarzenegger, Spiderman or Bruce Lee, prisoners always try to compare me to such characters. There is a lot of monotony in jail so they are happy to see someone who has done something new. In a way it brightens their stay. This may sound big-headed but it has often been told to me. Hey, I don't think I am a great hero, but I do think that people, wherever they come from, do feel an affinity with someone who does things out of the ordinary. It's natural to chase that buzz, that risk, that high.

Check out team-building events at the big corporations. What are the best ones? Are they those where people go through pie charts which are highly relevant to everyday work? No, they are the ones with bungee jumps, paint-balling or survival training, the ones which physically engage us in a raid against the bureaucracy imposed upon us in the first place. How much of this is about bonding with colleagues? And how much of it is a personal experience, the heightening of senses, self-control, and an exercise in bettering oneself?

We all dream of taking risks, of discovering what we are really capable of. Twisting an ankle in your home is hardly a drama or adventure, but twisting an ankle in the middle of nowhere will test you and draw out a supreme commitment. I guess my solo escalations are urban representations of the same thing. A life lived in a disinfected world makes us restless. We are all drawn to a challenge, even if we shun the risk. But not all of us decline such adrenaline. My fellow inmates are men who are willing to take risks, sometimes outrageous ones – just imagine what kind of man you must be to attempt an armed robbery – and when they are caught, there can be few places more sterile or regimented than a correctional facility. It punishes them but it also bottles up their frustrations and maybe perverts these personality traits into something darker and more criminal. I say, give these men a way of using these instincts positively. Maybe we should give them climbing lessons.

I am fortunate to have found my outlet. Who knows what I would have become without it? But regardless, it puts me on the wrong side of the legal fence, and after each ascent I know that I am entitled to a stay in prison.

My first jailhouse experience was in Chicago after my first climb. Despite colliding with the cold reality of a prison cell – an experience which could easily have been intimidating or could have conjured a sense of failure – I had the weird feeling that I was enjoying privileged access to a rare place, to be able to experience something exceptional. I was not at all prepared for detention, I had no criminal leanings or objectives, but for me prison was the cherry on my cake. This sounds a tad stupid, right? I know, but it is exactly how I felt.

In my cell, I sang, alone but happy. Happy to be in Chicago, happy to have made a successful and beautiful ascent, but especially happy to have reached my first objective. I guess you could say I was happy to be alive. As I conducted other climbs, I found myself back behind bars, again with a smile on my face. Prison was so connected to what I did that it became a necessary component of my dreams. It's something like the pain you suffer when you run a race and beat your personal best. It won't stop you running again, you accept it, and eventually you dream of that crippling stitch you know you must endure to reach new heights. My dream back in Chicago had just begun to take shape, deep within my subconscious. But I was totally unaware that I had just begun my world tour of prison cells. Lying there, I rediscovered a song about the French prison Fleury-Mérogis, by the punk group Trust. It was so appropriate to my new situation.

Fleury-Mérogis one day in September 1976
Where he existed so little, like he was a nobody
His food is slid along the ground
And a bowl of water that quenches his thirst
He is alone, without sun.

It sounds crap translated into English without the accompanying beat, but in my cell that night those lines struck a chord with me. I imagine the authorities would not want me to feel pleased with being locked up, they would much rather break me. When I am in jail, of course, I have been removed from society as a public enemy. But even if I am persuaded that I have no right to clamber up walls, I have a lot of difficulty feeling guilty. Besides, the other prisoners have always accepted me as different, as if it was evident that I was not part of their world. Prison for me holds no fear, no punishment, no 'correctional effects'. I quite like it. Remember New York? That magical experience of being thrown in the air like a hero could have happened nowhere else.

Being jailed around the world has given me great insights into various peoples and nations. You can tell a lot about a society and its culture by its policing, courts and prisons, its attitude to human rights or dignity, and the way the authorities treat you if you do not obey them or do something they don't understand.

In Malaysia, the police arrested me when I had just attempted to climb what was then the world's tallest structure. As the Petronas Towers had just been finished, I was covered with construction dust and other salty residue and grime you find on buildings in this permanently damp environment. In the tropics, or on a humid day, you find everything sticks to a surface. These cops meant business and took arrest much further than in other lands. Roughed up, I had to undress for a body search. I had to strip stark naked. They searched my body, hands rubbing and groping my most intimate areas. Then a creepy guy came to see if I had anything hidden within my body. Inside my mouth, my hair, in my ears, my nose. They even inspected inside my anus. What would a rock climber keep in there? A rope so I could escape? Climbing slippers? These space invaders were not professional proctologists, that's for sure. Alright, alright, it was not the worst thing in the world, but these hands touching my whole body left me the sensation of an abuse of power, maybe even a sense of rape.

After this unpleasant rectal investigation I was allowed to put on a tattered pair of swimming trunks. Was I heading to the shower due to my grimy and blackened state? Not at all, this was the prison clothing I was to be issued with. For security reasons the tightening cord and the tiny metal logo had been removed. Bare-chested, with these torn and ragged trunks ready to fall to my knees, I landed in a big murky cell full of Indian, Malay and Chinese prisoners, a typical reflection of mixed Malaysian society.

I have seen my fair share of prisons and certainly none is ever listed in *Zagat* or the *Small Luxury Hotels of the World*, but this Malaysian jail was something else... The ground was sticky, disgusting. Even the cockroaches had difficulty moving around. We would try to crush these enormous tropical bugs on the floor, often having to stamp on them several times, such was their armour and strength. The air was stale and thick with pungent sweat and urine. As the door slammed, all eyes were upon me. I could not communicate with these guys and they would stare at me endlessly. A Caucasian in prison? It just didn't happen.

I sat there for hours, staring at my gloomy new home. Eventually two snarling guards brought us the newspaper – how nice of them. The news was bad apparently. But this paper was not for reading, as it was soon torn and divided between the men. Then the food arrived. It was awful: a mixture of rice in some limp watery sauce, with fragments of things we could vaguely call 'chicken'. It could just as easily have been rat, camel or orang-utan for all I knew. Okay, maybe not, but it was not like any fowl I had ever encountered. There was no plate, nor a place setting, just an old tin can and a sheet of newspaper. I had not washed since my escalation and my hands were so dirty that I did not dare to eat with my fingers. I am not particularly stuck-up, but there are limits I find difficult to exceed. But I was hungry. It took me a minute or so, but once I had absorbed this cheerless scene, I decided to spread my page of newspaper over a tiny spare area of the filthy sputum- and cockroach-splattered floor. On my knees, my nose planted in the tin like a mongrel, I tried to eat. Do they not allow for human dignity here or is it considered a western or subversive concept?

Pitying me, one of my banqueting companions showed me how to eat 'properly' by using the main three fingers to scoop this bleak gruel into my mouth. I knelt again, with pleasure, shovelling this muck in as it spilt over my chin. My knees began to ache. This new method may have resulted in getting more into my mouth but it was hindered by the limited function of my wrists. What can I say? There are days when we really feel old.

Some suffer from rheumatism, and would not enjoy this experience. I am such a person. Indeed it is very difficult for me to turn my wrists at all, and this was exactly what was required by this Malay speciality. I reminded myself that there are countless peoples of the world who eat this way and eat food of this calibre if they can eat at all. I plunged diligently into this survival operation, but I was pretty bad at it. Half the food was being lost. Slowly, the sauce poured along my arm. Grains of rice fell on the foul ground or remained in the hairs of my forearm. Misery…

I began dreaming of Valence, its subtle scents, the serenity of family ballads in the Rhône vineyards. I wanted to drink a little of that famous wine I buy every year from a small fellow with a fine vineyard, a vineyard almost at the foot of the cliff which has inspired many of my finest challenges. But instead of the tannins of my favourite beverage, I was given only a worn plastic bottle, half full of a worryingly unclear water, doubtful and yellowish. Two weeks of this! Not eating is okay, but it is impossible not to drink in such stifling heat and humidity. And so I drank, even if I had not been entitled to the necessary vaccines in these tropical parts of the world.

My mind wandered elsewhere. I even dreamed about the five-gram pack of potato chips which had been given to me in a cell in the USA. Imagine holding such an item in such high esteem, to long for it, to marvel at it. Your mind does strange things in such a place. After a while, I even began to think that they had only looked inside my anus so I didn't smuggle any food in. I began to wish that I had perhaps tucked a chocolate bar right round the corner of my colon where it would be safe and hidden. It would be melted, perhaps, but how lovely it would be… Though despairing, I shook myself out of these increasingly unhealthy thoughts and decided to adapt for survival. I couldn't go without food and water for long in this environment, so I felt it was better to satisfy my hunger and thirst with an amoeba or a bug.

That was Malaysia, a country which desperately needs to look at its prisons and the welfare of its inmates. Prison food in Malaysia was woeful and in general the food I have sampled in the world's jails has been at best nondescript. In France, if someone is going to jail there is always a friend somewhere telling them "I will bring you some oranges!" I have heard this countless times, and today I still continue to receive oranges at the door of my home from mischievous friends. But once I did actually get some in jail! And they made a very nice snack for me and were most appreciated. So you see this story of oranges is not a legend.

Shared hardship does help forge bonds. The prisoners pretty soon find out why I am inside, and my fellow inmates often ask me to sign things for them. Even the screws ask for autographs. In Philadelphia, a guard approached my cell to ask me to perform my famous speciality – the board. He had discreetly opened a few cells nearby so I could show off my party trick to certain prisoners with whom he shared an unlikely affinity. I am always surprised by this kind of request, but I agree happily. I had often wondered whether such requests were a joke or some kind of provocation. Today, I recognise that I was wrong. My cellmates are no different to the people who gather at the foot of one of my ascents, curious, maybe bored of whatever routine they had been following at that given moment, and looking for a good show.

I'd really like to stress that I do not care for jail. People have told me they think I must like it if I keep on with my escalations, and that I seek imprisonment as some kind of masochism or badge of honour. This is not true! Prison just decreases the time spent pursuing new dreams. Yes, I am often happy to have made it to jail but only because it is a by-product of a climbing success, not for the experience itself, as interesting as it has often been. These successive confinements have allowed me to compose these lines, because after spending the first hours of isolation recovering from my efforts, the only thing to do is engage in introspection, trying to decipher the graffiti engraved on the walls or adding your own. You can count the inscriptions too, and this may take between one to four hours depending on the size of the cell. Then you count all there is to count. Furniture, bars, bugs. Finally, you sleep to escape. But when you have slept like a log for 48 hours, you remain awake for a long time. The ability to sleep has been exhausted, the ticking of the alarm clock is too loud, the wasted hours stretch on and on. I can compare this artificial wait to that I underwent in hospital, nailed to a bed and full of tubes. The only means of escape is through thought, through dreams... Dreaming about another life, happier times. Having lost some months of my life in hospital beds, it seems evident to me that there is a link between these wounded hours of dreams and my pursuit of the world's highest buildings. Maybe the waiting, the loss of time, must be compensated for. So I must be patient, whether in prison or in hospital, and make up for this lost time.

Two years after we first met on top of the Elf Tower, a still-fuming Le Floch-Prigent has me in court again. I will need to dig deep into my pockets to hire a defence, but fortune smiles on me. Since this is a unique case, with an interesting legal and media slant, I somehow manage to land a famous lawyer. Le Floch-Prigent meanwhile has diverted a significant amount of Elf's money and resources towards punishing me. He really will not let this go and therefore a lot of people find themselves gathering in this courtroom today. But in these two intervening years my fame has grown and so has my experience of lawsuits. I humbly enter the courtroom in a green snakeskin jacket over a black shirt and a pair of dark glasses perched on my irregular nose. My attire is enough to help the judiciary relax. Poor guys, they don't have many opportunities to have fun. The charges are read out, something along the lines of trespassing on private property, endangering the multinational company and responsibility for potential accidents.

The Elf corporate law firm are there and the case commences. It rumbles on for a while but it soon becomes clear to everyone that the prosecutor is in despair and really doesn't know what to do. Obviously, the jurists know that the prosecution is only supported by the stubbornness of their boss. It's a pretty weak case even with the best lawyers that money can buy. In a further stroke of good fortune, the prosecution forget to indicate that I could have potentially fallen on a passer-by and killed them – according to my hot-shot lawyer, my only legal weakness.

After fumbling through a series of unconvincing legal arguments the prosecutor sits down. My lawyer gets up and smiles – the case is already won. He addresses the court and advances my professional abilities better than I could ever have done: highly experienced climbing instructor, world record holder in solo escalation, famous high-level athlete, instructor to the fire and police services in climbing and rope training... the list goes on. Did I really do all that? It sounds pretty good. I have to say I feel pretty happy to have this guy around me. It gets even worse for the prosecution, and before long the trial descends into farce. The judge tells Elf's lawyers that instead of suing me they should have sponsored me!

The case collapses. Elf and Loïk Le Floch-Prigent have lost again. The onlookers applaud and joke as if it had all been a Sacha Guitry comedy. The magistrates relax and share in the jovial atmosphere. My trial has been a breath of fresh air for these guys. Some magistrates even ask me to sign autographs for them, to the annoyance of the lawyers of the following case impatiently waiting outside to use the courtroom. The prosecutor, resigned but human, approaches us and tells us he did not want to pursue this desperately hollow case. But as a member of the Elf corporate law firm, he had no choice.

And though it ends there for me, the court soon beckons Le Floch-Prigent. They say that the flutter of a butterfly's wings can trigger a hurricane. Maybe this is true, because events were about to take a quite implausible twist. I do not wish to overstate my role in subsequent events as I was quite incidental to it all. But it was exactly my public ascent of their building and the following trial that had attracted a lot of attention to Elf's wasteful decision-making.

Elf is a state-run company funded by taxpayers so the decision to prosecute me twice comes under scrutiny. With these matters discussed in the national press, an investigation is launched into Le Floch-Prigent's misuse of company money. Numerous people criticise Elf and their bosses for their folly, and demand answers.

Suddenly Le Floch-Prigent is on the back foot. He becomes evasive, ducking and avoiding journalists. In the coming weeks, wheels turn and it soon emerges that there are many more such irregularities, some of them increasingly outrageous. Elf is state-owned and so the issue becomes political. What started out as what many regarded as a total waste of Elf's and therefore public money soon spirals out of control and turns into a full-scale financial investigation into all dealings within the corporation! Elf's CEO is dragged through the courts in a blaze of publicity for misuse of company funds and property.

This monumental scandal shakes the French financial community and becomes news around the world. In the investigation it emerges that as head of Elf, Le Floch-Prigent is one of three top executives who illegally enriched themselves by creaming off huge sums from the oil giant.

An incredible web of political favours, kickbacks, mistresses, secret accounts, luxury villas and international bribery is uncovered. He is convicted on charges of corruption and embezzlement in a case *The Guardian* newspaper of Britain calls 'the biggest fraud inquiry in Europe since World War II'!

Elf is shaken to its core by the scandal, and 37 people are charged with embezzlement. It is nothing short of a sensation. The fallout claims Le Floch-Prigent, his deputy Alfred Sirven and another high-profile figure, André Tarallo – known as 'Monsieur Africa' because of his shadowy dealings with African leaders. It embroils members of the government and results in the former foreign minister Roland Dumas receiving six months in jail plus a not-so-small fine. The others are also put behind bars for several years.

Loïk Le Floch-Prigent, former CEO of Elf Aquitaine, is heavily fined and thrown in jail for his part in a $350 million fraud. The man who was so desperate to see me locked up is found guilty before a court of law and sent to jail for five years.

6

Fantastico!

In bookshop after bookshop, I comb through shelves hunting for information on Brazil, focussing mainly on Rio de Janeiro, Sao Paolo and Brasilia. Whilst sifting through literature I try to concentrate on these places but I also take in other South American cities such as Buenos Aires and Lima. It's all very scenic, but right now I am really fed up with endless pages about the Amazonian rainforest, or the samba schools about which a vast number of books have been published. I am sure a large area of rainforest has been felled in order to print them.

What I am looking for is a target, a skyscraper to climb. With its unstable economy, chaotic city planning and mediocre construction industry, Brazilian buildings are not the most photographed in the world, so it might seem inappropriate for me to show such an interest. The genesis of my ascents generally come about the same way – an image on television which snaps me out of my lethargy, resulting in me spending hours in bookshops trying to investigate the sense of pursuing an idealised project. If it looks good then I am on a plane and from that moment on there is little else.

But my sudden interest in Brazil has been sparked by an invitation to Rio de Janeiro by a Brazilian TV channel. It sounds like a great opportunity to personally acquaint myself with a fine Latin building, so here I am in the bookshop. I uncover nothing in the literature that appeals to me, so I decide to make my decision when I get there. The best buildings I can find so far are very boring, most of them average, drab or very ugly indeed. How can I climb something so lacking in passion, life or soul? My escalations should be a thing of beauty upon a thing of beauty. It is not worth risking my life for a boilerplate concrete box. The only clear and attractive challenge takes a human shape: the Christ of Corcovado, the famous statue dominating the bay of Rio. But, though I revel in climbing buildings, I have a problem with religious stuff. Having no particular religious conscience, these moods should not worry me, despite the omen in Milan. But I really do not want believers to be shocked. If a samba festival was organised in the heart of Notre Dame in Paris, there would be a wave of angry French voices shouting against such a 'heresy'. I am thus sceptical at the idea of honouring my commitment in such a quasi-blasphemous way.

Meanwhile things are in full swing with the media. TV Globo wants me, so they will have me. The primetime television show *Fantastico* is similar to our French programme *Ushuaïa* but it has a 45% market share, the world's biggest audience for such a programme. TV Globo wants me to enact a climb in Rio that can be broadcast live on *Fantastico* across Brazil. The channel has a devoutly religious audience with Catholicism at its core. So you will understand my hesitation to propose to the producer the escalation of the statue of Christ. It would be like suggesting to a Saudi channel the ascent of Mecca's Grand Mosque in front of hundreds of thousands of pilgrims.

Ten hours after leaving Charles de Gaulle International Airport our plane arrives in Rio de Janeiro under a low blanket of damp cloud. The city soaks in the greyness and mixes with the palette of the ocean. The climate catches me off guard. I thought I had left this weather in Paris! The sun is absent today and it is certainly not the carnival or bikini weather I had anticipated, but it doesn't matter. I would like to look around but orientation and exploration will have to wait for another day.

I jump into a taxi and head downtown to my accommodation, Hotel Everest. I wonder if it is coincidence or if TV Globo's guys have chosen this hotel for its apt name, thinking it would please me. Three quarters of an hour passes and the taxi progresses from traffic jam to traffic jam, sinking into the heart of this damp and sooty concrete octopus. The driver must think I am a weirdo because I dash around the back of his car, jaw hanging loose, pressing my nose against the panes like an overexcited Jack Russell. I desperately look for inspiration but only find commonplace concrete blocks which never exceed a hundred metres. There is nothing spectacular or aesthetically distinguished, just endless shitty buildings which welcome me with nondescript faces under an anonymous sky.

Chewing my lip I pull in at the hotel, a magnificent five-star establishment, with no solution to my problem. My agent Julie organised the stay, made the contacts, signed contracts and she is waiting to greet me. I collapse on my bed while she presents me with the schedule of the week. The first piece of news is that the highest building in South America is the Edificio Italia. It is not in Rio but Sao Paolo and stands 160 metres high. The news is dispiriting, as this Edificio Italia is not really the dreamlike object I am looking for. The second item of information she has for me is that I am famous! I am suddenly a true star in Brazil, *Fantastico* having teased the country with tales of my previous escalations over three consecutive weekends. All the TV channels and magazines want a piece of Alain Robert! It is quite bewildering. She continues with more details and appointments but it is time for honesty. I interrupt her and crowbar out the crucial question which constricts my stomach.

"But what am I going to climb?"

Julie makes me understand that this is not her business, but she calls TV Globo to advance the scouting hours and ask them if they can find something really interesting, as climbing an ugly block does not interest us. We were doing a lot for the channel and we all know that if the story is successful then it could lead to more stories and opportunities. Certainly we will honour our agreement, but come on, there is a minimum to be respected.

I join Julie, Alexis the photographer working for Gamma, the cameraman, and a TV Globo journalist in a people carrier and we hit Rio. We pass through a hive of activity. The journalist takes me down several avenues and shows me various possibilities but nothing jumps out at me. Every time he turns a corner to reveal the next one, a pout of resentment congeals across my face. The journalist does not need me to explain my opinion. Nevertheless, he knows the city and does his best. It's not his fault that Brazil never built the Sears Tower. But we have to find something for me to get my fingers into. After a circuitous exploration of Rio it becomes clear that nothing is really good enough, but we come to agree that a glazed medium-sized structure, archaic and filthy, is the best option. Aesthetics cannot come into it in Rio so we have gone the other way. The battered façade is dirty enough to be slippery, making it unpredictable and thus dangerous.

Not to be beaten by the other television channels who could easily scoop them, TV Globo prefers me to climb by night, lit only by a brilliant spotlight. A team of technicians will install camera positions and broadcasting and lighting equipment on the opposite building – by bribing the guards. In a country where corruption reigns, a few green notes can perform almost as many miracles as the Christ of Corcovado.

I leave everything up to the TV guys in the run-up to broadcast. Between two interviews for television news, I look around this city where exaggerated misery and luxury live together. Social disparities exist naturally in my country, but in Rio an elite minority live surrounded by an enormous majority incapable of earning a living. They cannot eat properly and countless masses live in shacks tacked together from broken ends of corrugated iron, without tap water or sewers. They no longer speak about social division in the big cities of Brazil but more about two worlds which many fear can never unite, just as two magnets inexorably repel each other.

The poverty is such that it is difficult to walk the streets of the city. My media overexposure makes me instantly familiar to the poor and the down-and-outs. As far as they are concerned, since I have been filling the airwaves, I must earn a lot of money. Wrong. Yes, I am on TV, but I am a rock climber, not a rock star… When I climb I get fined, I don't make money! Sure, I have a deal this time with a TV channel but it is not much, enough for my family until my next climb perhaps, but certainly not a big sum.

Legions of Cariocas – Rio natives – come up to me to ask for a small banknote, the classic exchange of small change for a dose of good conscience. My financial means are not unlimited, far from it. I pass in front of a church where thousands of wax candles burn outside on an immense steel sheet. A woman carrying a two-month-old baby begs me to help her. Sobbing, she tries to make me understand that her child suffers from malnutrition, that he needs milk, that I am his only chance. *Quelle dommage!* It is a distressing and heart-rending sight, but when people ask for your help all day long, you eventually have to protect yourself. I have no ambition to be a saint. Nevertheless in that momentary glance I can see genuine pain in her eyes and I decide to take her hand and bring her to the closest pharmacy. In two bags I put some powdered milk, nappies and other basic products. It has not cost me a lot, just a couple of reals and a little bit of time, but it makes me feel good! I know that from now on in Rio, a woman and her child know that Spiderman is a friend of their family.

To please, or to be pleased? The fact that I gave on some days a little respite to someone and, maybe, a little bit of hope, enriches me much more than a bunch of reals and centavos. Nevertheless, that little look in the eye, that humanity, is not always there. In New York one day near Exchange Park, a young guy asked me for five dollars in an extremely aggressive way. Without a doubt, this sum was for him to buy his dose of crack or heroin. Sponsorship of drug dealers is not my thing at all. I like speaking with people to whom I give a little bit of money, I like exchanging a little more than a scrap of paper with a curt nod of the head, but that day, no way… it was impossible to communicate. Although he was only in his twenties, he already lived on another planet, something like the one described in the Beatles song *Lucy in the Sky with Diamonds*. Without my five dollars, I was quite sure he was going to attack the first grandmother he would meet. So, even if it was only to prevent the next crime, I pressed the note into his hand while searching in his empty eyes.

Every man, woman and child of the streets has their own story. Some souls are lost to drugs, prostitution or crime, but others turn to enlightenment, religion or entertainment to help them cope. In a Parisian subway, while the city folk left their cosy homes to head to work, an old man begged. He sang, and beautifully so. His melodious voice spread through the crowded train as the song of a blackbird marks the arrival of spring. His face shone. His voice was strong, reassuring, moving. Repeatedly, I had got up to put some coins in his cap on the ground. And I observed how, as it is often said, people are afraid to meet the glance of the poor. They prefer to ignore it, to see nothing, because their eyes speak to us. I appreciated this old man's efforts and tried to lead by example. But nobody followed. He was nothing, his plight meant nothing. I found this mixture of contempt and indifference unbearable. I erupted. I berated the carriage for their stinginess and insensitivity. They raised eyes towards me, surprised, then began again to shrink behind newspapers and look at their shoes. This old tramp was a man, a man who had decided to try to bring joy to society as best he could rather than turn to criminal means of support, surely something to be admired. As much as society may try to overlook it, human pain and misery will exist anywhere, be it Paris, New York or Rio. None of us can save the world but likewise none of us has the right to ignore those who have had less luck. Do not forget that the wheel of fortune sometimes turns.

Twice in my life I had the occasion to beg, just to see what it was like. The first time was in Paris. For gloomy but now-forgotten reasons, my sister did not want me to stay at her place during my trips to the capital. The following day, I had to climb a building for a charitable event for homeless people, in partnership with the newspaper *Le Réverbère*. Naturally, I would have been able to settle down comfortably in the hotel, but I did not want to miss the occasion to share, on this December night, the life of those for whom I was going to climb. At the foot of my sister's building, my best friend Claude and I took two or three boxes and settled down. Automatically, as if it was a necessary prop, I held out my hand. The more I extended it, the less I seemed to exist. A rather curious paradox emerged: the more you appeal to others, the less you are helped. In the dark of night, when the cold intensified, I stripped off and sat bare-chested, just for a touch of provocation. Still no reaction. I had no idea the world could be so blind. Claude and I shrugged and eventually the numbers of pedestrians dwindled. We cannot claim we spent the most comfortable night of our lives there, but the next day I climbed with a new determination, my will multiplied.

My second stint as a beggar was in New York, on Manhattan between Broadway's neon and Times Square's huge advertisement hoardings. It was there that I saw him, a Navajo Indian asking for 30 dollars to join his tribe, in the west, on the other side of the continent. His incredible face was so tanned and lined that Hollywood's producers would quickly have cast him in the role of a wise elder. This man of more than 60 sat at the foot of a marble tower and waited for luck or whatever else to come his way. I approached, I discussed. I admire the Indians, the true forefathers of America. Those who had the luck to avoid the extermination of the pioneer days have come to build, astride girders of steel, the cities of their invaders. Native Americans have held a strange fascination for me since I heard about my prior lives from a medium in the alleys of Bangkok. I begged alongside this Navajo with little success in the heart of one of the most important business centres on the planet, surrounded by shops selling luxury goods to millionaire yuppies. But in two hours this man from another century was able to join his tribe.

Homelessness is one of the easiest miseries for society to alleviate, as at any given time the city teems with more shelter than kerbside. When I climbed in the Champs-Elysées it was partially to highlight the initiative of scores of long-empty flats being used to house the homeless, a rather obvious solution to what is after all an immoral problem.

On another trip to New York I got to practise what I preach. I was spending a few days in the Big Apple in the spring. On a random street I had met John, a homeless black guy in his forties, who would wander around reading the Bible to other homeless people. Three times we met and he read me some verses. We had discussed them, then each of us had returned to his everyday life, me in France, him on New York's pavements. At Thanksgiving at the end of November, I was again in the concrete maze of Manhattan. I was in transit for a few days after a little trip to Las Vegas where I had scaled the Luxor pyramid. One night, while the winter bore brutally down on the Eastern Seaboard, the apologetic desk clerk pulled me out of my sleep. Somebody was asking for me at the reception desk, at two o'clock in the morning. Half asleep, I threw on some clothes and headed down to see what the fuss was, and discovered John shivering in the lobby. I don't know how he had found me, though I guess he had probably read in the papers that I was in town and staying at this hotel. John was frozen. Famine tormented him and hypothermia constricted his face. In spite of the good relations I had established with the management of the hotel, John could not settle in the establishment. As the McDonald's on Times Square never closes its doors, we spent the rest of the night there as he scoffed no fewer than four Big Macs and swigged back two litres of watered-down but nevertheless hot coffee. In the early hours, when my eyes became bloodshot and bleary and I had difficulty propping up my eyelids, I left him with enough to stay a few more hours. When the shops opened I found a nearby sports store and browsed around inside. There was only one sarcophagus-like sleeping bag which could support a climber in extreme temperatures, and it was slightly torn. Citing its blemished state, I asked for a discount. The salesman seemed quite open to the idea. Patiently I explained to him the purpose of my purchase – John. The streets. The cold. The salesman's shocked outburst? "No way!"

I only understood later that it was an error to reveal my true intentions, because he may have gladly granted a discount to Spiderman, but cutting his profit margin for a simple tramp annoyed him. He was quite clearly offended. Sickness squeezed my throat as I bought the sleeping bag from this oaf but when I gave it to John, I received in exchange the same glance as the one from this Brazilian woman, a mixture of happiness and gratitude.

From the snowdrifts of New York to sunny Rio, the poverty of some, and the absolute indifference of others, are the same.

Jogging in the morning on Copacabana Beach with the hot sun, fine white sand under my feet and a turquoise sea – this is more like the Brazil I had envisaged. What a unique stretch of sand this is. Holidaymakers and the homeless make for a kind of tourist paradise for people with social blinkers. In spite of the background of poverty and strife, everybody smiles. And all sorts – rich and poor, fat and thin, old and young – come towards me to ask for autographs, or simply cry out *'Homen aranha!'* which means 'Spiderman!'

My word, I hadn't expected this on my morning jog at all. Julie was right, it seems like the whole of Brazil knew I was coming! There's a lot of flattering attention as I try to continue jogging. A few kilometres into my run I am joined by three cheeky kids from the nearby favela of Rossigna. They want to play with me on the beach. Why not? I am not too old to fool around on the sand. We muck about and have a fantastic time.

In the evening, having spent a good part of the day together, I invite them to a fancy restaurant. At first, the idea seems brilliant. The kids are as excited as if it were snowing in Rio, running in front of me trying to climb anything vertical. Suddenly, just for a blessed moment, time pauses. Life is absolutely beautiful in the sweetness of this winter evening, when the temperature does not fall below 28 degrees and I am Spiderman, a hero to little kids and the superhero of my own childhood. I enjoy the fantasy for a little while, then ground myself. Believing yourself to be someone you are not is an egotistical honey trap, a delusion, the same as forgetting the reality that this is a city which kills half a dozen street children each day. But I am enjoying the company of these mischievous monkeys and feel lucky to have lived such a day as this. Fortunately, I am of a simple nature, and this allows me to mix one day with the movers and shakers and the next day with the penniless urchins of the favelas.

The four of us arrive in front of the restaurant: a beautiful façade of stately stone, big glazed windows decorated with purple velvet curtains which, slightly parted, give a preview of beautiful raised tables laden with three glasses, three knives, three forks and all the other posh trimmings. Exactly the type of bullshit that rich people find compulsory. Three different forks for kids who have never used a single one? This extravagance might seem a bit stupid, as stupid perhaps as the aristocrats of 17th-century France who felt it equally essential to apply copious quantities of powder to their faces.

We enter and I smile and ask the waiter for a table for four. He looks at me as if I had ordered him to put a live lobster in his underpants. He is wearing a strange strangled expression, a painful face which evokes a misfiring contortion of comedy and tragedy. A few seconds of this face doesn't help anyone. Even the kids do not seem comfortable. As they have entered the establishment barefoot, I understand their reaction, but I explain to them that if they want I can also go barefoot. Immediately I see smiles in their eyes. For them, this truly is another world. But I also feel a little ashamed to have put them in this unpleasant situation.

· I stick to my guns when looking at the waiter, holding his gaze as he almost implodes. This is not some members-only nightclub, just a fucking restaurant. The waiter is squirming but he cannot refuse, perhaps remembering that I had dinner here only yesterday evening with the top brass of TV Globo. He leads us in and we take our places at a round table.

I reflect and begin to understand. The problem is not really that they walk without shoes or money, but that they are favelados, they come from the slums. The kids, dwarfed by the embossed menus, peer over the top and tell me what they want. I flag over the waiter who, now trying hard, has stapled on a smile and stands attentively. I place the order and soon a sumptuous meal is served. My young friends' eyes widen in delight as the plates are laid before them. They pick up the alien knives and forks and make a fine effort to eat correctly and with dignity. Will they have the chance to eat dinner in a restaurant like this again one day? Probably not. I watch them finishing off the food, smiling so much. I am happy to have pleased them, and also happy to have broken a sort of taboo. But deep inside, I know that I can do little more for them. Nevertheless, a bond has formed between us and they eagerly await more from me. To be indifferent now would be difficult and would taint the whole experience. So the deal is on. I shall go to visit them in their favela.

I return alone to the hotel. Night has fallen on Rio. After sunset, the pavements empty, as if a curfew is decreed. I stroll down the darkened streets. Groups of people remain here and there, chatting, smoking cigarettes or wheeling and dealing. The noise of my cowboy boots resounds on the tarmac, amplified by the hard walls. This time tomorrow I shall be ready for battle, hanging onto my life by my fingers. An oily pock-marked guy in his forties approaches me from across the street.

"Maconia (marijuana)? Cocaine?"

The sale of drugs is severely punished in Brazil but the consumption seems to be enormous. A line of cocaine or a cigarette, there seems to be no difference. I smile and answer that I can get stoned or high on adrenaline. He does not understand and melts away. A Crocodile Dundee character from Europe walking around Rio late at night but refusing to buy drugs? He must be hiding something. As the guy walks off he mutters an inaudible sentence that does not need translation. I don't care, he will find plenty of other customers tonight. When I get back to the hotel, I ask Reception for my key.

"You have messages, sir," the desk clerk says, passing me two pieces of paper. They must be from Julie or the guys at TV Globo, worried that I have not returned to my hotel during the day. I tear open both scraps of paper. And guess what? Two girls want to visit me in my hotel room! Groupies? Amused, I crumple them and leave them with the receptionist. What a day. The clerk is worried to see the crumpled messages lying on the marble counter.

"Did you receive bad news, sir?" the clerk asks in a hesitating voice. I walk to the elevator and respond over my shoulder with a wave.

"On the contrary, the news was excellent!"

The following morning, after a series of interviews, I leave to do some shooting with Alexis and a cameraman. They will either use the material in the news broadcasts or, if need be, use it in edits after my ascent this evening. In the street, people call out to me. This sudden popularity amazes me. We get our shots but for two hours I am mobbed. I sign autographs on anything: books, diaries, family photos, visiting cards, scraps of worn paper, fragments of boxes found in dustbins. I even sign arms, backs, faces and cleavage. Ernesto, the cameraman, tells me that Brazilians are strong on keepsakes. They will keep these recollections stashed safely away in a drawer or a box amongst a pile of other signatures for their whole lives.

Time shoots by and already it is time to return to the hotel. As we head back I begin to retreat into myself. I need to isolate myself before climbing, concentrating on my task and my state of mind, whilst making a conscious effort to avoid external pressure. I take the elevator and lock myself away in my room. As much as I try to escape it, the prospect of being filmed live for millions of viewers can only put me under stress. People often wonder, what would happen if I did not feel well at the foot of the tower? Or if I suffered a bad day, as can happen to any sportsman? How about if it was this evening, live on air? Unlike most other sportsmen, a bad day at the races could be fatal for me. Every time I approach an ascent it is the same – my brains and innards begin turning in my head and in my stomach like they were in a washing machine. My state of mind before climbing must be similar to the stage fright of a rock star panicking before confronting thousands of expectant fans. Maybe this is the real reason why so many of those bands are as high as kites when they take to the stage. Sure, I am in the habit of facing pressure, but this evening, climbing by night and live on air, my heart drums so hard and fast it is as if I had taken a kilo of Rio's best cocaine.

Fifteen floors below, at the hotel lobby, a car from TV Globo pulls up. It's for me. It's time. They all know I am in my zone. Nobody speaks during the 15 minutes it takes to get to the building. Slowly I get ready, lace my slippers, and begin once again the eternal ritual so familiar and so important to rock climbers.

The car arrives at the scene and I cast my eyes upwards into the darkness. The production team scurries around. The countdown is well underway, the scene is set and the pieces are all in place. At a set time, the projectors dramatically ignite, revealing the façade in its entirety. This razzmatazz is like a boxing match – Robert versus Rio, David versus Goliath. The scene is great for the audience but does little for my frayed nerves. Adrenaline courses through me. The clock ticks. We are going to air within seconds. All eyes are on me as I sit in the car cocked like a pistol. I focus. I am ready. I watch for the signal... *Now!*

I burst out of the car and in haste launch myself at the tower and speed through the first movements. In seconds, the pavement fades away. I try to find a good rhythm, the method I will repeat right up to the summit. Suddenly, the technicians begin to yell and wave their arms frantically. They are telling me to get down again! My throat tightens. What's going on? Have the cops arrived already? I redo the movements back to front, and despite the confusion I try to retain my focus. Back on the ground, they indicate that we aren't ready, as the previous broadcast has not ended yet. I return to the car to isolate myself again, then someone comes and knocks at the window.

"Okay, okay! That's it, go quickly!"

I dart out again, a little disturbed and alarmed, and once more begin to climb. When I climb, I count only on myself. Reliance on others is something I must keep to a minimum. This time I decide I will leave the pavement in a blur, and nothing can stop me, not even a power cut. The technicians will have to be as effective as I am!

Once I am away I think of nothing but the escalation. I lose my awareness of the ground crew and audience, and become absorbed and engulfed by the building. It is as if I am part of it. The brilliant spotlight accompanies my progress, like an enormous anti-aircraft searchlight tracing the path of an enemy bomber. The setting is not particularly discreet and starts to attract curious onlookers. They accumulate on the pavements, and soon cover the whole avenue.

Thirty minutes later, only two floors separate me from the summit. As usual, I sense the presence of the police. How many are there this time and how are they going to operate? I don't care, I have plenty of time to find out. I place one hand, then the other, on the low wall at the summit. This tower has not really given me any problems. It could become a classic climb if this sport attracts followers in Brazil!

I poke my head over the top, throw a heel over, and get both feet on the ground. A dozen policemen are waiting for me, not so calm at the sight of a guy clambering over the façade. Every time I get to the top, no matter where I am, I see the same look in their faces. Handcuffs secure my wrists and the sober policemen take me down to the ground floor. The lift doors open and they take me outside.

On the flight of steps beyond the entrance, more than a thousand people applaud me. A thousand! I am tired by the exertion of the climb, from the released flood of adrenaline that accumulated in me during the day, but I am so happy to be warmly welcomed and appreciated by such a wonderful people. To stand there in the middle of such a scene is quite overwhelming and the emotion of this special moment chokes me. Frankly, I really do not remember if I cried or not. I didn't realise it then, but it was so crowded that evening that the police presence was more for my protection than my arrest. The people push in towards me and I almost drown in a sea of appreciation. If anything, dealing with the surging crowd is more hazardous than the escalation! It is quite difficult to explain unless you have been in the middle of something like this. But I now understand that the public can quickly become frenzied, hysterical, utterly crazed. I would like to find other words to describe the intensity of such an unbelievable moment. I can't.

The cops don't enjoy it as much as I do, that I can tell. After we have fought our way to the car, the convoy starts and tries to clear a passage through the massed crowd. On each side of the squad car, dozens of Brazilians stick their faces against the glass, tapping the rooftop of the car which resounds as if in a hailstorm. Revolving lights swirl, sirens wail, the crowd applauds. After a few hundred metres, peace returns. My head is still spinning as we pull in to the police station. And here also, a new experience – a pair of slick lawyers from TV Globo are already here fussing around to bail me. For once I shall make only the briefest visit to the police station. I am in and out within minutes.

That evening, I am invited to a luxurious apartment with bay windows looking onto Copacabana Beach and Sugarloaf Mountain. This immense lounge is artistically decorated and every object within it is perfectly placed. A large number of people from high society are gathered. I just had the time to take a shower and here I am drinking flutes of champagne, speaking with two snappy dressers. One of them wants to sponsor me and the other worries about the management of my interests. I know these odious loud-mouthed types, typical salesmen who take me for an idiot and try to impress me with glitter and bullshit. Just for fun, and maybe also because of the champagne which my body is readily soaking up due to my earlier exertions, I play along with the conversation. I eventually tell them that now, because we are such good friends, it is okay – I shall go and climb the building where they work and will dedicate the ascent to them, to show my friendship. Have you ever seen somebody swallow an entire mouthful of champagne? It is particularly disturbing at this kind of party.

Enough is enough and I take off towards the buffet. The offerings? Ham, roast beef, smoked salmon, *petits fours*, cocaine… Cocaine? If somebody had not stuck his nose in the salad bowl, I would have sweetened my strawberries with the narcotic. I am way too naïve! More snorting takes place amongst the party nibbles and clinking of glasses. I guess everyone needs some sort of stimulus to lift his mood but I shudder to think what I would be like on drugs – I am already considered unhinged enough without them.

The next day, Julie wakes me with a pile of newspapers. I monopolise the coverage as never before. Too bad: if I could read Portuguese, I could have stayed in bed all morning finding out how my escalation had been received. In spite of the TV channels which all now invite me on air, I choose to spend this one day far from lenses and microphones. A promise is a promise and my young friends from the favela of Rossigna are waiting for me.

Rossigna is a maze of muddy and stinking streets, sheet metal, stray animals and trash which shelters 300,000 inhabitants, and there are other such favelas in Rio. The taxi drops me at the entrance to the shanty town. The driver urges me not to venture in, certain that I will be molested. I give him a handful of notes and sink into this impoverished labyrinth. As if the inhabitants all had walkie-talkies, the news of my arrival quickly circulates. Rossigna is a big place and I wander around aimlessly. The area contains countless thousands of people, little or no infrastructure and certainly no tourist-friendly signposts. When my three friends had suggested meeting them there, they had simply told me: "Come to Rossigna, and you will be our guest," as if it was possible to say to someone that you'd have a meeting in Paris without specifying where or when. I was a bit sceptical but they had insisted.

I meander around, half-expecting to spend fruitless hours searching for them. Yet they find me within ten minutes! At first, a favela looks like a real shambles. But in fact communications are very well organised to defend against police raids, and also due to permanent gang wars and drug trafficking. As princes in their palaces, the three kids lead me to a meeting with the leader of Rossigna, and a complete tour. As they proudly show me around their neighbourhood it starts to rain on Rio. The shanty town is filled with mud and pollution. And yet the happiness of these magnificent, ever-smiling people is contagious and heart-warming – even if it is necessary to press myself against the walls from time to time, to avoid a squall of gunfire not far off. I am told there is some disagreement going on, almost certainly drug-related. I can barely believe it as I have only heard machine-gun fire in movies. I should be terror-stricken, but my tour leaders seem mostly unconcerned, as if a neighbour had dropped a plate or something. Here, gunshots are a part of daily life, just like samba schools and football.

Our group stops in front of the highest building in the favela, only a dozen metres high and made from irregular red bricks. It looks like a mottled collection of rubble from demolished buildings stuck back together again. Okay guys, no need to say anything, I know what you want! Two hundred kids stare at me wide-eyed and expectant. Some of them have broken teeth due to extreme consumption of cocaine, others wear weapons slung over their shoulders. I pull off my waistcoat, remove a few loose bits of mortar, and then go up the broken wall as I would a cliff, climbing slowly to prolong the pleasure below. I whip up the crowd and they are in delirium, going absolutely wild, as if I had performed a miracle. When I eventually get back down they surge and engulf me. When I look back over all my climbs, all my achievements, this climb is maybe the most beautiful recollection of my life. The joy in bringing something special to these kids was a dream for them. But even more so for me.

The day begins to fade and a samba evening starts around a fire. The Cariocas are justifiably proud of their samba schools. Every year, the elaborate costumes take thousands of working hours to create, and the results are amazing. Sat beside the town leader and my three friends, I admire the spectacle, dazzled. The dancers, almost naked and adorned only with vivid yellow feathers, approach, then take my hand and invite me to participate in this syncopated dance. I dance like a demon and enact an abominable mixture of samba and wayward French boogie. It's neither well choreographed nor attractive, but I really get into it. The samba allows for pure physical joy, like an escalation. Everybody claps their hands, whistles or dances to the primal beat. Bodies writhe and costumes glitter by the fire which crackles and lets fly airborne orange embers. Few people can party like the Brazilians! The hours pass and all too soon it is time to head back.

My friends transport me back to my hotel in one of the only functional cars in the favela. The lopsided box splutters and rattles back to the hotel in a noxious cloud of black diesel. The rust is so extensive it is impossible to guess what brand of car it once was. The vehicle judders and wheezes to a stop. On the steps outside my sparkling five-star hotel I feel shame; shame because of the insignificance I attach to this luxury. The people of Rossigna live a hard life but keep smiling through it all. They face utter poverty, the presence of death, disease, bullets flying from machine guns and pistols, and the scorn of society. In the middle of all this are kids just like these, who by the age of eight carry weapons almost as big as themselves. We stand for a while. This minute of farewell seems endless to me. Cariocas, this is just *au revoir*. One day I shall return to Brazil, to Rossigna and to my family there who have made me feel so very much at home.

The next day, the guys from TV Globo tease me with a little information. Apparently there is a very suitable building in Barra, a district of Rio. It is under construction and still unnamed, but I have to conquer it.

The cameras accompany me as usual, but today there is a police presence in the area. I take a sneaky look around and assess the incomplete tower and the cops on the ground. The building has no windows yet, but it looks okay and shouldn't pose too many problems. The site is not properly sealed off and I can see the bottom of the tower quite clearly as it is just a stone's throw from the road. Discreetly, I get ready in the car. I get past the slack gatekeeper and enter the premises, having only to walk about 50 metres before I can attack with my first movements. But already, policemen are pouring towards me like an army of angry ants. Naturally I break into a run. But within seconds I am away, off the ground, and the cops are floundering in my wake. They run in all directions to try to intercept me and cut off any escape. As the building is not yet finished, the work of the police is made much easier. With no window glass, the hollow building's inside is still largely outside. But who cares, let's go for it! Let's play a game of hide-and-seek, or rather policemen against thief, in three dimensions!

As I ascend, a head would pop out next to me and cry out as I passed by unperturbed. If I saw the cops above me, I would move across a few metres, then pass them, much to their annoyance. More running and yelling. More cat-and-mouse stuff. This game lasts until the eighth floor, where I finally surrender, totally encircled by angry cops.

They bring me down the stairwell but do so without having placed me in handcuffs. They lead me outside to the street, where their police cars await. But the street is filling with journalists and spectators. As we exit the construction site the crowd surrounds us and I am shoved through the hustle and bustle. I pick my moment and take advantage of the scrum to escape, slipping out of the grasp of the guards and cops. I slalom through the crowd as uniformed arms claw vainly at me. I emerge from between someone's legs and dash back, a cop and a guard in pursuit. By the time the others have realised what is going on, I have already climbed two floors. Below, the crowd applauds. A human chess game resumes on a gigantic vertical chessboard for all to see. If they move a pawn to the right, I move my madman to the left. I move diagonally, sideways, all over the place, confounding my inept and uncoordinated opponents. The crowd loves it! They cheer as if it were a live sports game.

At the 12th floor, the numerous opposition finally corner my solitary piece. Checkmate. I climb in and I am firmly seized. I find my opponents were not very sporting players. They certainly didn't like losing the first game! Too bad, everyone else had a good time. Handcuffs are firmly fastened behind me this time and they curse me in Portuguese which, I must say, does not have the required effect. The more they get excited, the more I laugh. I am led out again to wonderful support from the crowd. With the cuffs on there can be no third round of this entertaining game, no best out of three. It ends in a draw.

As I am pushed through the crowd I notice the lawyers from TV Globo are on hand to help me. But first, we go to the police station for mug shots, fingerprints and the usual questioning. My lawyers are armed with fat chequebooks and as they expected I am quickly released. As I make my exit I get a big surprise. Several hundred people amassed around the police station applaud me! It's only midday but it starts all over again: interviews, footage of this strange 'Connect Four' escalation on the television, and coverage in the newspapers.

Although the game was fun and the media response is overwhelmingly positive I regard the escalation as a failure in climbing terms. With coverage of me at saturation point, and my movements very limited, TV Globo and I decide to try elsewhere. We shall pay a courtesy visit to the Edificio Italia in Sao Paulo, a megalopolis of more than 20 million people.

I fly over to Sao Paulo expecting to leave the crowds behind. But as in Rio, my stellar popularity precedes me. This is really getting over the top. Sometimes, the police have to intervene to evacuate people massed around me, and even block off traffic! My arrival in Sao Paulo has not gone unnoticed and the rumour spreads that my presence has something to do with the Edificio Italia. The paparazzi follow me, trying to confirm the rumours, snapping me whenever I dare to stick my head out. This misplaced stardom amuses me on a personal level, but as a climber it is annoying. More discretion would have been nice. After my failure in Rio, my self-esteem dictates it is out of the question to fail here. But how am I going to take the guards by surprise? Just imagine what you would be thinking if you were the chief of security at the Edificio Italia – having seen all the fuss in Rio, and then seen my arrival in Sao Paulo heralded by paparazzi and gossip columnists speculating that I am here to scale your building. And even without the publicity, the building itself raises one or two problems for me. A circular terrace on the fourth floor will enormously help the security guards. If I get past them on the ground, they can easily pluck me from the terrace. The following morning, I learn an order is imposed on the guards and on the police to do just that. If they let me through and I climb the tower, they will lose their jobs. Brazil is not a country like France, where such a threat cannot be carried out without the employer being taken to court. I have to take this threat as serious. I have no alternative than to give up, not wishing to put any families in difficulty.

But I do not have to work too hard to find another objective, and instead I attack the Centro Cultural FIESP on Paulista Avenue. The escalation turns out to be very easy and the police are unable to prevent me from making the climb. Nearby, a TV Globo helicopter hovers in a stationary position. A cameraman is perched on the edge of the chopper filming me while other cameras, placed hastily on the building opposite, also record images for the evening news. At the summit the police pluck me like an apple from a tree, whisk me to the station and then let me rot for a night in custody.

From my perspective I am pleased to have achieved an escalation despite the huge media, police and security presence. For Julie and Alexis, their contract ends here and they must depart Sao Paulo. But I can look forward to at least another week of freedom before my appearance in front of the High Court of Justice.

And the trial is marvellous. As soon as I sit down, charges are immediately dismissed and I am completely free – free to scale the Vermont Hotel. I happen to be staying at the hotel at the moment, an attractive building of only a dozen floors. I have struck a deal with the hotel owner, for whom this is the chance of a lifetime, an unexpected and far-reaching advertisement. I enjoy a few comfortable days at the hotel and then, the day before my departure, I attack the façade of the Vermont. There is already a group assembled below, but when I take to the building, hundreds of additional onlookers immediately block the avenue.

I progress with relative ease but, to my surprise, cops start opening windows in an effort to catch me! A window opening, a frustrated cop and a startled climber – the scene draws laughter from the audience. But why are they here? I have obtained a licence this time. The hotel manager produces it in a flash. The cops fade away and I make it up to the tenth floor where, before reaching the summit, I must cross a doubtful and extremely fragile air-conditioning unit. There is no way around this thing, and it is the only grip I can use to make progress. Battered and decaying, it sags at a worrying angle. For almost half an hour, I rise and reinspect it and then retreat, hesitating on what action to take. Ten floors below me the crowd cheers and sings my name, helping to drive me on and find my way out of this maze. For my part their rousing support works. Maybe I am bound to their collective will, hypnotised by their chants. There are not many options. Either I climb down again, which technically is not difficult, or else I make movements which will allow me to recover my position – at the risk of leaving the side of the building together with the air-conditioning unit.

Every time I grab hold of the flimsy aluminium box, it creaks, folds and spills a sprinkle of dust. Finally, pushed by the crowd, I make my choice. The exit is upwards, where it has always been. Yet I am frightened to let this box take my whole weight. It feels like it was placed here by Pandora of Greek mythology – death, envy, greed, vanity, despair and violence lie within. Do I really dare lift its lid? When Pandora's box was opened, all the evils of the world flew out and wreaked havoc, but one thing was left inside: hope. I am not sure if this is a good or bad metaphor under the circumstances, and the legend is hardly reassuring, but while hope remains there is always a chance.

In an effort to make myself feel a little lighter, I hold my breath as I reach out. There is no way of knowing what will happen until I pull the trigger in this game of Russian roulette. I catch hold of both brackets and gently let my feet hang free. I then make two quick moves to put myself on top of it. With difficulty I surmount the rotten box. The hardest part is complete: the unit held. I now stand on top of it, but I am far from comfortable with my new location. The unit has given a little with my weight and seems to have sunk a little lower. I am 20 centimetres shy of the concrete ledge above me. In this hostile zone the concrete is smooth, without grips.

Marooned upon this degenerate pile of shit, I tentatively try to extend myself 20 centimetres… No, it's impossible. I have no other choice but to jump. But, to jump, it is necessary to be impulsive. This is really scary. To push against this unit could very well detach it, along with me. If it goes, I might make it, I might not. Furious, and disgusted at the idea of bringing down this fucking machine in the middle of an overcrowded avenue, I try my absolute best to measure my effort. It is a question of not pushing too hard because without a shadow of a doubt, if I do that, the unit is going to fall. On the other hand, I cannot push too gently, or I will land upon it again and that would definitely do it. I also don't want to loiter here as the bolts keeping the unit from falling may splinter at any time.

I peer around for grips once again, hoping one will materialise out of nowhere, but of course there are none. Slowly I empty my lungs. Then I take my leap of faith... time stops in mid-air... an eternity later, my fingers seize the ledge. Hanging like a stick of salami, I wait in terror for the deafening noise of aluminium against concrete... but nothing! In the street below, the crowd is roaring, completely hysterical! I yank myself up to the summit, saved. I have done it and my nightmares are swept away by the euphoria of relief. I thank my lucky stars that I hadn't caused a tragedy for anyone beneath me.

Although I control my movements, I have no knowledge of the quality of materials of or upon a structure, nor their premature wear. With binoculars of course I may study a building but I cannot tell the solidity of these elements. It is necessary to manage this problem, to properly select escalations to give the best chance of survival to myself and to those below. From now on I must count only on my muscles and the gristle of industrial steel or reinforced concrete.

I tremble as the tension accumulated over the last half-hour is unloaded in around 30 seconds. And, shaking upon the rooftop, I am surprised to be disturbed by the police. I have a licence and I can't understand what is going on. The hotel owner gets involved and I learn that although he gave me his permission, he did not apply officially. After a period of negotiations in Portuguese, all of which fly over my head, the misunderstanding is resolved and I can shoot off to the airport in time to catch my plane back to the greyness and anonymity of Paris.

By the time my feet touch the ground on the other side of the Atlantic, I am already missing Brazil. I can barely believe all the things that happened to me in the short time I spent in that awesome country. What can I say about such a place? *Fantastico!*

7

LIBERTY BELL

L ife is a journey, a scrolling pageant of scenery. As we travel this road, events can pass harmlessly by or accidentally crash into us. If we are going too fast or not paying enough attention, we can spin out of control, fly off the tarmac. Sometimes a road hog shunts us out of our lane before a junction and we end up by chance on a different but equally beautiful road. Though we try to direct our lives, fate makes us ball-bearings in a great pinball machine, sailing and bouncing through permanent chaos between disaster and success. Philadelphia was the scene of such an experience for me – events conspired to drag me through the rapids of a quite unplanned adventure. Philadelphia was once the capital of the United States and was known as the city of freedom, as embodied by a bell cast way back in 1752: the 'Liberty Bell'.

It is the 1990s and I am scratching around for sponsors to fund my escalations. I bag Outlaw, and they agree to become my clothing sponsor. Their head office is in Toronto, and an all-expenses-paid invitation to fly out to climb a building in the city comes my way. Knowing the climbing potential of this modern Canadian city, I tell them I will be there. Many such invitations come to nothing, but Outlaw and I make good progress and I get ready to pack a whole collection of slippers in my luggage. Before location scouting, I never know which equipment I am going to use for an ascent. Some slippers fit better with cracks or gaps in a building while others provide superior adhesion to the surface.

To add another interesting dimension, I hear the escalation will tie in somehow with a performance by electro-rock group Hors La Loi. And then, a day before my departure, a late phone call from the boss announces laconically that the operation is – wait for it – cancelled, because of pressure from Outlaw's lawyers and some other legal advisers. The price of my plane ticket will be reimbursed. Thank you. Goodbye.

Sponsoring these kinds of escalations abroad seems to raise no problems for multinationals, but on their territory, in their own country, it is much more complicated. When you are a safe distance away it is easy to benefit from an outside news item, to hit and run. Coming from one of my reliable sponsors, this about-turn hits me hard, like an act of treason. I shrug and keep my plane ticket. My bag is packed. I am keyed up to go climb a skyscraper! Maybe I can achieve my own ascent of a Toronto tower. But still, I am not happy. I consider that risk-taking must be shared. I put my life and my freedom on the line and my sponsors should honour our agreements and support my escalation. Surely this is fair. I phone around to grumble and soon get through to Julie, my agent.

Julie succeeds in persuading me to 'let the matter drop' (What an inappropriate expression!) telling me instead of the advantages of climbing in her home city – Philadelphia. Cunning as a fox, she plays on my frustrations and delivers a good argument. What kind of outlaw is Outlaw anyway? More like 'Grovel before the Law' or 'Outlawyers' perhaps. Shit, why give my cowardly sponsor such an undeserved present – an escalation in Toronto – when supportive Philadelphia stretches out its welcoming arms? I get off the phone and pull out my bible, *The World's Highest Buildings*, flick through a few pages of flattering images of the American city and make my decision.

Goodbye Toronto, hooray for Philadelphia!

My face clamped against the porthole of a 747, I observe Philadelphia as we descend. The approach to the airport is less interesting than in New York or Chicago. Here, high rises seem scattered, and even if the aerial view is misleading, the concentration of tall buildings is weak. When Julie, a former model hardly 25 years of age – such a beautiful girl – meets up with me, she reads disappointment on my face. Put simply, as for many immigrants confronted with reality, the American dream is not as beautiful as in books. Partially responsible for my journey to Philadelphia, Julie foresaw this. She whips out some grainy photocopies of a building from her handbag. It is One Liberty Place, the city's highest building, standing at 287 metres. I cannot determine yet whether I can climb it or not, but even from this poor-quality image I notice that it has prominent architectural features forbidding any hope of reaching the summit. This is so frustrating. The tallest buildings cry out to be climbed even though they often have features or obstacles which prevent me reaching their true apex. The desire to reach the absolute top of a structure often drives me towards buildings of lesser scale. Beauty or status can compensate for any shortcomings when I decide to commit. Doesn't this sound like the way humans decide to commit to other relationships?

On the highway leading to the city centre, Julie tells me more about the 200-metre club. There are only five members. In other words, my options are very limited. But the locations are quickly visited so I head out to swiftly assess them.

One Liberty Place? As expected, beautiful but no way. It is far too complicated, and what really kills it off is that the summit is impossible to attain. But nearby, a more modest building of only 45 floors and a shade over 200 metres attracts my exercised eye. The Blue Cross-Blue Shield Tower is a beautiful crystal of smoky and particularly aesthetic blue glass, and looks 'easy' to climb. To the left, Two Liberty Place raises the same issues as its bigger brother. Blue Cross-Blue Shield though has a devastating design thrusting from the earth like luxurious geysers of blue ice, topped by a pyramid-like sloping roof. It is magnificent, irresistible... I catch Julie by the sleeve so we may have a closer yet discreet look at its feasibility. From about 50 metres, I have most of my answers. At this safe distance I can leisurely study the holistic structure without drawing the attention of the ever-present security services. I dissect my specimen with my binoculars. I spy on the building, tracing her lines, unlocking her secrets.

Facing the Blue Cross-Blue Shield from the opposite pavement, I do not want to cross the road. But not the slightest grip can be seen on this crystalline monument. It seems to be a block of pure glass. I pause then slalom reluctantly through the traffic, fearful of seeing my dreams dashed. Julie is on the other side of the boulevard, leaning against the mirrored surface of a nearby building which reflects and multiplies her image. Three smiling Julies are waiting for me. We walk a little until flanked by blue and I survey the foot of the building, silently looking for a fingerhold, a foothold, a weakness. Julie follows me, perplexed and curious. And then the miracle occurs – I finally find the Achilles heel, a fine crack which will allow me to climb. My fingers slip only with difficulty into the groove and as for my feet, well, essentially the chance of them going in there is science fiction; but at this moment, Blue Cross-Blue Shield is playable. Extreme, but playable. It is the tail end of the afternoon and the city-dwellers swarm on the pavements, making a test climb impossible. Not only that but I have no slippers. But my mind is made up – this building attracts me irresistibly, dangerously, as the maiden Lorelei attracted the skippers of the Rhine. I shall climb it.

I generally make a small trial attempt by night to test my theories and experiment with my moves. We return to the scene under the cover of darkness, to put into practice the method elaborated at Julie's place: ascent via two sets of cracks. But I have slightly overestimated my reach. Quartered, crucified backwards with my crooked nose pushed against window panes, I cannot move a hair. It impossible to move my feet. I have no choice but to pull on a single tiny crack which will not allow me to jam in my feet, a basic requirement in escalation. After multiple attempts and multiple failures, I reach, in agony, the first horizontal joint – a small concrete and silicone strip marking the border between two panes. There are 120 others like this. I do not dare to undertake the second phase as the percentage of risk is not in my favour. Exhausted, I drop down.

Back on the pavement, my brain bubbles: ideas collide, mix with doubt and uncertainty, and whirl in a maelstrom of frustration. I look up, look around, inspect the crack once again. I do not know. I do not know any more. And yet a prodigious force urges me not to abandon the project, to persist, to attempt the movements with various different slippers, to determine which pair will give the best results. I go through my whole collection. It's all in vain.

Julie advises me to abandon Blue Cross-Blue Shield. Deep inside (she will admit it later), she feels partially responsible and is concerned for my safety. A few yards away I attempt another tower, with equal success. But it is only a half-hearted attempt because my mind is elsewhere: Blue Cross-Blue Shield obsesses me as never before! Against Julie's advice – in these moments, I do not listen to anybody – I return to my nemesis full of determination and collide again with failure.

Finally, expecting nothing but defeat, I try to climb with my feet against the panes. I expect to slip, to judder downwards, something I would prefer not to do 200 metres in the air. But unexpectedly, and because every face of this building is washed thoroughly every four days, the adhesion of my slippers turns out to be firm, well beyond my expectations. I should have known from the sheen of this building that the glass was immaculately clean, but how many buildings are so pampered? This is an amazing stroke of good fortune. There is still an element of uncertainty as I cannot be sure the window cleaners are so attentive over the entire surface, especially high up where they might be tempted to rush the job and get down for their cup of tea. I doubt if many people go up to check their handiwork – let's face it, the only people likely are other window cleaners and the occasional French rock climber! But I have earnt some respite and the fight is on.

It is strange. Sometimes, a tiny hope of success leaves us greatly perplexed. When there is no possible way forward, desolation leads not to defeat but acts as an imperative to propel us onwards to victory. This can be applauded as a 'never say die' attitude. But on the other hand, when the mind does not succeed in reaching a resolution, and a weak light of hope still sparkles, how can we be persuaded that abandoning a sinking ship is not necessarily an act of cowardice? Does the captain go down with his ship or jump overboard to rally his men to fight another day? Blue Cross-Blue Shield is such a stricken ship, and I need bravery to make the best decision. I have a whole night to think about it, a night of fear, a night haunted by demons.

In the past I was sometimes obsessed by a target. The building or the cliff was so perfect that its only defect was that it hung in my consciousness without ever being able to leave me in peace. I would be hounded and harassed by this rock or building, without even a second of respite. These visions were so violent that I would often feel compelled to attack the target, almost as a form of self-defence. When vanquished they became my most beautiful sports successes as well as driving me through some of my most risky challenges. They were also the root of my most terrible fears... If performing a precarious movement over Verdon's green waters gives me a chill, the simple fact of imagining this situation, before even lifting a foot, terrifies me.

I lie in the twilight, staring at the ceiling of my room, sleepless in Philadelphia. I can feel myself being sucked in. I must find a way out... an exit if I am brave enough, or a solution if I have equal courage. The trial run was so clumsy apart from the last attempt and that was hardly a resounding success. This Blue Cross-Blue Shield building offers no other way, no alternative strategies if I need to switch. The design of the building also excludes any possibility of rest. Doubts creep in. The Golden Gate Bridge had been a close call: had the cable been a few metres longer or the paint a little more slippery, my miscalculation would have meant I would not be in this comfy bed now. Sometimes you must give up. But how to deal with failure?

Recently in Paris I had to climb the Concorde-Lafayette Hotel for a sponsor. There was little to worry about and the heat of the tail end of summer was no trouble. It seemed like it would be an enjoyable excursion. But on the day, after an advertising campaign and in the presence of the press, I opted to call off my ascent and climb down from the dozen floors that I had already put behind me, the structure being slightly moistened by rain. It took huge amounts of strength to get that far, and all my reserves to reverse and get down. By the time I had descended to the second floor I was utterly exhausted and had nothing left. I looked for the best place to jump down to. I landed safely on the ground before a crowd of cameras and journalists, utterly spent. I had no intention of committing suicide and had fought tooth and nail to get back down in one piece. The jump, though sizeable, did not injure me. But up there my body had reached its limit. Naturally, danger is a motivator, but all the will in the world cannot make a car go another yard if it is out of gas. I had known to turn back at the right time, estimating a fall in the neighbourhood of the 20th or 21st floors. Only in Hollywood movies are happy endings adhered to religiously. Reality is totally different. Even if we can run 25 miles, the 26th may be impossible. Any further effort is useless. Knowing when to quit isn't just wise, it is necessary, and it will be imposed upon us if we do not take the initiative ourselves.

Will I be able to adhere to the building's panes for almost 300 dramatic metres without sliding? I try to extrapolate various climbing parameters but it is clearly impossible to answer this question without trying it. In traditional escalation, the immense majority of solo ascents are always a little unpredictable. They can be difficult but climbers employ hooked grips which tell you at once whether or not enough hold exists to proceed. On flat surfaces or with fickle grips, you do not know what to expect. You can slide simply due to a tiny veil of dust, or because the push of your foot was too enthusiastic or not correctly anchored through its axis. This unpredictability has built my fame in the climbing world. It has formed the basis for my life, but also perhaps one day, for my demise.

As luck would have it, one of Julie's friends works at NBC as a presenter. Of course the television channel loves a story and the management have been informed of my upcoming climb. They are very keen to broadcast some footage, but as per usual they don't want to take any legal risks. So we wheel out a tried-and-tested approach which satisfies the channel's requirement to make it look like it is first on the scene due to the speed and tenacity of its journalists. Viewers might be surprised to learn how much of the media's reporting is stage-managed to create an artificial air of independence and distance from the subject. Sure, some of it is genuine, but the rest? Show business! Reporters with sole access to a story can often call the shots in much the same way as a documentary director.

I am told by the news team that NBC helicopters take to the air over the city each day at about 5:00pm, to report on the traffic or any unfolding events. Since the surreal live broadcast of the car chase involving O.J. Simpson, helicopters have been at the forefront of American news gathering. News has become more like reality TV, dramatic voyeurism showing things as they take place, non-stop, often with little explanation or analysis. It's all action. But in order not to be accused of collusion, the pilots must be able to assert that they accidentally discovered me scaling the Blue Cross-Blue Shield as they made their daily tour of the skies. If I attack the tower a little earlier, the timing should match their flight plans.

NBC decides to whip up some images in preparation of the escalation. The city in which the *Rocky* movies were set conjures up images of training to that heroic music. I am asked to jog up a flight of stairs, as in the movies, and then raise my arms to the sky in a triumphant and combative manner. They are going to use this as an intro to their report, soundtrack and all. It doesn't sound anything like the spontaneous report they were talking about, but okay, cue the music. After Schwarzenegger in San Francisco and Bruce Lee in Malaysia, I am now Stallone in Philadelphia.

Muscles, muscles, it's always about muscles. This symbol of invincibility in this city which fondly identifies itself with *Rocky* is too much for the producers to resist. Standing only one metre sixty five high, I admit that I have difficulty lending myself to this role. I am a climber, not an actor, the things I do are real.

But I go along with it. I jump through their hoops pretending to be a fictional boxer hard at training. Early in the afternoon, I need to stop. The TV guys try to get me to do a few more scenes but I am throwing in the towel. That's enough, I'm fed up! I want to be alone, I want to write picture postcards and, if my subconscious allows me, to sleep a little. I need to rest, to disengage. I have a skyscraper to climb later today.

Back in my room I lose myself as I scribble away on a bunch of postcards. Writing has always pleased me. Before a huge project, it is a sort of release. The senses sometimes conjure up unexpected sentences which take on other dimensions. When I travel, I cannot help filling the backs of postcards with thoughts for my friends. I write according to the humour of the madness or mounting stress levels I find myself with. Sometimes, I even write more cards than I have addresses. I like playing with the words, imagining that when my friend receives the card he will have a good laugh at my waffle – or that when he gets it the lines may have added irony due to the fact I shall perhaps not be around any more. Macabre? Not for me. Anyway, at this precise moment, having performed like a seal at the circus, rest is a profound need. I dream of the beautiful noise of handcuffs snapping around my wrists. It is a synonym for success, and for life. I slip into my bed and let my mind drift. Despite all these images colliding in my head, I succeed in sleeping for half an hour or so, no doubt facilitated by my earlier exertions and a lack of sleep the night before.

The hour arrives. It is time to go. As part of my preparations I choose a jacket with easily accessible pockets into which I can slide my special bottles, the ones used by athletes on the move. Where the structure permits it, I might snatch a drink and rest a moment. Regrettably this is a rare luxury as it is more often than not impossible to take a break. Next, I must choose my slippers carefully. I weigh up the factors affecting my decision: the construction materials, the architecture, the weather… I opt for my Bambas, flexible and comfortable slippers in a size a little larger than I usually use. Generally, rock climbers' feet are compressed in a fashion that would be unbearable for non-climbers. It may seem like masochism, but it is in fact physics. When the toes are compressed and unable to move, the precision of this small grip is multiplied tenfold. You can seek out a smaller groove or ledge and your rigid foot is more robust in this tiny area, the same way a metal hook would catch or snare in the rocks. But the Blue Cross-Blue Shield does not require such footwork. I have considered the complex adhesions required for this climb, and I choose a large size which enables me to roll and flex my feet. The loss in precision is inversely proportional to what is gained in adhesion. But I have to admit that beyond these technical aspects, I have also chosen these slippers because these faithful companions have already participated in the successful completion of numerous different challenges. I am unusually attached to these shoes. I guess it's a kind of foot fetish.

There is still one major problem which needs to be dealt with – the effect on my skin of climbing several hundred metres of a narrow crack. This is a glass building and the pressure and friction constantly pulls at the skin. If one of my fingers were to be sliced open, blood would act as a very effective lubricant and reduce my adhesion to zero. Professional rock climbers will often sand down their fingers with glass-paper to remove the thick calluses, sometimes on a daily basis. This fossilised skin can act like a comfortable glove and protect us from the pain of sharp or rough surfaces. But the thickness and hardness of this skin can also reduce the sensitive, pliable surface we need to effect a good grip. Worse, these thick calluses can easily split and crack, leading to bleeding and forbidding any escalation. To counter this risk, I protect my hands with unstretchable adhesive strips which are usually used in physiotherapy. Fingers must be mummified except for their tips, which are exposed for sensation and adhesion. Success depends on technique as much on training.

I take a call and then slam the phone down irately. I often find the duplicity of the press infuriating. After making an idiot of myself and running up and down stairwells for them, it seems NBC are happy to get all the footage and showcase their scoop, but offer me no cooperation whatsoever as this is an illegal ascent. They won't film me making the escalation live, they wish to 'stumble' across it in their helicopter. They want to protect themselves but they are happy to see me risk life and limb, and get thrown in jail, so long as they get their story! I almost always have some backup, people I can count on, but here I am alone. One of Julie's friends, a weatherman called John, does try to organise some ground footage but NBC shy away and will have no part in it. They do at least drive me to the building, but in the car leading me towards my fate, the silence is deafening. Nobody speaks. These fellows from NBC are awash with embarrassment and do not dare to talk to me. But what could they say? When you drive somebody to the hospital emergency room, you avoid small talk. You also avoid expressing support or encouragement as it would come across as fake. If you are wise, you keep silent. You drive.

I withdraw and try to control my cardiac pulsations as my heartbeat has already doubled in pace and strength even before I have moved an eyebrow. The tower is within sight. I am frightened, since without a doubt

Alain's climbing adventures began early. This photo taken by boyhood friend Pierre shows Alain with the young of a formidable eagle owl encountered halfway up a cliff.

By his early twenties Alain had established himself as a top rock climber. Here he tackles *La Nuit du Cauchemar* (rated 8a/b) in Buoux, southern France.

Alain's second urban climb in Paris put him on a collision course with Loïk Le Floch-Prigent. The enraged Elf CEO pursued Alain through the courts for several years until, in an ironic turn of events, he found himself in the dock.

Above: Alain's friends Thierry and Bambi wrestle with a security guard at the foot of TF1 before being overcome in a mass brawl.

Opposite: Climbing the sheer rock face of *L'Ange en Decomposition* (rated 7a) in the Verdon Canyon.

Top left: The ancient Luxor Obelisk in Paris lacks height but has an almost insurmountable base which required a novel approach.

Left and above: Alain is arrested in Rio de Janeiro after climbing for the hit TV show *Fantastico*. His ascents in Brazil caused a media sensation.

Above: Conquering *L'abominafreux* (rated 8a) in Cornas marked Alain's recovery from injury.

Below and opposite: Tackling the Petronas Towers in Malaysia, then the tallest buildings in the world. Alain was afterwards imprisoned in an appalling jail.

Above and top right: Seemingly impossible to climb, the Blue Cross-Blue Shield in Philadelphia drove Alain to the point of obsession.

Right: Alain nears the top of *L'Ange en Decomposition* in the Verdon Canyon.

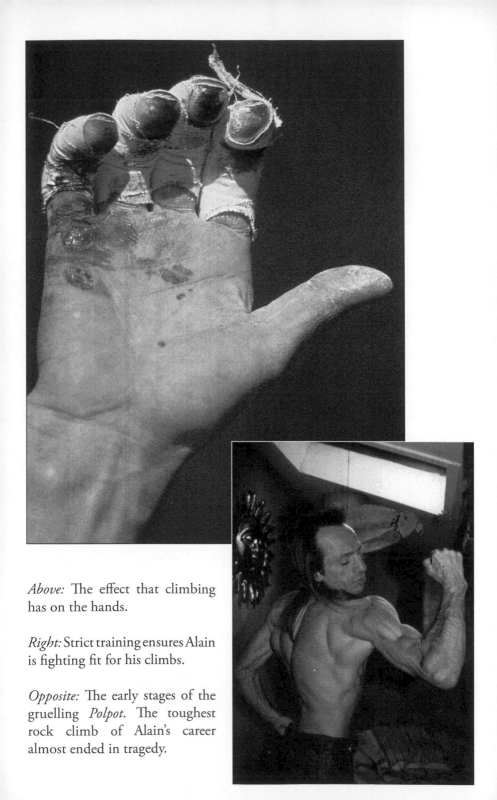

Above: The effect that climbing has on the hands.

Right: Strict training ensures Alain is fighting fit for his climbs.

Opposite: The early stages of the gruelling *Polpot*. The toughest rock climb of Alain's career almost ended in tragedy.

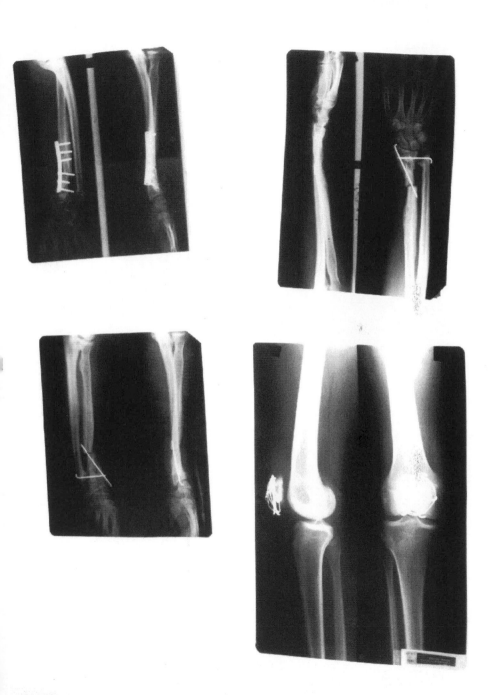

Smashed bones, a coma and the near loss of a hand have left Alain with crippling injuries and official disability status. Doctors continue to be stunned by his recovery.

Alain's ascent of the 180-metre National Bank of Abu Dhabi brought the city to a standstill and was watched by a vast crowd of people. He achieved this with a broken thumb.

Above: Alain negotiates the maze-like lines of the Etisalat Building in Dubai.

Opposite: Getting to grips with the varied angles of Hong Kong's Far East Finance Centre and the Sydney Opera House.

Top left: Meeting Sheikh Nahyan, the Education Minister of the United Arab Emirates, and Britain's Prince Andrew.

Left: Alain is carried aloft by a crowd after scaling the Warsaw Marriott Hotel.

Above: Alain climbs the Sabah Foundation in Borneo for charity, an event that drew over 15,000 spectators.

The view from near the base of Framatome, La Défense, Paris. On sheer glass buildings Alain must find an Achilles heel. Here a single vertical crack leads to the summit.

Opposite: Chicago. An unforeseen deterioration in the weather meant that the Sears Tower was Alain's most dangerous urban climb. *Above:* The clouds break, revealing the summit. The moisture made the glass tower incredibly slippery and perilous. Alain did not expect to survive.

Below: The Golden Gate Bridge was a punishing climb not helped by the wind and swaying cables. This stunt earned Alain time in a San Francisco jail.

Alain's youngest son Lucas learns to climb as soon as he can walk.

Taking on the IBM Building in Johannesburg, South Africa.

Posing for the cameras in Hong Kong prior to climbing the Cheung Kong Centre.

this will be one of the toughest buildings I have ever taken on. The fiasco of my trial runs flicker through my mind: the slipping, the exhaustion, the difficulty of finding a solution. I decide to lighten the mood and muck around a bit with these sober men. "We who are about to die salute you!" I bellow at close range, to their startled bewilderment.

At this precise moment, I spring out as a gladiator entering the Colosseum. I must now be a warrior, stronger than the lion. My zodiac sign? Leo, and in the Chinese horoscope I was born in the year of the tiger – great omens! A few strides and I regain both my self-control and concentration. My heart stops galloping and fear retreats deep within me. My doubts are erased, pulverized, and nothing can deflect me from my path.

The shouts of the security guards reach me in fragments: distant, irrelevant, incomprehensible. Anchored between two one-way boulevards, JFK Avenue and Market Street, Blue Cross-Blue Shield occupies a strategic position in Philadelphia. I have already decided it is impossible to climb the two outer façades, as it would lead to disrupting peak-hour traffic. In court I would have difficulty defending my case. It is also impossible for me to consider putting the lives of pedestrians in danger if I were to fall. I have thus chosen to attack a rear-facing flank of the building over a covered car park.

I jump against the tower and make my first movements. I move clumsily, revealing my restlessness. But as I engage the second pane, I regain my balance and control. I push on, away from the group of security guards on their walkie-talkies, and make my way up this glazed structure. This technique of walking directly up glass is new for me and I focus on the adhesion of my feet to the panes. About 50 metres off the ground, with my soles pushing against the glass, my feet slide! Before I can react or attempt to save myself, they stop... to my huge relief. But then I feel dismay. There will be others like this between here and the summit. I pause to re-examine the surface and find a totally unexpected surprise – this geometrically precise structure is not regular. Though barely noticeable to the naked eye, it undulates a little here and there, perhaps explaining why certain panes are marginally cleaner than others: they might have received more soap and water.

At the 35th floor, I find a more difficult anomaly. The entire ledge here – the grip I have been using to propel myself upwards – is missing. There is only a flimsy silicone join, barely a bump against the panes. I am wary of placing my feet on this silicone, to say the least. I look around but have no other option, as when I had to hang off that clanking old air conditioner in Rio. At least there is a join, some sort of feature to play with. If this had occurred higher but without the join there would be no reversing. I take advantage of the pause to snatch a drink, suspending myself by a single hand from the middle of the façade. Below are crowds of commuters and journalists. Apparently some people believed I was smoking a cigarette! How cool.

It is a mildly awkward posture and my supporting left hand begins to ache a little, distracting me enough that the bottle slips away from me. In my haste to catch it, I accidentally spray my right hand and the glass pane – and all around my feet – with my energy drink. Holy shit! As if the escalation was not precarious enough... Liquid, a lethal lubricant, trickles down the pane. I dry my hand against my body, as it would be impossible to restart climbing drenched like this. And I need to hurry, before my left arm starts to throb. I leave this deadly zone fast, in the hope that it will be okay. Without even thinking about it I place dampened slippers over the bumpy track of silicone and overcome this ledgeless obstacle to continue upwards. It must have been a very tricky move but I was so preoccupied with my accidental hosepipe effect that I didn't even notice it.

I gain several more floors and only then do I remember the missing ledge below. Strange, but it turned out to be fine. The smoked panes do not filter out what is going on inside the building and the deep blue surface acts as both mirror and window. The employees of the insurance company after which the building is named have already left for the day, except on one floor which still has its lights on. As I reach it, I see a chap studiously stooped over his desk. I bang on the window without really interrupting my progress. The man turns around. His face is a picture of utter shock, as if he had just seen a ghost. It is not exactly the right time for such a joke, but it lessens the pressure. Well, mine anyway. Humour is an escape valve in climbing just as it is in life. I keep going, and every now and then I take a look around. On the other side of the street, in a skyscraper of more classic design, I see people stuck to the windows of every floor. Hey guys, that is what economists would call a lack of productivity!

About 20 metres from the summit, one of the window panes has been opened and three figures appear. They are waiting for me. I realise that the escalation is nearly finished. Just like that, I suddenly feel very tired. The last ten floors, where the top of the building tapers inwards to a point, will not be necessary. The true summit is impossible unless I am dropped by winch from a rescue helicopter and such a finish, though technically possible, would not be desirable due to the downdraughts. No, this is good enough. I make another pane and approach the opened window.

"Hi!"

Greeting cops at the top of a skyscraper is one of my constant pleasures in life. I clamber through the window as they move in to arrest me. But before they react, I pull a flag out of my jacket emblazoned with the slogan *Eagles beat Dallas*, Julie's idea to win public support and hopefully soften the local justice chiefs. Philadelphia's American football team will be kicking off that very evening against Dallas. The helicopter has been filming me for a while now and records this moment for the evening news. At first, Julie had thought of honouring Princess Diana, but I had put an end to that idea at once. I did not want to hijack politics or tragedy in a way which could easily be interpreted as demagogic or at least inappropriate. The link with sport is much more suitable and effective. Even the cops smile beneath their bristly moustaches.

I give them my passport and picture postcards to prove that I am a professional rock climber and not a psycho or someone with suicidal tendencies. In my early days I used to climb without papers, thinking that anonymity would be my best protection. That was an error. Showing them who I am and that I know what I am doing reassures the police.

Handcuffs. Elevator. Exit. Cameras. Before the cop car takes off I wave my flag in front of the crowd. The car streaks away in a whirlwind, like something out of *Starsky and Hutch*. Invoking the fiery sporting allegiances of Americans cannot leave Philadelphia unmoved. I sit and enjoy the ride, but having not dared to stop for another drink since my squirting incident at the 35th floor, I am feeling a bit thirsty. I am used to handcuffs now and I succeed in getting my bottle out of my pocket and sipping from it. As I do this, the cuffs pop open at one of my wrists. Hmm... It is quite comfortable to sit in the back of a cop car unrestrained for a change. But on second thoughts, arriving at the police station hands-free is not such a good idea – cops really aren't too pleased if you keep pulling circus stunts and Houdini acts around them. I desperately try to put my handcuffs back on. It's easier said than done. There's a series of clicks as I wrestle with the cuffs but finally I manage to restrain myself on their behalf.

We soon arrive at the city's main police station. For once, the cops are nice. They simply go about their jobs, recording in minute detail the facts for their report. It will be the court's job to decide the gravity of my act and mete out the proper punishment.

"Are you the French Spiderman?" Rather than the usual lecture on the stupidity of my escalation, these guys ask for my autograph. In single file, they wait respectfully for me to sign my postcards. As usual the media has broadcast the images of the ascent across the whole country.

My cell door closes with a metallic slam. Stretched out on a blanket, I savour my hard-fought victory with a rare satisfaction. The technical difficulty of Blue Cross-Blue Shield was extreme and the level of commitment required was very high. All things considered, the climb went superbly well. My previous trip to the USA was to San Francisco, where almost everything had gone wrong. I had followed it up with a little illegal jaunt up the famous pyramid of the Luxor Casino in Las Vegas. While I was incarcerated I read the prison graffiti with interest and patiently engraved my name in enormous letters into the bench. At no time did I imagine the cops would not appreciate this kind of sculpture. A hulking woman twice my size, the worst type of person you can possibly meet in this man's world, discovered my hieroglyphs and erupted in fury, roaring so loud that I could not understand a word. I guessed what she was trying to say from her facial expressions and the way the whole cell vibrated as if the San Andreas fault had ruptured. But for God's sake, woman, shut up! I took my turn and abundantly offended her in French, armed with my most beautiful smile.

This time the cops seem polite and friendly and I hope that everything proceeds just as well with the courts. My experience with Philadelphia's justice system so far seems favourable. Apparently the most likely penalty is a fine accompanied by a night or two in prison, a mere administrative formality.

A clanking in the lock makes me jump. It's Julie and she is overexcited. Her enthusiasm is contagious but her tone alarmist. She too was called in for questioning during the ascent, betrayed apparently by electronic surveillance cameras. John had to go to the cops to bail her out, in the process revealing his connection. So the press were in on it! There's a scandal. Furious, the boss of NBC demands that John publicly explain himself during an exceptional press conference. John explains to the cameras that there was no premeditation on the part of NBC, and that his motivations were of an entirely private nature, Julie being his partner. It's all broadcast on the news and further complicates my situation. And since bail has not been set, I must stay in prison for the night. Tomorrow will be another day. I've had enough excitement anyway. My body seems to be adrift as I am washed over by waves of fatigue, sinking to the seabed of deep contented sleep.

A guard pulls me out of my dreams. Is it morning already? My muscles are heavy, aching. The night was not enough. Groggily, and with one eye open, they transfer me to another large cell where a group of policemen and prisoners are watching a news broadcast. All eyes are riveted to the screen. I then realise it is midnight, and after the adverts, the nightly news begins with images of my ascent. From the ground it looks pretty impressive to have climbed this featureless glass façade. My public applauds me warmly, and I thank them for their support. Praiseworthy congratulations indeed, but a few more hours of sleep, even on the knobbly board I have been given, is more appealing to me right now. With a few slaps on my back which almost topple me I shuffle blearily back to my cell for much-needed rest.

Five hundred and ten dollars. That's the price of my freedom. It's pretty cheap considering everything. Julie arranges for ABC to settle this amount in exchange for the scoop of my reactions and release at the police station.

Once I leave my cell, Rob, my lawyer and a friend of Julie, tells me more about my case and its modifications during the night. It has shifted from penal to criminal code which means it is no longer treated alongside minor misdemeanours such as traffic offences. Criminal code, I am told, is serious and this is where it gets nasty. After my brazen escapades in Chicago, New York, San Francisco and Las Vegas, the judiciary is angry and requires a punitive sentence... apparently of up to two years in prison! This is indeed bad news.

Since I have promised the scoop to ABC, I leave the premises with my face masked under my T-shirt, probably giving the impression that I am an ashamed and disgraced criminal. It doesn't matter though, there's time to talk to these guys later, so I forge through a journalistic mêlée and dive into a car. Once we are away, we look at the lawsuit. Rob is a specialist in penal lawsuits and yet he seems subdued by the dimension of the task. Reassuring... In spite of this sword of Damocles above my head, we decide to go out and forget about it all, gyrating in the city's nightclubs.

The news comes through – the criminal lawsuit will take place in three weeks. In the meantime, I return to France while leaving the country is still permitted. I admit that the idea of leaving the USA forever, to be sentenced in absentia and become a fugitive, did flash through my mind for a few seconds. Two years in jail is not something anyone would wish to fly back for. I can think of other places I would prefer to go to for the same ticket price. But though I am not a fan of some of their cops, I just love the United States. Few countries if any can offer me so many vertical adventures.

Before I get on the plane, Ted Simon, a famous lawyer, suggests taking on the case and defending me free of charge. According to Julie this is a great stroke of fortune. This brilliant man of about 40 is a pedigree lawyer with a glittering record, his reputation further enhanced by winning a lawsuit against the police of Singapore for their torture of an American citizen. As I fly over the Atlantic Ocean my imagination runs through all conceivable scenarios but I fail to find a definite solution to my predicament. At the kiosk at Orly Airport in Paris, I pass time by leafing through the newspapers. A name catches my glance... it's no less than Simon again. The American lawyer makes the cover of Le Monde, one of the most respected French newspapers. This guy must be good! His repute crosses the borders of the USA and reaches the shores of France. My imagination works overtime once more... Alain Robert and Ted Simon, a double act of impact!

In a few weeks I am back in America and back in court, facing a two-year prison sentence. The prosecutor is really going for it and the charges laid against me are drastic. With visible anger, the prosecutor accuses me of putting the lives of pedestrians in danger and disrupting law and order. Which lives had I put in danger by climbing over the concrete roof of a parking lot? And as for disrupting law and order, by choosing this rear façade, neither of the main avenues had been closed to traffic, nor could drivers see me and become distracted. Against a man of Ted Simon's stature and acumen, these deceptive arguments quickly crumble. Simon tells me though that there is no way the court will let me off scot-free this time. As it turns out, a fine of $4,000 is enough to forget the dispute, a compromise

I am happy to accept given the state of affairs a few weeks ago. With relief I exchange warm handshakes with Simon as the court dissolves.

In an unexpected twist, the boss of Blue Cross-Blue Shield makes a personal approach towards me, not with the aim of seeing me condemned but with an offer of sponsorship! Not long afterwards, the two of us visit the top of his building and I nip over the edge to show him how I did it. For an insurance company, the image of risk versus safety, of the guardian angel, is a powerful one. The severe charges laid against me came exclusively from the prosecutor, not from Blue Cross-Blue Shield, and discovering that this man wants to explore a partnership leaves me dreaming of new ventures. I have fought for freedom to pursue my path and Philadelphia has embraced it. The Liberty Bell will ring a little more clearly this evening.

8

ALAIN AND THE KING

As a kid, I used to imagine that a king was a man before whom we should kneel down naturally and respectfully. Certainly the story of good King Dagobert, the 7th-century monarch of the Franks, made a big impression on me in my childhood but I also remember images of the flowery-bearded emperor Charlemagne, meditative and majestic, in the magnificent Gothic cathedral of Reims. Today, despite the erosion of monarchy and ceremony around the world, the decorum and pomp accompanying this tradition remains appealing. Not so in France though of course, as we rather dramatically ended all this by guillotining our last monarch, Louis XVI.

In the stifling humidity of tropical Kuala Lumpur, I am going to meet a real king. My first king and also my first queen as well as my first princess! And for this regal occasion, I want to do my absolute best.

From my suitcase I delicately remove my most beautiful black leather trousers. And now I hesitate for ages as I try to select the perfect top. What should I wear in such circumstances? I don't meet kings very often. What does protocol suggest? I know that it would be absolutely rude to have dinner with a king dressed in too casual a way. After trying on multiple tops, and after having spread them all over the floor of my hotel room, I finally make up my mind – my lizard-skin sleeveless waistcoat is just the thing for this very special event. I slip it on and size myself up in the mirror. So posh and trendy... Bare-chested in a lizard-skin waistcoat and black leather trousers... The result is very tasteful and will create a great stylistic splash for sure.

As I prepare for this remarkable meeting my head spins. The more I think of it, the less I succeed in understanding the sequence of events which will lead me, in less than an hour, to spend the evening with the highest personalities of Malaysia. Three days ago, I was rotting in a gruesome dungeon: a malodorous and gloomy hole besmeared with filth and grime, infested with cockroaches the size of bars of soap, and filled with a multitude of wretched and mistreated souls who slept on the bare floor. I had seen them beaten and physically abused, sometimes severely. I had myself been kicked viciously and needlessly by a cop. And I still hadn't forgotten the episode with my anus. I have gone from the misery of eating what is supposed to be 'food' off the ground to attending an exquisite banquet in the very best restaurant in Kuala Lumpur, and it really took only one step. Just like a fairy tale…

It was in Valence one day that due to a lack of projects I could not stop brainstorming. Beautiful stories often begin this way, during an aimless afternoon. For the thousandth time I had gone through that fat book which holds images of the world's most skyscraping architecture. I read a passage under a nondescript picture of a pair of concrete-and-steel skeletons surrounded by cranes, a picture I had not bothered with before. And then, a thunderbolt! These two immense towers, still under construction, were poised to be the tallest in the world, exceeding the current record holder in the States. The record holder was Chicago's Sears Tower, a stupendous structure that I had long yearned to climb but which had appeared all but impossible. The final height of these twin record breakers? A staggering 452 metres against the 443 of the Sears. These young giants were the Petronas Towers in Kuala Lumpur.

But Malaysia remained too distant, the idea of climbing too expensive as well as too vague. The buildings were not finished in the photo, so I did not know what texture they would possess. I could not be sure what I would be holding onto. Also, from a climbing perspective, it was pretty hard to distinguish the actual base of the building. Architects hamper me when they choose, especially for ambitious projects, to build the first ten or 30 metres with marble. Alright guys, marble is an attractive material which enhances the impression of height and adds a semblance of grandeur. I have nothing against marble but it occasionally prevents me from achieving some magnificent challenges.

Sometimes, if I am lucky, the top floor of an adjacent shopping centre allows me to avoid these impassable zones. It may be connected by a bridge, or it may simply back onto the tower I am chasing. Using these detours I can bypass the marble sections and access the rest of the structure.

From what I could see, the Petronas Towers had some of this marble but maybe, just maybe, I might be able to find a way past it. What a fantastic slap in the face! I have been inspired. Have you ever told yourself that a course of action is not feasible, that it would be better to wait until the next day to act? Have you ever found, just a few seconds later, a perfect excuse to abandon it altogether? And still does it not disturb your sleep at night, your subconscious mind angrily prodding you to remind you of your cowardice? Immediately I seize the phone and call the Gamma photo agency.

We enjoy some small talk about interviews, projects, life, Kuala Lumpur… Conveniently one of the agency's photographers has just come back from the Malaysian capital with a complete report on the impressive Petronas Towers. Ten minutes later, I give my wife a shout and I am in my little VW Golf, in fifth gear heading straight to Paris.

The white lines on the highway scroll into a flickering blur, which is good, because I have only one point left on my driving licence and I must evade the cops. I drive without a tax disc, dragging an unenviable trailer of several thousand francs of unpaid fines. I really don't want the cops to catch me and must ensure this journey is as brief as possible, so I push down on the accelerator. In Brazil, you can pass your licence if you are really pernickety, but the most common practice remains to forget about it and hand over a few notes when the cops catch you. Whatever happens, whether your papers are in order or not, you will have to pay a bunch of dollars to resume your journey. The concept of what is right when faced with a man with a gun and the law behind him is not discussed. What do I have affixed to my windscreen in place of my tax disc? The only thing I have ever had from the French state: a disability sticker which comes in handy for parking.

In the bustle of the agency, I meet the photographer who saw my towers. He answers all my queries but is not really able to guarantee that the base can be overcome. But a good piece of news is that he confirms the Petronas Towers truly are the highest towers on the planet, after a ruling by the CTUBH – the Council of Tall Urban Buildings and Habitat. The CTUBH has the final word on such matters and has ruled that the antenna of the Sears Tower in Chicago cannot be counted as an architectural feature. An American speciality for much of the 20th century, skyscrapers have been part of the brand image of our transatlantic cousins and they do not like sharing it. The Americans asserted that the Sears' immense broadcast and plane-guiding antenna made it higher than any other building, whilst competitors stated that this was a crafty addition with no purpose other than to claim the title. The Malaysians countered that the Petronas' concrete spires were an absolutely integral component of the structure, just as the mooring mast and depot for Zeppelins at the top of the Empire State Building was accepted as part of the Manhattan structure. All very contentious and a tricky battle of expert opinion. It is an argument that continues today as even taller buildings such as Taipei 101, the Shanghai World Finance Centre and Burj Dubai sprout up and overtake them, each vying for the distinction.

If Malaysia still remained a dream, another project was a concrete reality. For some months, I had been trying to scrape together a budget to go to Australia, where I hoped to climb Centrepoint or the Sydney Opera House. As is sometimes the way, a chance call opened the door. Suddenly the required finances materialised and I had only to fly there, some 24 hours from France. Seeking to kill two birds with one stone, I researched air routes and various fares to see if it was possible to grab a stopover in Kuala Lumpur. I had vaguely spoken to my photographer Alexis of my desire to go and see the Petronas Towers at close quarters during a brief visit there. But first things first. We had a few things to attend to in the land Down Under.

Sydney is a picturesque fairground with numerous attractions for the urban climber. The clear air quality and sharp light, not to mention the striking city backdrop, will make for some pretty escalating photos for my holiday album. Centrepoint, the city's observation tower, is the tallest free-standing structure. The slim stem of the tower section sits on top of an 11-storey combined office building and shopping centre. Since I have no way of inspecting the tower section itself until the actual ascent, I conduct my reconnaissance from a useful vantage point in the nearby Hilton Hotel.

From the hotel I observe a circular base of white cables, anchored at the foot of the main trunk section, which lead all the way to the top. They seem to cross over one another on the way up. The cables meet the edges of a circular disc-like platform halfway up, and then converge in a neat and tight ring against the stem some 50 metres or so above it, before fanning out again to join the cylindrical section at the top. The cables at the top half of the tower give the impression of forming a tautly pulled net, though this is just an optical illusion caused by the sight of cables upon cables from a two-dimensional perspective. I know I will only be able to get as far as the underside of the cylindrical top section containing the revolving restaurants and observation decks, as the enormous overhang and the smooth featureless exterior makes the crown of the tower impossible to reach or climb.

I return to Centrepoint the next day and quickly scale the 11 storeys of the concrete building at the base. I make the rooftop without incident – there is little evident security and I climb up unimpeded. The rooftop is deserted. But when I approach the giant trunk of the tower section and come face to face with the cables, I am immediately struck by an obvious problem. They are huge, much larger than they appeared through my binoculars. I had no idea the cables were going to be this large – they are wider than my thigh. Not only that, but they are painted with white gloss paint and slippery: significantly more slippery than the thinner rope-like cables of the Golden Gate Bridge. Back then, I had a square space between four cables in which I could wedge myself and climb, but here I have just the one fat pipe-like cable. I am hesitant at the thought of trying to climb these enormous glossy cables after the difficulties I faced in San Francisco, but I decide to try it.

I wrap my hands around two crossing cables and push up with my feet. My hands don't feel so secure, due to the dimensions of the cable, but my feet seem to hold okay. I climb cautiously at first to acquaint myself with the cable then decide to ascend as if I were harvesting coconuts up a 305-metre palm tree. The escalation is tricky and tiring, demanding much energy, but I feel optimistic about my chances of success.

Soon I have ascended high enough that I am visible from ground level, and it doesn't take long to realise that scores of Sydneysiders are pointing upwards. A news helicopter is encircling the tower and a few heads are peering over the edge of the top. As I near the disc at the halfway point I become aware of some activity up there. There are several cops awaiting me and it is clear that I cannot avoid them. Sadly it seems the climb will end here.

At the disc there is unfortunately little room for humour today as amongst the cops is a female one, and a woman cop is of course even more terrible than a man. I am unsure why this is the case – perhaps they feel they need to overcompensate to match the natural authority their male colleagues possess? I really don't know, but all over the world I find there is almost always a bitch inside the uniform of a woman cop. And this Australian one, whinging and whining sarcastically through her nose and threatening me with physical violence, is horrendous.

I am arrested, held in a cell for a day, then swiftly taken to court and fined. The climb was always going to be problematic or perhaps even impossible to finish so the outcome is not that much of a surprise. The reception from the antipodean press is warm, even if this escalation was ultimately a failure.

To end my trip down to Oz on a positive note, a few days later I decide to nip up the Sydney Opera House early in the morning. It is certainly iconic but the Opera House does not pose a significant challenge, standing at a modest 183 metres at its apex. More importantly, it lacks verticality and is more of a walk up a hill than a climb. This little diversion is more about enjoying the famous scenery. Plodding up its curving roof to catch the sunrise over Sydney Harbour makes for a splendid morning. Once I have absorbed the sight I drop back down off the roof in around 40 seconds, totally unnoticed by anyone and totally satisfied.

Alexis and I make our way back to France, but en route our 747 touches down in Kuala Lumpur to enable us to disembark. As soon as we pass through immigration and customs we get down to business. Our schedule is tight with no time for hanging around.

Straight from the airport I jump into a taxi, a pair of binoculars in hand. The car slaloms through a river of traffic gushing into the capital, a gigantic sprawling construction site with more than four million inhabitants. Far off, in a haze of humidity and pollution, my towers are already outlined. As we approach them I gasp. It is often said that a skyscraper tears the fabric of the sky. But here they rip it, shred it, pulverise it! New York's ill-fated twin towers can be compared to these giants. The World Trade Centre buildings seemed high, but hugged by a multitude of nearby skyscrapers, they did not dominate the sky as much as their measurements would suggest. In Kuala Lumpur, the Petronas Towers erupt from an area of parkland and lower buildings, emphasising their height more starkly.

The taxi stops close by, and I pay my rip-off rate after a bit of a battle with the driver. At the base of the towers, at the world's biggest construction site, the builders hammer, clank and mix away in a rush to complete the immense shopping centre which forms part of the complex. Around the edges of this enormous site a corrugated fence forbids access and I cannot find a point from which I can observe the base of the building.

The towers themselves are finished and handsome indeed. Clearly inspired by the minarets of Islam they are full of pride, purpose and identity. Many-sided and receding inwards towards their twin spires they look eminently climbable, at least at first glance. The two-storey sky bridge on the 41st and 42nd floors, which connects the two towers, is quite unusual and catches my eye although it will have no bearing on my climb. With my binoculars, I try to decipher this enigma. Thoughtfully I rub my chin. After the first 30 metres, invisible from this angle, the escalation seems to be quite straightforward. Still, it will be necessary to get that high in the first place.

Back in my hotel room the TV is on as I fiddle with some crap in my luggage. A news story abruptly jerks my head up. Images of my escalation in the land of kangaroos and boomerangs scroll before my dumbfounded eyes. It is like announcing to all Malaysia that my next objective will be the highest towers in the world, right here in their capital. And this is a nation that doesn't like people to challenge authority at all. Well, too bad guys, I have a little something for you! But already it is clear that this project has a whiff of danger about it. While in Sydney I had run the idea past my Australian lawyer. He told me straight that Malaysian prisons closely resemble the Turkish jails of *Midnight Express*. They are no picnic. According to him, the security forces have few scruples when it comes to putting the boot in or splitting a lip and the police force's reputation is terrible. Furthermore, Malaysia being a Muslim country, I do not really know whether the judges will enjoy my joke or not. I cannot be sure how my climb will look in their eyes.

The phone rings. I am asked to participate in two television shows in France, and this should provide enough time for the local authorities to forget about me. The timing is probably a good thing. I decide to return home and ponder this challenge. My photographer friend Alexis remains in KL to obtain a flying licence, without of course revealing our true intentions. But my hunch that the authorities were on my case appears well founded – during my absence, Malaysia's secret police pay an impromptu visit to Alexis demanding to know the purpose of my visit.

I walk merrily if unsteadily off the plane at Kuala Lumpur International Airport just ten days later, having got utterly drunk with my neighbour on the plane. In a bit of a whirl I hit the shower on arrival in the tropics to try to regain a more human appearance. I stand out a mile here. With long blond hair, leather outfit and cowboy boots, no secret policeman will get a medal for tracking me down. I hardly make it difficult for them with my nice clothes. As the water sprays my face I do my best to shake off the effects of the alcohol as MTV is going to interview me in less than an hour, and I climb very early tomorrow. The climb will be timed to avoid the overwhelming midday heat and the frequent tropical downpours in the afternoon. For such a huge tower, an escalation can easily last several hours or even more.

Semi-sober, I rush to my meeting with MTV. The interview takes place at the top of a tower, in a panoramic restaurant offering a magnificent view of the Petronas Towers a few kilometres away in the distance. In spite of the prospect of alerting the security services, I speak very freely about my plans for the next day. Whatever happens, the local authorities already know where I am and of course they must know why. No one is unaware.

Between two filming sequences, I slot a few coins into a telescope to look at the silhouettes on the horizon which obsess me. From here I can really appreciate the magnitude of my target. It's one big, big climb. I sip some water to continue rehydrating myself after the effects of the flight and the unplanned alcohol. Tomorrow, it will be necessary to carry some water to stay hydrated. Drinking hydrating fluids delays the onset of lactic acid, an essential precaution for such an effort and in such a climate. Maybe getting 'shit-faced' – as my neighbour described it – wasn't the best thing to have done but sometimes you meet people and things just snowball.

It is dark and I am finding it extremely difficult to sleep. Tomorrow is already today. At 7:00am sharp, still foggy with jet lag, I shall engage in a battle against the world's highest towers. Even if, according to my observations, the climb does not seem technically extreme, the scale, the heat, the dust, the doubt and the uncertainty of the subsequent punishment fill me with less than my usual composure. Nevertheless, it is from this acrid mixture that I find my strength, an immovable motivation which will push me movement after movement, onwards and upwards. I know that this pressure is a true ally, but feeling it pressing on my shoulders tonight pushes me into a world of nightmares. My Everest, my twin peaks will decide whether I live or die. I am humbled by them, drawn to them like a moth to a flame. They obsess me.

It's 6:00am. I awake, petrified. My alarm clock rings out like a shattering window. The bell catapults me as a battered contender into the middle of a boxing ring before a hungry crowd and a mountain of muscle eager for blood. It is a superfluous image, but at this moment, my tortured imagination summons this last fragment of nightmare. I must override my biological clock to break out of my lethargy. In spite of its frightening harshness I always pack my ancient clock with its shrill bell and terrifying tick-tock which fills the room. I cannot part with this menacing timepiece. It accompanies me in all my ascents, even if the noise of its mechanism is sometimes unbearable for me. I think I need this sensation of discomfort to dramatise the situation, to provide the stress which transforms a man into a wild animal; because in this mortal contest, I must give everything, I must fight to survive. To me it seems difficult to launch a survival operation without previously being tortured mentally or physically by an enemy.

Seven o'clock. A car drops me in front of the barricades of mankind's highest towers to date. I waste no time and just get out and run straight through the gates. The security services start running as well. It's that manic scramble again. I just love it – this is surely the best way to start the day. During this dash of two or three hundred metres, I have time to neither think nor doubt. Shouts ring out from all directions, the sounds of anger and panic assail my ears, and the multiple pounding of footsteps on the hard surface betrays determination equal to my own. But I can see salvation! And there is no marble at the base of the tower. I spring away and fly up the side of the building as fast as I can.

I am out of reach of the guys on the ground within seconds, but still I power upwards. Five minutes… Ten minutes… Breathless, I wait with fear for the first bark of an Alsatian from a window or for the blast of a firearm. I wonder why I have never been used as a human bull's-eye in certain countries. It really wouldn't surprise me if one of these days some security guy went too far. But so far, nothing out of the ordinary has happened. The guards surely must have known that a game of cops and robbers was on the cards for today but as usual they are a few steps behind me. The first point goes to Spiderman.

I am a few dozen metres above them, the necessary safety margin to pause to regain my breath. Conditions are hazardous as the towers are still an immense construction site. My slippers look more like workmen's boots than the graceful ballerina slippers of a dancer. One way or another I have to clean the soles, keep them bare and smooth. This mixture of rubber and resin, the same material which is used for the tyres of Formula One race cars, must fully contact and grip the building or else I will slide like a rally driver on a dirt track. The uninitiated often wonder why a climbing boot does not have a sole adorned with crampons, as a mountaineering boot does. The larger the contact area, the more adhesion one gains, provided of course that the surface is uniformly clean. Additionally, a flexible and slim sole allows for great sensitivity. The soles need to warm up to gain adhesion and efficiency, just like the tyres on a race car. Rock climbing boots have been developed from the same technology and the same challenges require the same remedies.

As expected, the structure does not raise insurmountable technical problems. Sure, the passage from one floor to the next requires full concentration, and the scale of the building in this heat is quite sapping, but a good rest after every section allows me to recover. I brought plenty of fluids in a squeezy pack and I grab a drink, hanging from one arm. As usual I rest by suspending my weight from one arm and then the other, letting my free arm dangle whilst shaking it to relax it and to lose the fatigue. Inside the Petronas, behind the grime and dust of the newly glazed bays, I see workmen between showers of fiery sparks. Construction workers are engrossed in their tasks, yellow helmets screwed onto their sweaty heads. I enjoy this moment of voyeurism, spying on this scene we are forbidden to see. None of them suspect that at this moment, the French Spiderman observes them from the outside. Behind them, just for a minute, they have a man-shaped interruption to the perpetual monochrome blue of the sky.

After 350 metres of escalation I am approaching the 60th floor. And here I face the thorniest problem, one which troubled me most during the night. The last section of the tower is blocked by an obstacle. It is a circular terrace, two metres wide with a balustrade, and virtually impossible to pass unnoticed. Hope being the favoured weapon of the ambitious, I remain optimistic. This is where they will intercept me for sure but I harbour a little hope that I can tiptoe past them. The design of the structure unfortunately does not allow me to move sideways, which might let me appear somewhere unexpected and dodge any welcoming committee.

I move in stealthily. Two floors from the terrace, a head pops over with a radio. *Merde!* That is it then. I have lost. Unless, as in Brazil, they forget to put me in handcuffs…

Still concentrating fully – nothing is more dangerous than to lose focus under pressure – I flop over onto the balcony where the guards seize me violently and all my illusions vanish into the humid haze. Objectively, I knew from the beginning of my journey that my chances of reaching the summit were slim. But still I cannot refrain from feeling profoundly disappointed.

Firmly grasped on the terrace I manage a glance upwards. Only 80 metres from the summit, I contemplate my Everest, now inaccessible. For those mountain climbers who want to reach the roof of the world, the weather report is their incorruptible watchdog; for them, fate lies in the goodwill of the skies. In my case, defeat results only from the inability of the cops or guards to appreciate the necessity of human triumph over adversity. Sometimes I have seen a sparkle in the eyes of the men whose duty it is to catch me. Those men can see it, they understand the poetry behind my climb. But these guys don't treat me so nicely – I am just a criminal, a guy who has stepped out of line and who needs to be overpowered and roughed up. I guess guards are just guards, we can't ask them to display intelligence or understand philosophy!

When I am brought back to the cracked mud of the construction site, I overhear that an official visit took place here today. So that is why there are so many guards! It is not my day. Alexis had been called back to France so Lim, an independent Malaysian photographer, has been arrested too.

Amongst the cranes, machines and scores of construction workers, the leader of the guards steps forward. I give him a smile as his henchmen clutch our hands behind our backs. He walks up to us and coldly stares at me from behind his shades as if he was some bad guy in a Bond movie. He does not seem to laugh with me and even less with Lim, who silently absorbs some painful and noisy slaps across his face. I am saddened by this. It really seems like this is the normal way to conduct business here. Oh, the malaise of Malaysia… Once he is done with his cameo, the Bond villain gestures to his henchmen. Grabbed by our collars, we are dragged to the nearest police station, where I immediately notice that everybody is wearing military fatigues. The atmosphere here is certainly not as nice as it was in Europe!

An angry fellow, rather big for an Asian, faces us. His authority is apparent in his build and manner and the fact that he is the only one wearing a cap. Bordering on hysterical, he roars at us in fury. Everybody takes a step back as he blows his top – the cops, the photographer and I are swamped by this tsunami. I don't understand a word of it but I don't need to understand Bahasa to know what is meant by this raging thunderstorm. A second officer gives me a report to be signed. Automatically, I ask to acquaint myself with the contents of it, but what is a basic legal right in Western countries seems to be considered an insult here. For the capped officer, this is too much. The violence behind his immobile face is convulsive and it is clear this is a man who enjoys terrorising people. There is an expression on his face… a desire to inflict pain.

Lim casts himself at the feet of the chief, on his knees, imploring forgiveness. The cops seize him by the armpits and drag him to another room. Lim, who had at our first meeting proudly shown me his visiting card bearing the embossed title 'Photographer – Fashion Designer', behaves now in a much humbler way. As I am dragged down the corridor past him I see his underpants lying like a rag on the ground and Lim cowering naked in front of the guards…

I have no idea what happened to Lim. I hope he was just beaten up and released, as he didn't break any laws – he didn't climb, he didn't trespass, all the poor guy did was take photographs. Me, I am left here to rot.

After two days in prison under the control of this diabolical despot, the French embassy intervenes and frees me from my cell. I had begun to think that I might be there for weeks or even months. The Australian lawyer was right about the grisly nature of Malaysian prisons. I was kicked two or three times by a screaming guard, molested during an invasive body search, and saw sadistic violence in that place. I knew that I would not be forgotten and that my release would come. But at that moment, I never guessed that news of my ascent would reach the highest echelons of power, falling onto the desk of the Minister of Transport – the Prime Minister's right-hand man – and that this dungeon episode would only be a prelude to five astonishing weeks.

I'm out. I'm free! Back at the hotel I savour my liberty. I appreciate simple pleasures in life the most. Something tasty to eat and a clean flushing toilet get me very excited. And so do the luxuries of air conditioning and clean carpets after the air and floors I have had to suffer, let alone the mod cons like kettles, TVs and mini-bars.

I catch up with events on the outside and learn that the Dato, this famous Minister who has become my guardian angel, has publicly announced that I will be granted a licence to reattempt my ascent of the Petronas Towers. From the moment the news breaks, the hotel is invaded by journalists. What is going on? The whole country drops by Room 7239: from the Dato to an entire delegation of deaf-mute Malays. I have very fond recollections of my unexpected meeting with the latter. With a sign-language textbook in front of me, I communicated with them the best I could. It was a warm and touching experience.

All manner of people pass through and want to meet me. The most incredible? A visit by the police chief. The same hysterical and detestable tyrant who had humbled me and Lim just a few days earlier now waits patiently in the lobby for me to accept his invitation to dinner! Apparently he wants to hear more about me and wants to tell me more about himself too. It is an offer that I obviously decline. After all, I had already had the opportunity to enjoy his hospitality.

Thanks to the Dato, I live like a prince. This man of authority, president of a humanitarian organisation – nothing is more fashionable for the elite than to be interested in the misfortune of others – is my pass, my guide, my magic wand. He opens every door. I have only to follow his lead as his orders cannot be discussed. Often, he offloads like a tornado in my room, no matter what time it is. He dictates my to-do list for each day, lining up a chain of press conferences and dinners with high officials. When you are caught up in this beguiling whirlwind, there is no escape. All you can do is go with the flow. I had moved from the violence of the prison's inner courtyard, where the guards looked forward to meting out random blows from their truncheons upon their fellow human beings, to the luxuriant splendour of receptions with the men who rule over the country and over those very jails. The inconsistency of the state's reaction to me filled me with bewilderment.

The Dato arrives in my room one day even more excited than usual, while I am engaged in an almighty session of body-building, not forgetting to sample a glass of wine between each series of press-ups. I am French after all. Even in the privacy of a hotel room, it is necessary to know how to be a little sophisticated… With a huge smile, the Dato announces that the royal family wants to have dinner with me. My reaction is to choke on my wine. I look at this man without understanding his motivations, nor what urges him to introduce me a little further into his world every day, as if he had a mission. He has even provided me with a car and chauffeur, a gorgeous Mercedes-Benz limousine. An A-Class would have been more than sufficient!

For every invitation, I try to push the exuberance of my clothing a little further. They want the French Spiderman, the crazy guy who has never heard of stairs? Then they will get him. It is in this state of mind that I start this special evening, being simultaneously respectful and disrespectful.

My limousine stops in front of the Shangri-La, the hotel housing what is reputedly the best restaurant in the capital. The chauffeur removes his cap then opens the back door. I extend one leg, then both, to test my clothes on the photographers who have already invested in a place near the entrance. In case things deteriorate, I have brought along a black jacket in the back of the car. Certainly, nobody expected to see my lizard-skin waistcoat, but I consider the reaction positive enough. The royal limousine also draws up in front of the steps. Ready… steady… go! The Dato, surprised but resigned, lines up beside me and then introduces me to my regal hosts. One hour beforehand, he had insisted on my adherence to the protocol to be followed during the introduction. Of course, I had to say "Your Majesty" and so on. Naturally, I mix everything up, I muddle the polite phrases with incomprehensible gibberish, but nevertheless everything seems to go okay. A little bit of fun cannot do any harm. No premeditation or lese-majesty here, just a little bit of confusion… Later I shall be told that certain newspapers the following day criticised my clothing.

As we enter the restaurant, the diners stand up and wait for a signal from the King to continue their meals. Dressed in a dark suit and Malay-style hat, the King, a man in his fifties, settles down at the table, inviting us to do the same. In front of me sits the Princess, a beautiful woman in her early thirties dressed in a very chic Chanel suit. She is strict but smiling and relaxed enough to make me feel comfortable. She is also responsible for a charity organisation. For two hours, synchronised with the rotating tray of dishes, I answer the classic questions: Why do I climb? Am I afraid? Is Paris always Paris? The usual routine.

Armed with my chopsticks, I try to avoid two principle fears: turning the tray while the King or Queen are using it and, more likely, dropping the piece of fish clamped between my chopsticks onto the tablecloth. Imagine this moment of absolute solitude when your intended morsel splatters on your trousers or falls inside your waistcoat or upon the table, while the highest personalities of a country watch in silence. I believe I don't commit too many indiscretions unless, in an effort to eat only those things which I can capture with my disobedient chopsticks, it is considered bad form to eat a veritable vineyard of red-hot cayenne peppers.

The Dato seems to have so much influence that he does not doubt for a minute that his idea of an escalation for charity will go ahead. Furthermore, the King is interested. And thanks to our association tonight, his daughter would also like to be there. The dinner finishes on this inspiring note of optimism. I will be able to climb my Everest. What an evening!

Sunk into the leather upholstery of the limousine, I cannot help but marvel that life is full of unforeseen developments. But things take a little twist. While I am watching TV in my hotel later, I see an interview with the Chairman of the Kuala Lumpur City Centre (KLCC), the complex which includes the shopping centre as well as the twin towers which sit beside it. He formally refuses to grant a licence to organise a show on the towers, and says there is not the slightest chance that I will obtain one, no matter who my supporters are. Apparently, he is not kidding: my lawyer makes additional enquiries regarding the proposed climb and is assured of my immediate expulsion to France if I make a second attempt. The Dato has free rein over state matters, it seems, but no right of intervention over private property.

The previous year, the Chairman had refused to let a Hollywood director shoot a scene near the towers for a James Bond movie. All this in spite of the financial rewards, the marketing spin-offs created by the world fame of Ian Fleming's hero, plus indeed the knock-on benefits this could have on national tourism, and on top of all that the presence of Bond girl Michelle Yeoh, a prominent Malaysian actress! Could I sleep after this news? No way. I was condemned to stare at the ceiling, mulling over the decreasing chances of seeing my project succeed.

The next day, a TV channel contacts me for my reaction to the rather austere intervention of the Chairman. I have nothing to say, apart from proposing a direct confrontation between him and me on a talk show, so that each of us can express his point of view. Such a duel will not take place, the Chairman having neither the time nor the inclination to face me, since his inflexible position, radically opposite to public opinion, will not increase his popularity. For now the climb really seems impossible. I could make another attempt but the terrace will only be overcome if the security guards let me pass, or if I pull off an improbable escape act. My goal of climbing the Petronas Towers seems destined to failure. I must try to put it to the back of my mind. This assault remains shelved, but not entirely buried in the innermost canals of my cortex. Maybe one day...

Disappointed but not discouraged, I look around for another target. Thanks to the Dato's invitations to many high-profile functions and banquets, plus a number of interviews I have given, I am sailing high in the media. There is an air of expectancy. Malaysia needs an escalation. Also I am aware that there are figures out there who will not react so stuffily as the Chairman of the KLCC. I suggest to the General Manager of my hotel, the Melia Kuala Lumpur, that I climb his building legally. He almost falls out of his chair, the unexpected publicity exhilarating him. In an instant he declares me a permanent guest of his establishment. My lawyer insists with the police that the traffic is regulated, to avoid any complaints. With everything done above board there can be none of the shenanigans I had at the police station – nor in prison.

The ascent of the Melia Kuala Lumpur is relatively difficult, requiring a lot of technical know-how and really testing my mettle. A good crowd look on in delight, applauding and cheering like a bunch of school kids. It warms me that my climbing is truly appreciated in Asia.

When I get down to the ground for my post-escalation interview, I assert that this escalation was technically more difficult than the Twin Towers, a remark not greatly appreciated by the KLCC. This is no idle statement. I repeat again to the interviewer as I have done around the world: the height of a building does not proportionately influence the intrinsic difficulty of climbing it. A modest three-storey building can be more complicated and dangerous than a 400-metre tower. Recently, during a dinner in France, some restaurateur friends of mine asked me to climb the façade of their establishment, just for fun, as if the comparison between the highest skyscrapers of the planet and their modest shop window made the climb laughably easy. Visually, and also in terms of psychological commitment, there is absolutely no comparison. I thus went to inspect this locally famous façade. Spiderman or not, I am definitely no gecko. I need grips, even tiny ones, to resist the gravitational pull of the earth… Levitation would be a useful skill for a climber, and I am working on it, but so far I do tend to go to hospital when I get detached from a cliff. If there are no grips then I can't climb an inch. Height is a lesser issue – the dimensions of a building only become important later on when they start issuing a broader range of strategic and risk management concerns.

This momentum of this hotel climb helps drive on the prospect of the charity show we had originally hoped for, though now it seems to have shifted its location away from the capital on Peninsular Malaysia over to the state of Sabah on the island of Borneo. The Chief Minister gives his consent for me to climb a 34-storey tower which belongs to the government. The building is named the Sabah Foundation. The charity project is finally taking shape, though I still need to verify the feasibility of scaling the building.

I jump on the first plane for Borneo and head directly to the Sabah Foundation which, surprisingly, is outside of the state capital Kota Kinabalu. Instead of sitting among the grey streets of the city, or even its suburbs, it sits in green fields on the edge of the ocean. A few kilometres away I can already make out its silvery-blue cylindrical form. It reflects the ocean, the sky and the vegetation, situated along the shore of a dreamlike beach. The Sabah Foundation stands proud and alone in a quite improbable setting. There is nothing here except nature, the sands and a shiny cylinder gleaming in the sun. Why build a skyscraper in a rural area? There is no premium for land here and any remote project like this would also require new infrastructure to support the staff who work there. Not impossible of course, but just plain weird, especially when one bears in mind that Kota Kinabalu is a small and relatively flat city. It's almost like a helicopter with a winch had flown into a crowded metropolis and stolen a building, then dropped it off on a random beach. For the office workers it must be difficult to pop to the bank in their lunch break or hide in a bookshop. And where do they all go for lunch?

None of these issues are my concern. I am here to climb, not to consider the dining habits of the building's secretaries. My success rests on the shoulders of the architects who conceived it. Did they leave a fault, a weakness for me to exploit? More than my safety is at stake – this climb is for charity, for people in need. Because of this I approach the building with a rare degree of stress. The shiny cylinder begins to grow and grow, my eyes darting all around her. About 500 metres from the tower, many of my doubts fly away: there is a long vertical crack leading to the summit.

Three hundred people wait for me as I exit the limo. There is also a ludicrous number of photographers. This spiral of people shifts along with me at its core, and a trail of other press and onlookers follow in my wake. From above we must look like a giant sperm cell moving towards a huge egg. Engulfed by the crowd, I progress towards the flight of steps. The sperm reaches the egg and the DNA packet, me, is injected inside. The ascent is conceived.

Where am I going? As usual I must see the summit. From the roof, I jump over the edge of the building, to the dumbfounded stares of my companions, dropping down the top two floors, then going back up them. I bound back onto the roof and confirm that I am 110% sure that I am able to climb it. There's no problem with the building and the charity show will be excellent.

There are just over 72 hours before I climb the Sabah Foundation. Unfortunately it is too short a time to arrange the merchandising operations which were originally bandied about as a useful method of increasing the day's takings. For my part, I only have to have a minimal discussion to establish the payment I will receive. But this discussion takes place in a rather indiscreet setting – before the cameras.

During a press conference, surrounded by various ministers, I am asked what my fee will be, so I announce that I would like to keep ten percent of the earnings. What are the costs? Obviously, I have no idea of what those are, but ten percent seems to be a suitable figure. My lawyer, who is absent this particular day, calls me. He is furious, absolutely raving! According to him, my earnings should be aligned with the percentage taken the previous year by Michael Jackson. When I tell him that the gig is not the same – Jackson has to perform on stage and this requires much more management – he replies that the risk-taking, too, differs strikingly and adds that the absurdly rich singer does not have these kinds of scruples. Well, I hadn't thought of that. My lawyer is most pissed off. I guess he is pounding the table because this reduces the fee he can levy on me. But anyway, thanks to his intervention, the government waives the taxes which I would have been subject to.

All this money talk is a bit disconcerting. Fees, taxes, percentages; who cares? Even if I am not the sort of man to be repulsed by cash, this sort of gold-digging at a charity bash seems a little out of place to me. In the past I have climbed for humanitarian events without ever asking for financial compensation. It seems logical that if an artist wants to advertise himself by putting himself in the 'shop window' at a charity show, no problem, but if he is paid… well, we are at odds with the principle of the show. Surely there's a time for earning and a totally different time for offering your services to help others, a time when it's not about personal gain.

Sometimes I wonder what is going on at these charity events. For ATD Quarter World I was once invited to go down a façade on the Champs-Elysées which had been especially decorated for the occasion. Bernadette Chirac and Geneviève de Gaulle were there, along with a plethora of actors and famous personalities. My role was to open a succession of windows to represent the opening of vacant Parisian apartments for the homeless. Unfortunately the cold had frozen these windows shut, and instead of opening as expected, they splintered and shattered, broken glass raining down upon the pavement. A political commentator could interpret that metaphor in any way he liked. The event was a success but the press conference had been held in Fouquet's, a very swish restaurant where the slightest glass costs an obscene amount of money. Hey, what is this all about? The plight of the homeless? Or the ability of Fouquet's barman to make magnificent cocktails? It didn't feel right to be clinking glasses in such luxury while the homeless froze outside. So I went out to climb the façade again.

The first time I had the chance to help a charity was on Christmas Eve in my home town, Valence. On December 23rd I had been chatting with a doctor friend who devoted some of his spare time to The Children of the Caravan, an association which tries to rehouse homeless people in old and specially converted trains. The next day, while everyone was fussing about with last-minute Christmas shopping, I found a paper mill among the pedestrian streets of the city centre and asked the boss for permission to repeatedly climb three floors of the building. Meanwhile, my wife, my children and a few good friends were selling my picture postcards to raise funds for the association. Being late December it was bitterly cold. An icy wind rushed through the alleys, robbing the colour from passers-by. Twenty times or so I climbed this mill, much to the interest of passing onlookers. They were captivated by the ascent but little motivated by the idea of spending ten francs. At midday, I was getting nervous. We had made next to nothing. As indifference appeared to be in fashion (I even saw my own parents carefully avoiding me), I ripped off my top and climbed the frosted mill bare-chested. What did that achieve? Well, nothing apart from a raging fever the next day. The operation brought in 1,500 francs. Not much really, considering the effort we all put in.

But Valence did do a little better another time. On behalf of Kiwani, an association which buys wheelchairs, I climbed the beautiful City Hall. The boys at the football club had sold tombola tickets the week before and the prize draw at the escalation generated enough money to buy three fancy wheelchairs. My T-shirt went under the hammer and was sold for 200 francs. Not bad at all for a second-hand shirt!

And there are times, unlike that chilly Christmas Eve in Valence, when people really get behind you. My climb of the Montparnasse Tower with *Le Réverbère* was an agonising but ultimately successful ascent in terrible conditions with gusts of wind reaching 100 kilometres an hour. But I received plenty of support and it galvanised me to battle on. Abbé Pierre himself, a member of the French Resistance in the Second World War and the founder of the homeless charity Emmaus, gave me a call to convey his thanks. The newspaper salesmen were all at the foot of the tower egging me on; the firemen, worried but supportive, were with me all the way. Even the cops did their bit, clamping small 'thank you' notes under the windscreen wiper of my car rather than parking tickets.

It's the day of the climb in Borneo and the fire brigade tell me that they are determined to install a safety net at the base of the tower. My response? It's completely useless! No net can save me from a 100-metre fall! If you want to slice and dice me into little cubes for a Spiderman casserole, then sure, the net is fantastic. The effect would be like making a serve with a worm instead of a shuttlecock in a game of badminton.

After half an hour of discussion, having explained the uselessness of the thing, I am running out of words. Increasingly exasperated, I decide to draw a line under the affair. If there is a net, I tell them, I shall deliberately avoid it and fall on the ground. Firstly, I would prefer my corpse to be stretchered off the concrete rather than swept up by firemen with a dustpan and brush. But more importantly than that, people are coming to see me, the urban climber, the guy who climbs buildings without ropes.

They will come from all around to donate their hard-earned money to our fight against AIDS and cancer. They deserve a spectacle deserving of their enthusiasm and support. I don't mean to sensationalise myself, I just want the good people below to be given the thrills and spills that we used to enjoy at the circus in years gone by.

Also I feel I owe everyone a bit more. Maybe it is stupid, but the idea of taking money from this operation makes me ill at ease and I am anxious to realise this ascent correctly, as if I had done it for myself, illegally. Coming from a humble background in France and being dunked into this jacuzzi of gold in Malaysia over the past weeks has reminded me of my luck and fortune in life. I really have to give something back. I feel like a footballer in a penalty shoot-out at the World Cup. I have to put everything I have into it. Eyes are upon me, people expect and hope.

The fire brigade reluctantly relent. But I must also respect the wishes of the locals in other matters. Apparently basing this show on a Frenchman risks inflaming certain old-fashioned types and politically motivated xenophobic critics. To mitigate this, a Malay stuntman will join me halfway up to exchange a handshake. Those who may take offence that a foreigner gets the top billing at the bash will be placated by this face-saving move. Actually I quite like the idea as it gives the audience a little variety and something to cheer about.

This morning, the sky is an unchanging blue, symbolic of optimism and success. Usually quiet, the road has become an immense traffic jam which our limousine has to forge through if we are to kick off on time. The crowd is enormous. More than 15,000 people are gathering at the foot of this isolated tower! Fifteen thousand… It's incredible. As we arrive I can see a brass band playing on the square around Miss Asia as well as politicians taking turns on the podium to spout rhetoric. Our car breaches the security cordon and crosses this great flood of people. Hardly out of the car, I am totally mobbed. Always smiling, their appetite for photographs is insatiable.

"One more picture, please!"

My concentration is shot down in flames but I don't care right now. Armed with two felt-tip pens I sign autographs two at a time. I am not ambidextrous but curiously I can write just as well (or just as badly, as those who have read my writing will agree) with my left hand as well as my right – but back to front. To decipher my scribble, I tell a few confused autograph hunters: just use a mirror.

After an hour of this I need to escape for some solitude. The crowd may want more autographs, but I can't do 15,000 of them if I am to do my climb today! They probably don't realise that before an ascent I do not revel in the publicity, nor can I enjoy the endless session of autographs, no matter how wonderful they are to me. Fear stabs my abdomen and twists a blade in my stomach. I would honestly rather lock myself in the toilets.

Composed and equipped, I emerge through the automatic doors. To keep my nerves at bay I do not dare look at the spectators as I walk to the departure lounge of my escalation. I already have all the butterflies of tropical Borneo in my stomach, including those massive ones with one-foot wingspans, and I do not need any extra pressure.

As I cast a final look towards the top of the structure, silence spreads like a Mexican wave throughout the crowd. The brass band also wheezes then dies. It is time… I rub my hands together in a puff of magnesia. I pause. Then I attack.

At first I ascend with ease. The base of this building is rather unusual, like the lower half of a cone. In fact the bottom half of the tower looks rather like a rocket sitting on a single booster. This part is a cinch but after a dozen metres I reach a tough obstacle. The cylindrical body of the building is now on top of me. A sizeable horizontal overhang blocks the route ahead. Without the typhoon which ripped through Sabah two months earlier I would not have been able to continue, but the wind has torn away panelling, laying bare the steel girders. I wrap my hands around the steel and bring my feet upwards. Then my hands start walking along the beam as if I were a monkey. I let my feet swing free. Dangling like an orang-utan, I make my way across to the end of the overhang. Whether on buildings or on rocks, the exit from an overhanging zone is always the most unpredictable and most difficult part. The position makes the hand grips more central than the feet, an intense position for a climber to sustain. Gaining height using the hands is difficult, and bringing the feet back into the game even more so, as they tend to skate around aimlessly until they find a foothold. If you can't find footholds, you must pull yourself upwards further still to prevent your body from swinging, and of course so you can find those invaluable grips with your legs. It is effectively one almighty chin-up. It looks easy on paper but it most definitely is not, and for a precious few moments you really do hold your life in your hands.

The overhang demands a great deal of muscular power. For a while my complexion shifts to a shade of scarlet but the footholds are exactly where I imagine the architect would have put them and I recover my vertical position. The escalation from now on will be less radical, but since I have only a crack to work with, there will be no horizontal grips to offer me any rest. I must place my fingers in the gap and pull vigorously on them, as if I were trying to pull a pair of closed elevator doors apart. Theoretically I should climb slowly to maintain the precision of my movements up this 120-metre edifice but this cruel lack of horizontals forces me to accelerate the rhythm. It's tiring. Speed enhances the risk of error but I must climb swiftly in order to conserve my strength.

Halfway up I wedge a foot in the gap and squeeze the Malay stuntman's hand which, carefree, extends towards me. Applause wafts up from below. I hang off him a little as he sits happily in his harness. It is so hot up here! Maybe wearing leather was not such a good choice. Exposed to the equatorial sun, as well as the heat emitted from the building, I am perspiring quite a bit. My clammy fingers are losing adhesion against the glass and steel. I peel off the unique turquoise leather waistcoat I picked up in Rio. Just like Madonna flinging her G-string to the hysterical public, I lob my leather waistcoat down to the crowd below. It spins and flutters on the breeze like a leaf. After a series of pirouettes and spirals, it disappears into a swirling sea of outstretched hands. I feel cooler now, both in terms of bodily temperature but also in terms of acting like a bit of a dude. Yeah man, rock 'n' roll…

Satisfied with this interlude, and having caught my breath, I switch back to the ascent. This time I peel up the building rapidly. Very rapidly. Out of respect for the crowd and the cause for which I climb, I endeavour to put everything I have into it. Even though my life depends on my adherence to safety margins I cannot bring myself to do the bare minimum. The success of the event is based entirely on my success and I have a duty to surpass myself. It may seem idealistic and melodramatic, but it is still possible to put your life on the line for ideas, or to die for them. I race upwards as if I were trying to break a speed record. The first half of the climb took me twelve minutes or so but I need only two or three minutes to make the summit.

As I draw a breath near the top, I spot someone in the middle of the crowd. One of the young deaf mutes I met in Kuala Lumpur had written to me saying that he would be in Borneo and would be among the spectators. He told me he would be easily recognisable since he would be dressed in lively red. In his letter, he had asked me to make a peace sign from the summit, arms raised, fingers spread, except the ring finger. Up on the ledge, I comply before collapsing, dead beat as ever I have been after an ascent.

I slump back and take in the blue sky. I have done it. But the heat, coupled with my exertion, has taken a lot out of me. On the verge of illness, I remain sat at the top of the tower, gulping down whatever liquid is passed to me. Recovery doesn't seem to be coming. I gaze around and see a photographer snapping me furiously. When I made it to the roof I had suddenly seen him a good ten metres back from the rail. As I clambered over the top, he obliterated reels of film. I hadn't seen him earlier and it occurred to me he had only captured me at the summit, missing the escalation itself. His vertigo is obvious. As I sit breathlessly recovering he continues snapping away as if making up for the lost action images. I tell him that a fear of heights is very common and it is a necessary evil to overcome. I explain to him how he can do this: by rationalising the situation, focussing and seeing the reward for his courage, which in his case will be some great action photos. He laughs nervously, then edges closer to the drop on hands and bended knees, as if the tower would collapse if he reached the railing.

Half an hour has passed, and although my breath and muscles have returned to their baseline, I don't feel much better. I have a throbbing headache and feel listless. Right now I don't feel especially in the mood to climb down the exterior of a building. I do not feel fully recovered but I know there are 15,000 people down below staring expectantly up at the top of the Sabah Foundation. The show must go on!

I rise to my feet and peer over the edge. Cheers ring out and I give a big wave to the crowd. I beckon the photographer towards the edge. He almost crawls over, but appears to reach an invisible wall… My ascent was so fast it made me feel a little unwell so I decide to exercise more restraint and descend the building slowly. After a deep breath I throw a leg over the edge and start making my way down.

The ascent was not easy, but the descent turns out to be downright difficult. I need to conserve my energy since I must keep enough in the tank to overcome the treacherous overhang, a dozen metres above the ground. Initially I climb down the same way as I went up, hands jammed in the gap, pulling it outwards as if it were a chest expander. But after a few floors I realise that this technique, though effective, is too demanding. I cannot face the overhang in an exhausted state and neither can I rest on my way towards it. So I decide to change strategy and squeeze my feet into the crack and slowly slide down it. I must admit that this unorthodox technique is unanimously forbidden by my doctors for it is far from the safest way to go down. But it is highly energy-efficient. I could get down this way within two minutes, but I wisely opt to descend at a reasonable pace, pausing from time to time to savour the sweet sensation of my controlled fall.

I slide to the overhang and with some difficulty and strain I overcome it. I hop down and submerge myself in the crowd, awaiting the final donation figure. As the morning wraps up, the figure is announced – we have made just over a million francs. The event has been a resounding success.

The limousine procession starts up again and sets off towards the hotel for a slap-up lunch. A restaurant is reserved for our sizeable party and boisterously we all take our seats. Pleased that I have not disappointed anyone or let them down I order a bottle of Dom Pérignon. As a good Frenchman, I enjoy drinking on special occasions. Rotund bottle in hand, I make a tour of all the tables one by one, to each of the banquet guests. I offer everyone a tipple of this fine vintage, which to my surprise no one seems to want to try. Maybe they are just being polite? Still, I make a tour of the entire restaurant, offering everyone a liberal dash of the good stuff, trying to nudge some of them into acceptance. Strangely it looks like they don't appreciate my offer... And only then do I realise my *faux pas*. In the euphoria of the moment, I have forgotten that Muslims do not drink alcohol! Sheepishly I take my seat with my full bottle. As a result, I drink the whole thing alone, guzzling rather than savouring it, totally aghast at the idea of letting a bottle of this price die so pathetically.

I awake the next day with an absolutely horrendous hangover. The equatorial daylight is painfully dazzling and my body aches like I have run a marathon. My stomach is delicate in the extreme. The place is quiet. The tension and drama has evaporated, leaving an eerie calm like the silence following a fierce battle. Over a late breakfast that I can't actually bring myself to eat I go through the newspapers and catch the news of my climb.

Two climbing propositions have also reached me. The first comes from the Sunway Lagoon, a gigantic and ostentatious hotel outside Kuala Lumpur designed by Las Vegas architects. The General Manager there wants me to fly over and climb it. Having seen my climb televised, the Roman Catholic Church would also like to organise a charity event on their modest but aesthetic cathedral, also in the capital.

A day or so later, I make the quick flight over the South China Sea back to Kuala Lumpur. Regrettably the plasterboard decorum of the Sunway Lagoon cannot be climbed – there is almost nothing to hold onto, and even where there is, this fragile material could easily crumble and give way. The church however turns out to be easy. Just to be sure, I climb three-quarters of the irregular building and study every section to consider technical solutions to the problems posed. I have only three days before I must head back to France but the bishop assures me that on the eve of my departure, everything will be ready. After my success in Borneo the church looks favourably upon such an event. Malaysia is a country where Catholicism represents only a tiny sliver of the population, and consequently funds garnered through donations can be limited. Personally, I am ethically okay with it if the church does not mind, and they let their flock know they feel this way. The last thing I want is to offend anyone. To be given the seal of approval to climb such a monument interests me enormously, particularly after the caper with the Duomo in Milan. But sadly I never get the chance to go up there, the highest authorities of the clergy at the last moment preferring to refrain. The bishop seems to regret the change of heart as much as me, but I depart Malaysia with his blessing.

And how can I be disappointed after the intensity of the last few weeks? I feel like I have lived an entire lifetime here. Malaysia has been a maelstrom of vivid experiences and adventures, a thrilling rollercoaster that I could have stayed on forever. I have tackled the tallest building in the world and experienced wildly contrasting scenarios, having met wretched dungeon dwellers and vicious perverts one day, and then powerful ministers and exulted royalty the next. I have had an absolute blast in Malaysia. It's truly been a right royal visit!

9

SPIDERMAN

When you choose to reject the status quo and follow your heart, you gain an astronomical degree of freedom but it comes at quite a price. Contentment cannot be bought and sold. But essentially, by pursuing your dreams you risk a life of destitution. It may come as no surprise to hear that there aren't many jobs in the employment section of the newspaper for people who climb up the sides of skyscrapers. And while the prisons do occasionally feed and house you, no one would consider this a way of making a living. I too have to make ends meet but my way of life puts me well outside the system. In fact, very few professional rock climbers succeed in making a decent living off escalation – no more than twenty or so of us in France, a paltry number for a sport at which the French excel.

For a number of years, I have been earning from climbing, but how much do I have left over at the end of the year? Very little! Once my travel costs, international telephone bills, fines (these can be quite substantial sometimes) and lawyers' expenses have been totted up, tens of thousands of Euros have fluttered away.

I conduct the occasional motivational speech, and do a little instructing on the side, but these are nowhere near enough to support myself, let alone a family. Sponsorship remains my only real means of earning a living but it imposes certain constraints – constraints which are not always easily swallowed by rock climbers, usually individualists jealous of their freedom. To support oneself by escalation is paradoxical. By looking for the financial autonomy to free yourself from traditional work and pursue your calling, a vocation if you like, you lose a certain core freedom as well as some purity. Imperceptibly, sponsorship tends to urge us to deviate from our road, to gently push our journey off course towards the materialism we renounce. Commercialism and press relations ensures that the route of the professional rock climber is littered with pitfalls, especially if, like me, he has chosen an even more specialised niche where the media circus remains the only possible window through which people will see you and then move in to support you financially.

For me, the very principle of climbing for money is impure and tainted, and I am not especially comfortable with the idea. I am not very proud of what I have done commercially, but at the same time I disown none of it. There are times when you are roped back in by the material world, a world that many who live there would call 'the real world'. The real world? Everyone's reality is based on their own surroundings, circumstances and perceptions, and my reality is no less real than that of anyone else – a painter, a banker, a tramp or a child. Each of us has our own realities, our outlook and judgement being forged by our life experiences.

In those moments when you climb not for art, but for cash, you try to think positively of what this bizarrely gained money will allow you to realise. It can be distasteful but maybe you should not ask too many questions and just take what is offered. Because, ten years after your career, who is going to remember you? Who will meet your needs?

In France the artists have an applaudable system of unemployment allowances to support and nurture their work. But not so for us sportsmen. Representing France at the highest level, receiving high distinctions, awards and accolades, making the national anthem resound – all this sometimes leads to a medal, or a fax of congratulations on behalf of the highest dignitaries of the Republic, but financially, peanuts... I am not saying money should rule the sporting roost. Undoubtedly sport must not be corrupted by money. Sport must be pure! But at the end of the day, the price of bread stays the same for each of us. And for a sportsman or woman it can be a real struggle to pay the bills and feed ourselves or indeed the little mouths that depend on us. Sportsmen are not idle layabouts and we work hard and contribute to society. High-level sports impose demanding regimes for numerous rigorous years, years full of discipline and moderation, pounding away endlessly on the treadmill, thrashing in a pool, or gritting our teeth in the shade of a cliff.

Of course some sportsmen become superstars and earn fabulous wealth. French athletics star Marie-Jo Pérec has retired but how much of what she earned will support her now she is out of the public eye? She would never have amassed the riches of an extravagantly paid football player like Zinedine Zidane for instance. Of course the Zidanes and Beckhams of sport are few and far between. The rest of us have to be a little more realistic, but still we shouldn't have to live like monks.

It's generally accepted that a sportsman has around ten years to ensure his pension. This is all well and good if he is at the top of his game, but even if he reaches the award podium and finds himself second, financially he might just as well have been last to cross the line. Oh, I do not speak for myself. I am outside competition or contest. I am not going to ask for a pension from the state for deciding to dash up the outside of internationally famed architectural works, having disturbed the public and disrupted international diplomacy. I just want sports to be better supported, financially speaking, for the good of sportsmen as well as society. Sure, we get some nice slaps on the back sometimes. I was presented with an Olympic medal, for example. Juan Antonio Samaranch personally bestowed the medal of honour upon me on behalf of the International Olympic Committee. Everyone knows that rock escalation is not an Olympic discipline but the IOC was keen to acknowledge the sporting accomplishment of my solitary ascents. I choose to define myself as an outsider, as an extreme sportsman on the margins of sport, so this gesture profoundly touched me.

As proud as I was to receive the award, I flew back to France facing the same old bills. It may not be ideal but at least sponsorship gives me the opportunity to get paid for doing something I love to do, and fortunately I have a good relationship with several sponsors willing to connect their brands with my vertical events. Even though there have been a few conflicts of interest along the way I heartily thank them for this happy association which has run on now for most of my adult life.

But such attention does lead to some criticism from other climbers. They go up alone in the mountains and don't get the sponsorship or the headlines that I do, and I understand how that can be frustrating for some of them. Some of my detractors accused me of taking unnecessary risks for money, just to seduce financiers. At first, I was amazed by this. Deep in my heart, I know that sponsorship is purely a question of survival, but these criticisms resulted in people questioning the motives behind my climbing. I was suddenly put in a position where I had to defend and justify myself. The media are very happy when I create stories for them. But sometimes, with little to write about and a deadline looming, it may be easier for them and more interesting for their editors and readers to gossip about me or attack me. As the years have passed I have grown to understand that justifying myself, whether in light of critical remarks from the media or from other climbers, has never advanced things. We cannot prevent anybody from having a negative opinion of us. Often the whole affair is not about getting at the truth – it is more due to the fact that it is in their interests to make such comments.

So why do I waffle on about all this? Maybe to help exorcise the ghost of the dollar which haunted me in Singapore, an experience that posed this very dilemma…

After a month of very high-profile media exposure in Malaysia, the management of a famous Singaporean shopping centre asks me to perform a live climbing demonstration at the inauguration of their complex. The job description? Climb up and down their building four times a day, with a rope, for a particularly interesting fee. No risk, no expenses, no sweat. In brief, the chance of a lifetime. My initial reaction is positive and I respond accordingly. The sponsored climb cannot go ahead immediately however as there are all sorts of legal angles which must be looked at and tackled. These negotiations with the government end up lasting several months, as Singapore is not just any country.

At first, for me Singapore is only the name of a distant place, represented by wonderful towering architecture and a comfortable pay cheque. Negotiations eventually pave the way for a deal and my flight tickets arrive in the mail. I feel rather satisfied to have seized this opportunity because I hope I will have the possibility of pursuing a real escalation after the show. A nice cash injection will allow me to travel the world and do battle with other buildings, in South Africa perhaps, and to discover other horizons. My most memorable moments result from unexpected meetings connected to my ascents. I have met some amazing people when mixing in circles on the opposite side of the world.

As I pass through customs at Changi Airport I am greeted by my smiling hosts. And the reception is princely. A limousine sweeps in to collect me and I am checked into a suite in the best hotel in the city. Glowing with prestige, it is immaculately designed and put together with every convenience. Personally I would have preferred less luxury and a little more human warmth. But never mind.

This tiny city state is a modern and engaging metropolis, famed as a melting pot of Asian culture. Shiny and corporate, it has some of the toughest laws anywhere, coming down hard on criminals. The island state has some very tough rules and regulations, some of them legendary. Some proponents state that this tough line on law has produced a safe and harmonious society with crime rates that other countries can only dream of. Critics however say that living in Singapore is like being at school. Singapore canes vandals and passes legislation punishing its citizens for chewing gum, so hoping to obtain a licence to climb a building is like asking the headmaster if you can abseil out of the chemistry lab window!

It is no place for a hippy or a rebel but there is no denying that this is a very attractive, safe, orderly and friendly city. Okay, it is also not an urban myth that in Singapore it is actually illegal to walk around your own home naked, but how many countries are populated by people who are as honest as the Singaporeans? Later I would be told by my Singaporean friends that if you dropped a banknote on the floor, no one would pick it up, even if it appeared to have no owner. It sounded like idealistic patriotism to me but they assured me that this was indeed the case. So, to see if this was true, I dropped a banknote on the ground and stood back to see how long it would last before being plucked from the ground. How long would a reasonable sum of cash last on the ground in any country of the world? In France it might only last a few seconds, and surely the first person to notice it would snatch it with the speed and hunger of a chameleon's tongue. Stunned I watched on as dozens of feet walked by my free cash prize with not one individual stooping to collect it. I had assumed that I would be able to return to my friends and tell them that after a while someone had swiped it but eventually I grew bored of all this honesty and went back to reclaim it. Rather bizarrely I felt more than a twinge of shame in doing so.

So it was true. But then so are many of the other quirks about this pimple of a country. I have to say that Singapore is an amusing little place. While walking around town I saw imposing signs in toilets threatening a large fine if I did not flush after myself. How on earth would they know if I didn't flush the commode? I actually find it a little weird – these signs imply that I would leave excrement floating in the toilet bowl if it weren't for the edict of the state. Do we really need to be told such a thing? Other signs forbid rather obvious things, such as explosives on the metro, as well as more surprising objects such as durians, a rather odorous tropical fruit.

After freshening up I am escorted to the site of my escalation, which is not far away – but nothing is far away in this tiny country. At the edge of the Orchard Road shopping district, the Great World City Centre rises a measly 18 floors, somewhat ridiculous when compared to the other concrete arrows around the city. And from the summit of the shopping centre, I still have the impression that I am on the pavement, the skyline teems with such vertiginous towers! While inspecting the mall and thumbing through the insurance paperwork, an urge scales my spine and enters my brain. I have two days of exhibition climbing, but it should be possible to disappear and nip off to a more ambitious project. Having four million people perched on such a small plot of land forces developers to build upwards. Since this is one of the world's most modern cities, it is blindingly obvious that the island nation has much more to offer than this humble shopping centre.

Furthermore, climbing a building with a rope seems to me like a bit of a swindle. These poor people will come to see a real-life Spiderman, not a marionette hung by a rope from a miserable 18-storey building! Where's the thrill in that? I feel embarrassed at this situation. It demonstrates to me that with a handful of dollars, you can buy anything, anyone, even those who have the ignorance to believe in their own incorruptibility. If the charity show in Malaysia had perturbed me a little, the prospect of my Singaporean performance almost makes me sick. Why does the lure of money compel me to break the rules of solo climbing that I have imposed upon myself? Solo climbing is about you and nature, or in my case, architecture. When climbing you develop a very personal relationship with your environment. It is an absorption into your surroundings, a symbiosis. It may be described as a spiritual quest, the very antithesis of pursuing material gain. When did I begin to betray myself? Was this the price of success, this taming of my soul? I am not a circus animal, not a puppet, but a rock climber who has consciously chosen freedom! But now I find myself in a cage, eating from the hands of unknown people in suits who have bought me for two days. The softest pillows and quilts in the world cannot help me sleep through hours of guilty introspection.

It's time to climb and a new experience confronts me: six grim bodyguards arrive at my hotel! At first, I honestly believe it's a joke or a misunderstanding. But these Terminator dudes do not laugh at all. Hidden behind ebony shades, they play their action movie roles with aplomb.

Permanently murmuring into their radios, they seem to have many grave concerns. I ask them if they have caught the marksman wanting to kill me. A bodyguard spins around, walkie-talkie poised to report an assassination attempt. I have to explain that it is just a jibe and it takes a while to calm him down. It is clear he doesn't find my quip especially funny. He switches back into 007 mode, checking for bugs and booby traps, speaking solemnly with his colleagues.

We leave the hotel as in a movie with me heavily protected as I step into my limo, just in case the doorman decides to pull out a revolver and blow me away, or the gardener is actually a sniper. Flanked by my army we make our way cautiously to the mall. I really wonder what is going on. This is ridiculous. I am just a normal guy heading to the shopping centre, not a Russian mafia boss arranging a rendezvous to sell weapons-grade plutonium. This pantomime is totally unnecessary but I play along with it.

A hundred metres from the mall, the first police cordon is in place, closing off the avenue. Traffic has been forbidden to ensure pedestrianisation – not because I might fall on someone and kill them, which is usually why they cordon off buildings when I climb, but because a good crowd and good press coverage is a must for the mall management. The publicity stunt is going according to plan, with all sorts of Singaporeans, especially families, crammed behind the barriers awaiting me. There is a good turnout; the advertising staff of the mall have organised the event well. Then it hits me that several thousand people are soon to be disappointed. It's a shame. I would have liked to have offered the good people of Singapore a much better spectacle than this.

A buzz of excitement runs through the crowd as we are let through and I exit the car 'covered' by my ultra-protective guards. I must admit I find it quite peculiar being protected by guards at the foot of a building, as I am more accustomed to being chased by them! A chill runs through me. Alain Robert protected by guards at the start of an escalation? Is this another nail in the coffin of my once untethered soul?

The performance can now begin. The first floor of the mall is made of featureless shop windows and cuboid pillars which are impossible to climb. So from the rooftop I attach my rope and throw it over the edge, then go down by the conventional elevator to ground level before preparing to commence the escalation itself. On the red carpet before the crowds

I feel ashamed: ashamed to have tied my soul down with my own ropes, ashamed to have been corrupted. Remorsefully I pull myself upwards on the rope. Curiously, the public react with the normal fervour. As I climb upwards they wail and cheer and jump up and down. Making an ascent with a rope disappoints only me, it seems. Nobody else there seems aware of the enormous difference between a life-threatening solo and an escalation made with a rope. If they are aware, then they don't care. My feelings are mixed. Naturally I am relieved that the public is satisfied by the performance but I am also disturbed by this discovery. During my escalation it becomes clearer than ever that I climb solo purely for myself, as I always have, and not to please curious onlookers. The media attention, the crowds, the reaction of police, judges and fellow climbers are all irrelevant. The rope which scrolls past my eyes is an ethical problem only for me – no one else.

Of course, I make the summit! I descend the building again by a flight of steps, to a thunder of applause. Then for half an hour, I answer public and press questions, but never directly – the bodyguards and the police preventing any crowd surge, or the slightest personal contact. It is hopeless... What is the point of organising this PR exercise if the slightest personal exchange is not possible? The whole operation is a dazzling Singaporean contradiction. I melt away for a break and then return to the carpet and to new crowds. Every two hours, the escalation starts again in an identical way, with disorder and passion reined in throughout. Warm applause, crowd control, ropes.

Before the shopping centre show I had got in touch with a local lawyer to find out more about the exact risks I would incur if, inadvertently, I ventured up the magnificent high rise which had captured my imagination ever since my arrival – the OUB Centre. Standing proud at 280 metres, the OUB is equal to the maximum height permitted by the Singaporean Aviation Authority. It houses one of the region's biggest banks and remains one of the most majestic skyscrapers I have ever seen. The design is bold and unique – from the ground level an eight-storey cutaway floods light into the base of the building, gently opening onto Raffles Place and inviting one inside. The angular tower is composed of two triangular prisms separated by the most slender of gaps, giving the impression that it has been sliced down the middle with cheese wire. From almost any angle it looks like one structure; it is only close up that one can see the magnificent fissure running up it from foot to peak. And what a fissure for an urban climber!

It is immediately apparent that it is possible to climb the OUB Centre, but what about the punishment? My lawyer looks over the top of his spectacles as he delivers the answer – a minimum of three months' detention plus a caning. Not surprisingly, it's a harsh penalty, but too harsh I believe. I try to rationalise it but it would be impossible to take such a risk without clearing a three-month window in my diary beforehand to do the necessary time inside. I need to reflect and consider the effect on my family and whether I can afford such a luxury.

I admit that the idea of fighting against this polished state of limited liberties arouses my spirit. Poking this wasp's nest, just to gauge the reaction of the powers that be, motivates me enough to take the risk of being jailed. I have always had the conviction that it is in these kinds of tests that you define yourself. Living in luxury, dying in the same, none of that is my stuff. I need to partake in other matters, to change, to move. I do not want to ruminate over my regrets every evening, sat in the same armchair, coping with the misery of everyday bullshit. Some people will say that my approach to life lacks pragmatism and maturity, and that I try to live by proxy the heroic adventures seen in Marvel Comics. Maybe they are right. Others think that I take advantage of the system without accepting its rules and constraints. Well, perhaps I am not one for falling into line. But never have I encouraged the undoing of modern society, nor have I wished anarchy to fall upon it. I merely use it differently, but without playing the social misfit or the rebel. I am too old now to believe I can save the world. If I can succeed in building the life about which I have always dreamed, to have stuck to my guns and to have followed my dream, I will have succeeded.

And so, as the limo takes me back to Changi Airport, I make a decision. I shall return to Singapore for a duel with this famous high rise, simply because I want to. I must remain myself wherever I am and not be cudgelled into conformity by shadowy figures who tell us who to be and how to live. Our leaders are themselves just ordinary men and women like me and you, with no right to enslave or subjugate us. No system should prevent us from artistic expression, from poetry or enlightenment.

A year later I return, having cleared my diary for the next three months. I exit Raffles Place MRT Station and, as planned, I immediately get to grips with the 63 storeys of the glorious OUB Centre.

I slide my fingers into the generous fissure between the two halves of the OUB and push off the ground. The building is warm to the touch in the equatorial heat, since it is clad in a smooth aluminium alloy of battleship grey. I feel her stealth and prowess. She is unsinkable. My feet find the aluminium surface kind and supportive, offering significant resistance. This resistance underfoot is strong and reassuring and will save me the potentially draining effort of having to compensate with my arms.

Within seconds a few eager Singaporeans stop in their tracks and start pointing upwards – and of course, some not-so-eager ones start running around and yelling in panic. For me though this escalation is pure joy. Few buildings if any have offered such temptation, such a splendid gap to work with. Right now I forget that wandering vertically astray may lead to a caning. The threat of a state-sanctioned spanking tests and provokes me, but the task in hand potentially offers a far worse penalty. Despite enjoying myself I ascend swiftly as this type of escalation affords no rest – both arms must be in constant opposing tension and I calculate that I must reach the summit in less than an hour, before my forearms give out. I expect to make that time very easily but one can never be too relaxed about such things as there may be unexpected obstacles or difficulties on the way up. On this precise piece of architecture I would be surprised if there are any major problems, as I can see the crack clearly all the way up to the summit.

But as I travel up the cleft one such unforeseen obstacle does indeed materialise, and does so at the 21st floor. Windows have flanked my route all the way up, only a metre or so away. As the crowd claps me on below, one of the windows swings open and two cops lean out, blocking any progress. Regrettably I am very much like a funicular train travelling up a vertical railway, the fissure offering me only one dimension of movement. Derailment is inevitable. The game is up.

I climb through the open window into somebody's office and into the custody of the waiting cops. I am taken through the offices to the elevator, past the huddled spectators and placed in a cop van. To be honest I am expecting the worst now, especially after Malaysia. In Singapore the people are pretty straight and preoccupied with making money. Not in a million years will my enterprise make its way onto anyone's pie chart. Climbing up the side of their nice important building and disturbing board meetings, or office workers attending to the well oiled production of Singapore dollars, will most likely rock the boat a little.

What will St. Singapore's Secondary School do about my indiscretion? I have been a naughty boy and I can expect a caning from the headmaster and several months' detention... Was it worth it? I think so, though I would be lying if I said I was looking forward to it.

Singapore is blessed with low crime rates for a very good reason. In Singapore the cane is not a harmless schoolyard spanking designed to make kids cry. The prisoner is bent over a wooden horse and strapped down with his buttocks bared to the prison guard. Padding may be put around the kidney or genital areas to protect the offender from permanent harm. Depending on the crime, the secured prisoner is struck a set number of times across the buttocks with a rattan cane. This cane is much heftier than those used in schools in the old days, and by law it must be over a metre long and half an inch thick! The guards who exact the punishment are trained to swing their canes at a speed of at least 160 kilometres an hour with an impact force of at least 90 kilograms. Multiple strikes almost always tear the flesh, leading to bleeding and bruising, and sometimes scarring. The pain is described by those who have endured it as 'beyond excruciating' and some men have actually passed out during the canings. Caned prisoners typically cannot sit, wear shorts or sleep on their backs for two weeks or longer afterwards. There are many documented cases where prisoners have described how they could not walk unaided out of the room afterwards, and that the canes were bloody with bits of skin stuck to them after the thrashings.

My buttocks tremble at the prospect. All in all it sounds terrible. As a foreigner, can I expect to be treated differently? It seems not. A few years ago a Hong Kong student was jailed for several months and received twelve strikes of the cane. And famously, despite enormous international publicity and huge pressure from abroad, American teenager Michael Fay was caned and also jailed for vandalism. Even the intervention of President Clinton didn't much help Fay, who in the end had his number of lashes reduced as a 'gesture' from six to four. What Malaysia did to my posterior was most unpleasant but what will Singapore do?

I am fingerprinted and go through the usual processing and am taken to the lock-up. Despite the shared border with Malaysia, and many cultural similarities, I am pleased to find that the prison and treatment is far better than the hole I was placed in when I was imprisoned in Kuala Lumpur. It's not good, but at least it is sanitary. The judiciary, immovable and severe, I expect will be another matter.

But as the day progresses I discover I am in for quite a surprise. The prosecutor visits me in my cell and gets down to business. She tells me that I am well known in Singapore for helping to promote local businesses, and they know all about my climbs around the world. It seems they also know of some of the work I had done for charity. She declares that my escalation was an offence under Singapore law. And then she tells me I am not to do it again. She leans forward and tells me to heed this warning, for next time they will definitely prosecute me and any punishment dished out will be stiff. That is all. I am free to go. The prosecutor collects herself and leaves.

I am stunned. Is that it? I was mentally and physically prepared for so much worse. Rather surprisingly, the day ends very well for me with a fair and reasonable reaction on the part of the Singaporean authorities. In actual fact Singapore, so often criticised abroad for its draconian laws and austere judiciary, has ultimately turned out to be more lenient and sensible than just about any other country I have been arrested in. Three months in prison waived… and my buttocks have been spared! I spring out of the station a free man. Feeling fortunate and blessed, I take in the humid equatorial air and exhale in joy and relief. I really can't believe it. Quite literally, the prosecutor has saved my ass.

People often ask why I do such a thing as risk being jailed or caned, why I willingly walk into confrontation with the authorities, or why I relish the opportunity to put myself in life-threatening situations. I am not entirely sure, as there are a myriad of emotions and principles involved, but certainly at or near the core of it is that I enjoy a bit of mischief. The spirit of revolution and disdain for authority runs deep in the French national character and I guess my psyche has a larger slice of it than most. One of my most daring rock climbs – the 'Night of the Lizard' – illustrates well this impish spirit.

The Night of the Lizard is the name given to a particularly exhilarating and treacherous route up a cliff in Lubéron in southern France. It is ranked at 8a+. For those unfamiliar with rock climbing, an 8a+ is one of the most extreme climbs you can do, a simply fantastic ascent only for the fittest, the most technically gifted and the most experienced. An 8a+ also ranks as highly dangerous and demands great reserves of physical and mental strength, requiring an absolutely flawless performance from the athlete. And of course, using climbing equipment such as a rope is the usual way to do it! It goes without saying that taking on a climb in this category solo is a matter of life and death.

The Night of the Lizard was not unknown to me, as in my crazy youth I had already ascended this cliff in an academic manner on my rope. My knowledge of the route meant I calculated the chance of getting to the top alive, if I were to attempt climbing it without ropes, was quite reasonable.

Bit by bit, the desire to go solo up this magnificent 20 metres of calcareous convexity had begun to consume me. The Night of the Lizard fascinated me despite or maybe because of the fact that the final section is as smooth as a pane of glass. The face of the Lizard is almost mathematically convex, as if it had been cut by machine tools. Over the years it has gained a glossy and shiny sheen due to the scrambling hands and feet of slipping climbers. Only the gentlest pockmarks give the surface any texture. The most challenging part of the vertical zone is devoid of foot grips and can be traversed only by using two ridiculous hand grips, flared holes which cannot hold more than the first phalanx of two fingers. Moving here is akin to towing one's entire body by the hollow of a teaspoon up a vertical cliff side.

In spite of its modest height compared to my city ascents (20 metres does not compare with 400 metres or so) the Night of the Lizard is an immense climb of the most challenging technical nature and it does not forgive a mistake. A fall from this height onto the chaos of mixed rocks below is more than enough to end everything. There is no doubt at all that realising this climb rope-free will invest me in the most exclusive club of international solo rock climbers. I resolve to attempt the Night of the Lizard unaided, and bit by bit I prepare myself for the extreme challenge.

The day before the climb, the nerves start setting in and I grow restless and pensive. I know I can succeed but obviously I don't know if I will, and I also understand what failure will mean. As I pace around my home I decide to give the photographer accompanying me on this assault a phone call to inform him that at the foot of the cliff I may give up. My life is more important than a set of photographs, even if we both hope the day will provide some eye-popping images. Obviously the photographer is conscious of this uncertainty and he seems to fully understand.

A good photographer strives to be a fly on the wall, to be anonymous and invisible to his subject, and fortunately for me I am with a real pro. I find photographers to be completely different to directors of either film or television who are always instructing me what to do as if I were an actor, sometimes oblivious that they are asking me to do things which are impossible, inconvenient or highly dangerous. Control freaks? Maybe not quite, but additional outside pressures prevent me from attaining perfect concentration. A solo of this level is a conflict between me and the cliff, and nothing must disrupt the serenity of this decision.

The next day, I leave my home and head out to face this 8a+ in Lubéron. The photographer chats with me amiably, pretending he is not trying to settle my nerves. Conversation is light and optimistic but at the forefront of my mind is the daunting cliff. The Night of the Lizard has devoured many a climber wise enough to scale this monster with ropes. No one has been foolish enough to take it on solo.

As I get out of the car I battle to focus and control myself. But as we approach the foot of the climb, my dread suddenly evaporates into the clear blue sky. Why? A new and distracting problem appears – a German climber is up there tackling the cliff. With the route occupied there is little we can do except kick around, rest and wait a while.

More than an hour goes by. The sun gradually moves across the sky. The face will soon be truly impossible to climb solo! Adhesion to the rock is distinctly superior in the shade, while the slumbering cliff still breathes the coolness it has stored from the night. Impatiently I watch the German climber ponderously inch his way along the cliff side, in the methodical manner of his brethren. Not surprisingly he is fully kitted and equipped and anchored securely by his rope, his red helmet occasionally scraping the rock as he cautiously (and wisely) checks his position and fiddles with his karabiner. He makes hesitant attempts, sometimes abandoning them for a while before moving onwards. From grip to grip, every two or three movements, he takes a breather and rests on his rope. Judging by his movements and his progress I don't think he will be able to make it, especially the formidable final stages.

Yet more time passes. The sun continues to creep across the sky and the sunbeams approach the face. I am running out of time. I pace around, tensely aware that I cannot wait for the German to finish if I am to climb today. At the last minute, as the first sunbeam grazes the edge of the cliff, I shout up to ask him if he can remove his rope just for a minute, while

I make my way up the cliff. Half cooperative, he removes it with a pout which does little to mask his lack of enthusiasm. Obviously this guy does not know me and cannot imagine that I am going to make a solo on the very route he has been wrestling with all day. The photographer, who has been kitted up for a while, now hangs a third of the way down the cliff, waiting for me in silence. I scrape the soles of my slippers under my thumbnail. Optimal adhesion. No obstacles. I am ready. Nearby, the German lad is looking at me, behaving superior and cool, as if he had just donated his balls to me on a platter.

I pounce out of the blocks and fly up the face with the intensity of a startled squirrel. The first part of this almost impossible climb is a long section with its own uncertainties and difficulties, but with a focussed effort I make it through. On the middle section I have to pull off a quite incredible movement where I must scale across to the left with my foot and finger pressed hard into the slenderest of grips. But the worst is yet to come: the smooth, flat, unpredictable exit.

I pass the photographer as his camera whirls and clicks frantically. I am entering the curved section and the cliff now starts to overhang, making tremendous demands on my body. I must maintain my grip on the cliff face through these tiny points of contact as gravity pulls me not only downwards, but outwards and away from the cliff.

I catch the teaspoon-sized hollow and insert as much of my two fingers into it as I can, bringing my feet up high in the hope of being able to push against this featureless surface to make the final grip. Although I have already given every step of this climb my maximum commitment and concentration, I need to double my efforts here. I take a deep breath and aim at the final grip. My strain is at an absolute maximum as I reach upwards... and then both my feet start to slide! A millisecond later I squeeze my abdominal muscles and lock my back, hanging exclusively from my two fingertips above the jumble of jagged boulders below. The skid of my slippers is arrested before I am claimed by Newton's laws and the graveyard of Valence. For a split second it could go either way. The exertion is truly phenomenal but in a light-headed and dizzy state, without the time to be afraid, I reverse the slide and steel myself for the final grip.

I will only get one chance to get it right. I pull upwards with all my might... it is only inches away, millimetres away... and I catch it! I pull myself upwards and exit the cliff. I have made it!

Almost overwhelmed, I collapse panting at the top, my head spinning with joy and also with low levels of oxygen due to the effort I have expended, especially at the end. I almost pass out but manage to exchange grins as wide as the Verdon Canyon with the photographer. The canyon is truly beautiful, the sky, the sun, the brush, the breeze. It is just so good to be alive!

Overcoming the Night of the Lizard is one of the greatest successes of my entire career. I can tell you that my penultimate move was very, very extreme. Some of the best rock climbers in the world have fallen from this section, and they climbed with ropes. Doing it solo was unthinkable, unbelievable, and I successfully managed it!

Later, the photographer tells me of the utter jaw-dropping bewilderment of the other climber, dismayed by my escalation! Dangling from his rope, the red-helmeted German throws his hands down in frustration, an action that the photographer sneakily captures. I guess I can understand how he feels. Despite all his efforts, he is unable to complete the climb – then someone comes along and asks him to move his rope, and shoots past him with only a bag of chalk for equipment. Poor guy, it was really too much for him.

The famous red-and-blue costume is only half finished. The costume makers need to add a few things to it, such as web patterns and a spider on the chest. But already it emits an aura of invincibility. I like it. The fitter chats to me in his thick Spanish accent, joking about life and politics.

I am here in Venezuela due to an invitation from the hugely popular TV show *Super Sabado Sensacional*. This five-hour variety show is broadcast at peak times on Saturday nights and is perhaps the flagship of the television channel Venevision. It takes well over half the viewing audience in Venezuela and is broadcast internationally across South and Central America, the Caribbean and the United States. The typical fare is family entertainment with musicians, international celebrities, comedians, magicians, daredevil stuntmen and various other glitzy performances. For South American TV executives, a guy who scales tall buildings without ropes obviously fits the bill. A decent tower in Caracas has been selected and they have negotiated a climbing licence.

Skilled in the art of sensationalism, Venevision asked for my measurements while I was still in France. Why? Because they want this Spiderman guy to make a big splash across the airwaves. They want me to look the part and are making me a Spiderman suit.

The Theatre of Caracas' costume department has made me a close-fitting costume of Lycra for maximum mobility. The fitter asks me to try it on. As soon as I slip into it I feel myself transforming, my alter ego surfacing… yes, this feels good, this feels right. There is one problem though, and it is quite a big one. When I slip the hood of the famous costume over my face the lights go out.

"You like it, Alain?" asks the costume maker with a smirk, a smirk I can only hear and not see. Of course I don't want to be rude, and I try to respond as amiably as possible, but the costume has a major flaw that needs to be addressed. I give my muffled but frank response.

"It's very nice. But how do you expect me to climb this building?"

"You can move okay? It fits nicely, huh?"

"Yes, it fits. But I can't see anything. And I can't breathe!"

My hands claw at my nostrils, eyes and mouth concealed inside the Lycra. It is impossible to even walk across the room. I feel like I am in some sort of bondage hood, a gimp mask or something equally restrictive. Only tiny dots of light make it to my deprived retinas and every time I attempt to inhale I suck taut Lycra into my nose and mouth. I flounder across the room, colliding noisily with furniture. The offer of a costume was very kind but I am exasperated. Am I supposed to climb a building in Caracas blind?

"How can I climb like this? This is… this is shit!" I lament sightlessly.

The fitter seems to grasp the problem and guides me back towards a chair. He parks me in it and helps me regain access to daylight and oxygen. As I return to my senses I note thankfully that the guys can see my point, and they set about making some holes in the mask.

When I return for the second fitting, things are much better – I have holes for both eyes following the contours of the Marvel Comics character and additionally, and somewhat importantly, there is a hole from the tip of my nose to my mouth so I can breathe. It doesn't look exactly the same as the real Spiderman's mask but it is a vast improvement in practical terms. I still have problems with the zip at the back – it runs from the top of my head down to my waist, making it hugely difficult to put on and take off, especially if I need to remove or replace my mask while hanging off the side of a building. But anyway it looks good, and maybe I can make some wardrobe changes later on, for very soon I am going up a building. Everything is legal and stage-managed and I need to scale the building live on television before millions. I must climb one of a pair of identical towers which are the highest in Latin America. The Parque Central Torre is an attractive stack of 56 storeys standing 221 metres tall.

On set, all looks good. As in Brazil I must climb according to the broadcasting schedule but at least this time we don't need to wait for another programme to finish. The escalation starts a lot less chaotically. Cameras roll and images go out to the hemisphere. Spiderman lives!

I get off to a cracking start and to great enthusiasm from the assembled crowd. I ascend steadily as I explore my relationship with the Parque Central Torre. The climb turns out to be technically modest, but I take my time making it to the summit to make a show of it for the cameras. I feel pleased that all over Venezuela, families are enjoying this entire climb live on air, that in this little moment in time I am making millions of kids smile in this corner of the world.

The reception I get from the audience during my interview afterwards as conquistador of Parque Central Torre is rapturous – I am treated like the real superhero! The timing could not be better, as with the impending release of the first Spiderman movie, cinemas are filled with enticing trailers for the upcoming Hollywood blockbuster. I request a second mask that I can wear just on my face, that can be pulled off separately for comfort and ease, and the friendly costume guys kindly oblige. Back at the theatre I admire my suited reflection in the mirror. The second mask is much better, much more practical. And like a real superhero I now have a costume I can whip on when duty calls.

Although I prefer to climb in my own choice of clothes, without the restriction of a costume and wearing fabrics after my own heart such as my nice lizard-skin, climbing as Spiderman is great fun. The coverage of my escalation in Caracas is very positive and spreads far beyond Venezuelan borders. Everyone loves the sight of a real-life Spiderman on a building.

I continue to climb in my own clothes throughout 2002, as the blockbuster film is released, but every now and then I don the heroic costume for a bit of a laugh. With the movie out and retailers churning out toys, T-shirts and other movie spin-offs, there is a surge of interest in the character. The new interest leads to a few calls – not for me, but for Spiderman! Spiderman is very popular it seems, much more so than I am!

One nice opportunity comes up in Puerto Rico, a US territory which also receives the weekly *Super Sabado Sensacional* TV show, and a place where people remember the Caracas climb with that Spiderman guy. So when I get their call, an invitation to fly to San Juan on the little Caribbean island for a fundraising gig, it is just too good to turn down. Without a moment's hesitation I book my ticket and board an airplane for the balmy capital.

Wearing my famous suit I crawl up a building in front of the local media and a keen crowd which includes hundreds of delighted kids. This climb is legal and fully supported by the community as we are doing it to raise funds for a cash-strapped children's hospital run by wonderful, dedicated staff. Most of the little boys in the hospital are orphans or abandoned, and many are physically or mentally handicapped. The day after my climb I visit the boys in my Spiderman costume – and they are absolutely ecstatic. I prance playfully around in my costume, shake their hands, joke and fool around. I will never forget the expressions on their faces. It was a marvellous day.

The following year Spiderman gets another call, this time from a potential sponsor in the United Kingdom, and their request is a little different. This call comes from the British and Irish satellite television channel BSkyB. The company tells me that one of their channels, Sky Box Office, will soon air the British television premiere of the Spiderman movie, and they would like a little publicity for their broadcast. I ask a few questions, and as usual the sponsors do not wish to involve themselves legally in any escalation, but they do offer a nice fee. So I head to London and find an innovative building: the Lloyds Building at One Lime Street in the financial district, a district known rather confusingly in the UK as the City of London.

The Lloyds Building immediately reminds me of the Centre Georges Pompidou in Paris, another structure which appears to have been built inside out. Features which are ordinarily housed inside have instead been placed on the exterior of the building. The lifts, the staircases, the piping and electrical conduits are all on the outside to free up the interior and also, of course, to make an artistic statement. To me it looks like someone has dissected a building like an animal, exposing the veins and organs for all to see. It is also rather reminiscent of the industrial minimalism of an oil refinery. Either way, with all these features stuck on the outside of the building, it is extremely accessible to the urban climber who has lots of lovely pipes, brackets and props to hold onto. This will be my third climb in London. I made two attempts to climb what was for a while the tallest building in Europe, the Canary Wharf Tower. My first attempt to climb Canary Wharf, or technically speaking, One Canada Square, was in 1995 and it was successful – but my second attempt, just six months prior to this attempt on the Lloyds Building, was thwarted when I got to the three-quarters mark but was bludgeoned into submission by the cold and pervading rain.

This morning I have better luck with the British weather and I get off to a good start with the spring sun on my back, a little after the employees of the insurance giant have settled down at their desks. In my Spiderman costume I vault easily up the side of this mass of pipes, struts and beams, though not as nimbly as the somersaulting and spring-loaded character in the movie.

The escalation is very simple and of course with such an abundance of glass I am spotted very early. Soon I see security guards emerging from the building, looking none too pleased, with walkie-talkies pressed to their lips. Office workers are popping out of their chairs as if a multitude of toasters were all going off in the open-plan offices. Many of them point and I get a few waves and thumbs-up.

The press, obviously tipped off by my sponsor – which is after all a television channel seeking maximum publicity – are on the scene in no time at all. Cops too are there in a flash. The Lloyds Building is a very interesting climb which allows me to pull off all manner of moves. I make the summit and give a wave to everyone below, and then descend this unusual building to the bottom. I am arrested by the police at the foot of the building for 'causing a public nuisance'.

"Hey, this is not a nuisance, it is entertainment! If you want to arrest people who are causing a nuisance, then arrest those noisy city boys who shout into their mobiles on the train, or maybe those people who allow their dogs to shit on the streets for us all to step in. That's far more of a nuisance. People like what I do!"

Well, people who are not in uniforms like it. The cops are having none of it and I am taken to the station where as usual I have my details taken down, my prints and photos taken.

And something new – they take a sample of my DNA! I am surprised that of all places this should happen in England. Why have they taken my DNA? I have been arrested, sentenced, fined and jailed all over the world and no other country has done this, even the most authoritarian lands or those with less than ideal attitudes towards human rights. It's a new and worrying development for civil liberties.

The London cops are not too happy about my climb and I am held in a cell overnight. The doors clang shut and I have to spend the night in jail in my Spiderman costume, which is not too cool, and then the next morning I am taken to court.

I stand before the judge dressed as Spiderman and I am fined for my caper up the side of the Lloyds Building. I am also told that if I climb again in the City of London I will get a £50,000 fine! Fifty thousand pounds? Are you serious? I would have to rob the Bank of England to pay that off! It makes me laugh a little, but all in all I note that the authorities in Britain take a pretty tough line with my stunt, and they do not dismiss the case out of hand. Nor do they see the climb for what it is – a guy climbing up the side of a building dressed as Spiderman for a bit of fun and publicity. And in actual fact it is not even my publicity.

The political mood seems to have changed in the UK over the past few years and maybe they are getting a little paranoid over there. But anyway the good news is that I am not jailed and I am free to go.

The escalation makes a big splash in the newspapers and on television, and BSkyB have the scoop they wanted. The jaunt also does me no harm at all in terms of future sponsorship. I return to France via the Channel Tunnel with my Spiderman costume in my suitcase for when I need it again.

I wish to continue climbing as Alain Robert and do not want to tie myself too closely to this powerful and iconic costume. But every now and then I will jump into it, for a contradictory blend of anonymity and celebrity. Whenever I don the mask I become the legend, the man without a face, the superhero. An ascent as Spiderman is always a blast. But in a way I lose myself. If I continue to climb purely as Spiderman and not as Alain Robert, I may forget who I really am. What you wear can dramatically change your identity, the way others perceive you, and also your sense of self. I need to remind myself who I really am...

Who am I? Do you really want to know? I'm the *real* Spiderman!

IO

FEARS AND THE SEARS

Those who know the region of Alpes-de-Haute-Provence take time to stroll around the village of Moustiers and then continue up the road to the section of the Verdon Canyon beyond the little village of Palud. You don't need to be involved in extreme sports to appreciate this glorious cliff or what it represents for a rock climber. For this is a site of inspirational limestone, splendidly sculpted by water and wind. Flecked with ochre, the chalky-grey underbellies of limestone overhang a flowerbed of foliage and scrubland. As you walk towards the cliff's edge the land opens up before you dramatically. Non-rock-climbers approaching the edge of the abyss tend to do so crouching or crawling on their knees, for fear of being snatched by the empty space. Staying steady away from a precipice is obviously not a problem but keeping your balance at the edge of an abyss requires mastery. If you think about it, that is pretty weird.

Across this magical landscape I have achieved many trying solos, many of them for magazine pieces. Glorious scenery, compulsory dizziness, and a guaranteed fear of morbidity, all so people may be entertained for a few seconds before they turn the page. But still I have had to overcome my own demons at the edge of this vacuum in the ground. Sometimes I want to prove that I still have the heart of a rock climber – that I have not lost my love of nature's grand spectacles and challenges. I do not wish to lose touch with my roots but of course urban escalation is now my career, my means of supporting myself and my family. It's a sad thing to say but the media will not come knocking for an old rock climber. Not unless he is ridiculously old and decrepit… a centenarian hanging above a precipitous drop might make a good story.

With my success in urban climbing, or 'buildering' as it is sometimes known, several rock climbers had started to attack me for scaling buildings instead of cliffs, as if this was some sort of betrayal. At other times such figures have tried to dismiss my climbs as some sort of retirement, a game for an old man being put out to pasture. In your thirties you start to face certain questions. Some of them come from other people but the trickiest ones come from yourself. On occasion we feel we need to prove to those snapping at our heels, as well as to ourselves, that we are still young, full of sap and that we are still in the game.

A rock climb again? Why not? I decide to seek a meaty challenge and 'Polpot' emerges as a perfect antidote to these troubling thoughts.

The Polpot I seek is the extreme rock climbing section halfway up a cliff in the Verdon Canyon, and not the Cambodian dictator. This Polpot is a popular abseiling route and is given a rating of 7c+ denoting an extreme climb. It is renowned for posing a highly physical and technical challenge. The best climbers in the world know what this climb means and it draws numerous experts wishing to prove their mettle on the ropes. Polpot is historic, unpredictable and full on. And there are no fire escapes – this isolated section of cliff face is treacherous and totally unforgiving. In brief? It's utter madness to climb this solo.

At the foot of the cliff I wait all day for the camera crew to arrive. Nicole and the boys are here too, accompanying me as they usually do on my rock climbs. The fact that the film crew is not here though is distracting to my concentration and preparation. The problem is compounded further as the day passes and the temperature plummets. The wind starts to pick up, making Polpot even more antagonistic. Pissed off with the crew, I decide to spend a little time climbing Polpot with safety devices, to familiarise myself with it and to work out my movements. Mind you, this is not a route that you forget in a hurry.

Polpot forms the top section of 250 metres of sheer rock face. It provides only a modicum of friction for feet with miniscule ledges and grips. As I make my way up it, the climb reveals itself as extremely tricky, even when fully equipped. I am happy with most of it except for a truly dangerous section near the top known as the 'Crux'. Here I must support almost my whole body weight by clinging on to a tiny hole with a finger or two of my left hand, with virtually nothing underfoot, and then perform a full stretch to reach out for a tiny grip with my right hand. There is no safe technique to navigate this impervious Crux. It takes a prodigious effort plus a big leap of faith to get around it. A little disconcertingly, my climbing slippers don't grip the damp rock and I slip and slide several times, leaving the cliff face and jerking to a stop on the end of my rope. I repeat the attempt but I keep ending up dangling and spinning around on the rope. To repeat the movement yet again is useless. Instead it will be necessary to maintain the highest focus the moment my feet start to give way. I have climbed Polpot before (albeit with ropes) and successfully got past the Crux, so I know it can be done.

The TV team have finally turned up. Apparently they were lost but they waste no time and start preparing to shoot. Terrified by the sheer drop, they secure their equipment in position on a little platform over the edge. Pointing the camera downwards from here will give a superb perspective. They seem to have plenty of confidence in me and are seemingly unaware of the magnitude of what I am attempting. To the untrained eye, only the height matters – a cliff is just a cliff and there is little difference between an easy route or an impossible one.

Once everyone is ready I make my way over the edge of the cliff. On my rope I slowly descend to the departure point of the route, some 40 metres below the lip of the abyss and over 200 metres up the cliff. I unclip myself and watch as my belt and equipment is winched back up. Bit by bit it is hoisted up until it disappears. The wind whistles up the face, obscuring voices from above and below, further cutting me off from the rest of the world. I am all alone in this desolate place. For the final time, I thoroughly clean my slippers. The trial run had revealed problems with my feet and their adhesion will be vital.

I am ready. I calm my mind for a few seconds and then strike out to execute the first movements, movements which are initially easy. Despite this early success, my mind is carefully focussed as gravity is present at all stages of the ascent. I cannot allow myself to drift.

After this short section I reach an area from which I cannot retreat. My inaccessible and invisible starting point now seems so distant. It gets tougher, but still my movements remain fluid and confident, and all is going as planned. Plastered against this sheer cliff I inch further towards the top and salvation. I stretch and pull against shrinking grips, each movement more demanding than the last. It is incredibly difficult.

After great exertion the most testing passage, overcoming the Crux, begins. From here I can see the grips ahead – tiny, ridiculous. There is no other way but via these tiny dimples in the rock. But I feel good. Serene. The wind is my only companion, making flapping sounds in the small folds of my clothes. I know that this passage cannot resist me, that my focus and training will enable me to overcome this horrible obstacle. There are no grips either side of the Crux, no escape, no way out. But only three or four moves remain. In ten seconds, I shall be alive, I shall have won my game against the Grim Reaper. I stretch out now for the first tiny hole of this final section, the point of no return. It is do or die.

And then, without warning, it all goes wrong. Out of nowhere I lose my focus and find myself racked with doubt and confusion. It is impossible to know where this sudden negativity springs from. Just like that, I drop out of my concentration and realise where I really am. My situation seems grotesque, stupid. Wind rushes hundreds of metres up the cliff through my hair and clothes, sweat trickles out of pores on my forehead. The grips oppose me and they start to recede into the cliff. They want me to plummet onto the rocks 200 metres below. And under my slippers, I feel my tread diminishing...

Frightened, I look around trying to find another hold, but I cannot even see any of these famous grips, let alone reach one. They are missing! Gone. Vanished into the haze. I am stuck in a prone position on the side of Polpot and I will soon fall. I start to panic. The team above and below thinks I am okay and fighting the cliff. I shatter this casual calm by roaring out to them.

"Gimme a fucking rope!"

Pandemonium. My wife is white with terror. She knows that I can hang on for a few minutes, but she also knows my end could occur here and now, before her eyes, before our children's eyes. And it is not a happy situation for me either. When hanging on for dear life, time plays tricks on you. It is not only that it ticks past, each passing second stealing a moment when you could have been saved. Time tortures you. Minutes become elastic, seconds stretch into what seems like whole hours. Later they shall tell me I clung on for three minutes. One hundred and eighty seconds. So little! What were you doing three minutes ago? That's how brief and insignificant this period is. Nevertheless during this time I am paralysed with fear. Pressed against the cliff, my life is slipping away. I can feel it going. I feel compelled to exorcise this acute fear by writing these lines, as Polpot's ghost still dwells deep within me, haunting me. Fear is a survival mechanism and it should not disrupt action – it encourages perfect reflexes. If the brakes of a car fail while driving downhill, then you pull up the handbrake and, if you can, steer the car uphill. As a last resort you can jump out of the car before it gathers too much speed, or just dive out and hope for the best. In this situation I really have no possibility of jumping. I am going to crash head on...

I owe my life to a cameraman who, fortunately for me, is experienced with ropes. It takes an eternity as he hurriedly organises my lifeline but from his rickety platform near the top of the cliff he manages to drop me a cord. To ensure my grip on the rope is secure and controlled enough for me to let go of the cliff I have to wrap it around a single hand, a dexterous operation particularly difficult when pressed flat against a rock face hundreds of metres in the air, fatigued and stressed by an emergency. Luckily I keep my wits and swing free of the cliff, recover my grip on the rope above the abyss, and pull myself up it to safety.

Sat on the ground and propped against a tree, still trembling, I recover my life. I soak it back in through my lungs, my eyes, my ears, my skin – all of which by rights should be dashed on the harsh rocks beyond the cliff's edge. Lactic acid has claimed my forearms and it is impossible to curl my fingers or even to speak. I am petrified, still paralysed by this fleeting eternity, this departure point of the tangents of time. It does not escape me that being thrown off into this tangent, life rather than death, was beyond my control. I was fortunate that those around me knew how to act. Standing around me, my wife and my two eldest sons can barely contain their understandable anger. Further away, the youngest is playing, oblivious. Life goes on. For the cameraman, the scene is potent. He captures a few images of the powerful non-verbal communication in my family.

"We had more than enough images for the article, Alain, why get into a panic?" he cracks.

"Those images are useless! I did not complete the climb!" I respond angrily.

My wife storms off, furious. I know that I have hurt her, but in these moments I am visceral, crude. My heart is still pounding, my muscles gelatinous, and I am still shaking. Up there I felt something terrifying. I felt my mechanism jamming, grains of sand blocking the well oiled components of my climbing machine. Searching questions flood into my mind. It is vital to know when to quit, even if it seems totally unacceptable. Am I really past it now? Do I have to stop climbing? Did I go too far?

As everyone packs and heads for home these unanswered questions torture my spirit to the point of obsession. On the silent drive back they fly like phantoms in and around my head, more and more of them cramming into my crowded mind. Finally, as the car pulls up at home and my sulking family gets out, the questions find the only possible answer – I need to go back up there to find out.

Five days later, accompanied once again by the photographer and my family, I return to the same point of the canyon. As they are not climbers, the others will not really understand if I am in trouble, unless of course I call out for a rope. To an observer, everything would look fine, even if I was in mortal danger or my grip was failing. Unless there is a catastrophic failure no one will know how well or badly I am doing.

The kids seem cheerful enough as they mess around in the sunshine. Little if anything has changed over the last five days. The air is maybe a little heavier. After all, it is summertime. As we approach we take in the daunting sight of Polpot towering above us. Recent tracks of magnesia are fading on the cliff face. They trail upwards before halting at the Crux, mocking me with my harrowing failure. It is clear to me what lies above on that rock. This is the crux of my career now. All roads lead here. All my answers will be found right here, upon these rocks. Today's climb will be my road of self belief or my doom, an endorsement of my way of life or the full stop to my career.

I approach Polpot. It glares down at me. I jump back into the saddle and kit myself up, climbing the route correctly again on the end of my rope. I clean the grips and grooves with a toothbrush to remove the surplus magnesia I left behind five days ago. This action allows for better adhesion between the rock and my fingers. But more importantly for me it is also the means of wiping the slate clean and embarking upon a fresh challenge. I check everything again, going over my movements meticulously. I must persist. After I feel I have completed every preparation possible, and my mind is calm, I signal to the photographer harnessed on the end of his rope that I will make a second solo attempt of this 7c+. This time, there is no television crew and no one to lower a lifeline.

The solo begins. My concentration and commitment is total. The photographer manoeuvres on his rope to locate the best angles. It goes exactly the same way as the doomed climb days before: the challenge is tough but I make it through the early and middle stages as I did last time, solidly, confidently. So far I feel good. And then I arrive at the impassable

Crux again. As it has for millennia, the Crux stands guard over the cliff top. It still looks formidable. But I cannot avoid it, and I attack it once more. I know that reaching for that grip is going to require a Herculean effort and that no rope can be lowered to save me. The wind flutters through my clothes again, but this time more gently, like a pleasant breeze. Okay – let's go.

The fingers of my left hand press into the tiny hole and I delicately push with my feet. I am prone, alone and hanging on with all my strength to the slightest of grips. But this time, as a camera shutter flickers back and forth somewhere diagonally above my head, the grip under the pads of my fingertips is firm. The cliff seems to support me, warm and steady. I reach across to the right, an almost impossible move requiring immense strength and the deftest balance and distribution of weight. Almost overwhelmed with exertion, I am on the very edge again. I grope around with my right hand. It takes an agonising few seconds, my fingers blindly groping… probing… and then I find it! The grip that escaped me last time was there all along, awaiting me, guiding me home. Still trembling with tension I pull myself across to the relative safety of a small but at least visible grip. My feet find the microscopic footholds and suddenly I am in the clear! I am ecstatically happy to have made it past the Crux. I lift my head and smile at the photographer whose camera is going berserk. The lower half of his face matches my own.

"I am completely crazy!" I shout to him, overwhelmed.

I exit the climb to an ethereal moment of jubilation with my family. I cannot describe the joy of these moments. This was and still is the most challenging solo I have ever completed, anywhere in the world and at any time. I still get excited and afraid thinking about it – a multitude of feelings spin around my head at the mere mention of this cliff. By achieving this mythical climb solo, and grasping a supposedly inaccessible grip for rock climbers of small stature, one of the most beautiful pages in the history of solitary escalation had been written. I had completed a stupendous climb. Polpot, the murderer, the tyrant, the torturer of souls, surrendered.

Fear aided my concentration as it will the next time I toil against a tough challenge that wants to get the better of me. For me, fear is indispensable. I would go so far as to say I actually enjoy my adventures because of it. It is a particularly subtle feeling. Fear interferes with your body but when you succeed in mastering it, it does not batter you into submission, nor does it propel you away from the object you confront. Without fear, danger is intangible, thus impossible to appreciate and respond to. The satisfaction of surviving danger is also non-existent without it. The workings of its sensations are much more complex than I would pretend to understand, but fear is hard-wired into us by evolution, and for good reason. And the ability to overcome it, also concealed in our genes, exists there too. But I grapple with buildings and cliffs, not Darwin or Dawkins, and I do it for the pure joy of it. The proximity of my mortal watershed offers an almost sexual excitement. Now don't misunderstand me, I don't get horny up there! Nor do I wish to join any architectural mile-high club. But I definitely experience a sort of ecstasy, an addictive thrill of the chase and the exhilarating rush of release. To realise an impossible movement makes me feel like I am able to influence the elements by the simple force of positive thought.

This feeling of fear does not pour through me only when I am caught in a literal cliff-hanger, nor while I hang off the 60th-storey window ledge of some skyscraper. It pervades every area of my life. Would my wife still love me if, from time to time, she was not afraid of losing me? Does she not worry and care about me more out of fear of a sliding foot or a forearm crippled by exhaustion? I don't know. I simply savour my two decades of marriage to this wonderful woman who has given me three wonderful children.

She understands why I do it, but many people ask me why I pursue such risks. Why risk losing my life, throwing it away? For me it is more about living than dying. Death is something we may feel protected from when we play it safe, but it is always there awaiting us at the end of our lives. Dying slowly from cancer, or as wrinkled geriatrics, or being cut down in the prime of our lives – it's all death at the end of the day and no one on this planet can escape it. The banker who has done the 'responsible' thing his whole life, the health nut who does everything to avoid cancer, we all die. The hardest thing for me is to accept the so-called sensible approach to life. I take risks, yes, but I have no death wish. I love life. My risks are carefully weighed before I act. Okay, sometimes I get it wrong and I end up spending a few months in hospital. But calculated risk-taking prevents me from having to live as a bookkeeper, nurturing money behind the blinds of some sinister office. I indulge in satire because I am fed up of being viewed as irresponsible. A little bit crazy, all right. Irresponsible? No.

Of course not. Playing life safe is much more dangerous.

I guess I can understand why people attach such meaning to wealth or other desires. Yes, a suitcase of money would probably make me smile. But far too many people dream of winning the lottery, convinced that money will make sense of their lives.

While I was illegally climbing the glass pyramid of the Luxor Casino in Las Vegas, what I saw surprised me. Under my hands and feet were thousands of people at gambling machines, trying to change their lives. Small players only willing to risk a few fucking coins, as if paradise could be bought and sold for spare change by vendors in ten-gallon hats. To me, gambling machines symbolise a mediocrity of ambition. If you are looking for a buzz, don't bother going to a casino and gambling only what you can afford. Risking everything you have on the spin of a wheel will give you a far more intense sensation.

"The bigger the fear was, the bigger the pleasure was," wrote Reinhold Messner, the greatest climber of modern times. You won't find him playing a fruit machine.

The other time fear almost got the better of me was when I faced a physical battle every bit as testing as my mental one with Polpot. The second ascent I made in Chicago was very special, one that still gives me goose-bumps when I look back over it. Before the Petronas Towers claimed the title, the Sears Tower in Chicago had stood as the world's tallest building since 1973. And what an incredible tower it is! Not just for its height and pure presence, but for its unique design. The Sears Tower is square at its base but as it climbs it tapers inwards with several receding tiers to leave the segmented core standing proudly clear of the impressively aerial city of Chicago. Cloaked in villainous black, there is more than a hint of Darth Vader about this awesome monster.

The first time I laid eyes on the building it never occurred to me to climb it. That was back in 1994 when I was climbing my first building for that Sector documentary, the climb that inadvertently started it all. At that time it was still the tallest building in the world and I was hugely impressed. Even before I got to the Sears I was astounded by the height of the other buildings in Chicago, and also taken aback by the completely vertical nature of them. The sheer glass fascinated me. But standing at 442 metres with 109 floors – or 110 if you count the mechanical penthouse – the Sears Tower was the zenith of the world's skyscrapers.

I remember I was especially aroused by its height when I visited the Observation Skydeck on the 103rd floor to find a building to climb for Sector. From my vantage point 412 metres up I could look down on a multitude of monoliths, as if I were sitting in an aircraft. Back then I was very much afraid of the prospect of climbing anything man-made and I was not as proud as I am now. Never in a million years would I have believed that anyone could climb that building – and I would have been astonished if I were to find out that the person who would attempt to climb it solo would be me!

But the Citicorp Citibank Building tipped the first domino and led me on a journey all over the world. Over the years, my confidence and ambitions grew and my eye turned towards the irresistible Sears Tower. I made five trips to the city to research the building. I kept delaying ascending it as I would decide it was too risky, too dangerous – but I would always come back for another look. I studied its structure with binoculars from the pavement or from neighbouring buildings, or indeed from inside the Sears Tower itself. I would approach it stealthily at night like a cat burglar and make a few quiet trial climbs at the lower levels to try to crack its code. By night I would study the shift patterns of the security teams and monitor the security cameras to probe for weaknesses. Watching the cameras is fair game, I believe, since they are always watching us. If they have the right to watch us, follow us, snoop around trying to work out what we are doing and where we are going, then I claim the right to do the same in reverse.

On top of my surveillance I had to canvass legal opinion around town to find a good lawyer willing to defend me. Step by step, my dream started to emerge as a possibility. As time passed I peeled further layers of wrapping paper off the Sears Tower and after exhaustive research I became convinced that it was technically possible to do it. It took time to get to this point. In fact it took five years of research and preparations before I was eventually comfortable enough to consider climbing it. Even though I knew it was a technical possibility I was still intimidated by the scale of the challenge – 442 metres plus the difficulties I knew I would face on the way up! This would put my other escalations in the shade. And I could not escape the hard truth that the nature of the technique I would need to employ, coupled with the scale of the tower, could well end with my defeat.

But there is something fabulous about continuously working towards your wildest dream. My relationship with the Sears was a love affair involving five years of flirtation and admiration, five years of passion and yearning. But as with true love, one is happy to wait. One wishes to prolong the intoxicating courtship so that when the magical night does arrive, when one finally gets one's hands on a lover, to explore her and reach those dizzying heights, it is beautiful, meaningful, perfect. I was in no rush to conquer my beloved. In between trips to Chicago I would climb buildings around the world to prepare myself for the biggest challenge of my life.

Finally I have set a date with my tower. My 747 lands at O'Hare International Airport and I check into a hotel downtown, somewhere I can be close to the Sears. I have waited five years for this, five years of keeping this long-distance relationship going. Everything has been planned meticulously.

In the early hours of the morning I leave the hotel and make my way towards the Sears Tower. I am running through my mental preparations as I approach the giant building in the silence of twilight. I can already see the Sears. What a sight! The black monolith is every bit as daunting as the mysterious black slab of Arthur C. Clarke's science fiction masterpiece, *2001: A Space Odyssey*. In fact in the silence of the dawn I can hear the rousing orchestral score of that film reverberating in my head as, like a hairy ape in the movie, I dare to approach the monolith and touch it.

I cast my eyes up towards the black beauty, utterly seduced by this angel. Her chastity beguiles me. But she is a complex character who can turn in an instant. As I take in her alluring lines I can't help but notice she is half-devil too. The black silhouette of the she-devil fills the overcast dawn sky and glares down at me. Her dark skirts, her hunched shoulders… Perched menacingly upon her crown, a pair of radio and television antennae form her satanic horns. How dare I try to mount her? She's not that kind of girl. Just because she is dark and demonic doesn't mean she is available to this foolhardy Frenchman or to anyone else. I know she will not make it easy for me, that I will have to earn it.

But then, before my eyes, she takes on a gentler angelic persona. She allures me. Does she blush a little with the gentle approach of the sunrise? It is hard to tell with this one, but I know that as a demi-angel she will also protect her virtue against my passions. She wavers back and forth just like a true woman. Half angel, half devil… I am attracted by both.

As I approach her sheer glass walls I am almost overwhelmed by the anticipation of a fierce battle. I know this will be my toughest urban climb yet and I will need to fight hard to see the rising sun set tonight. I feel the hairs prickle on the back of my neck, my heart pounding faster. As I approach I seem to shrink, becoming increasingly insignificant before this giant.

The horns of the she-devil are lost as I pace down South Wacker Drive. This is the only face of the building that I can climb, since it is the only side which leads straight up to the 110th floor. I will need to climb in the middle third of the building since it juts in with recesses on either side further up. To climb a face which is set back would allow me to rest before taking on the next leg, but of course it is the perfect way to get arrested and I have no intention of risking that. This escalation will be extreme and my concern had twisted into fear. Earlier I had called Nicole and told her of my state of mind. But as usual, she was more confident than me that I would succeed, and she reminded me of all number of positive things that meant I could make it.

It is 5:43am and I am poised like a sprinter in the starter's blocks. I just have to wait two minutes now as I know that at 5:45 the security guards change shifts. When the shift ends I will have two minutes alone for me to start my climb unmolested.

At exactly 5:45am the guards leave their posts and enter the building. For a moment the Sears Tower is unguarded, and apart from gentle birdsong, the streets are silent and deserted with not even a breeze. The coast is clear. Quickly I steal my opportunity and cross the road. I check left and right and then start climbing the Sears Tower in a relaxed, comfortable way. The first 15 metres are going to be complicated as I need to climb onto the roof of the main entrance, virtually under the noses of the new shift of security guards who could emerge for work at any moment. I must get away from my exposed position near the ground as fast as I can. With so much glass I am totally exposed to anyone inside the wide entrance lobby should they look towards the glass doors. The first few seconds are critical as I don't want to get collared before the ascent has even started.

The main entrance is tricky as I must pull myself up sheer glass onto an elongated triangular hood sheltering the entrance doors. It is not especially easy to navigate but I get around it and make it onto the top.

Now I am off the ground I can start ascending the sheer walls. Although I am on top of this glass veranda, I am not safe yet as I am still plainly visible to the whole lobby. I have to make a good ten metres before I pass out of view. Briskly but securely I scale the vertical glass walls by gripping the panes at their edges and driving upwards with my slippers. I do so with barely a second to spare, because just as I reach the safety zone I see the guards marching through the lobby. Although I can still be seen from inside, I am high enough that they don't tilt their heads up to view me. Below, a line of guards files out the doors. But it is still quite dark and the veranda partly shields me, plus I am quite well obscured against this ebony tower. Oblivious, and resigned to their daily routine, they split to take their posts. Well guys, I am going to liven your day up a little. Soon you'll be having your most eventful shift for a while!

My lawyer George Andrew is already in place nearby and looking up at me. He is ready to talk to the cops when the alarm is raised, which surely must be happening very soon. But by now I am away from the guards and steeled with determination. The doubt of the past few days is left on the pavement and I feel more like a tiger than the humble little mouse I was just a few minutes ago. Fire gushes through my veins now in place of apprehension.

I feel great and keep climbing, clearing several more floors. The escalation is proving to be quite difficult though, as during my trial runs I had only climbed two or three metres, making it impossible for me to gauge how I would feel climbing a substantial section of vertical glass. How will I feel after almost half a kilometre of this? I know already that I will be fatigued. I look for a rhythm but it doesn't immediately come.

Soon I hear agitated yelling below me as the security guards become aware that a figure is moving up the side of their building. As I survey the scene below I see George Andrew in the blood orange sunrise strolling calmly towards the guards to explain the situation. A few listen, hands on hips, while the others tear around pointing fingers and gesticulating. There is more yelling and anger, directed at me though, not at George.

On many of my climbs my partners-in-crime or associates have been set upon by angry security guards keen to vent their anger on someone, but in the USA no one dares assault a lawyer – even though they seem to be as universally disliked in this country as tax inspectors or traffic wardens in other parts of the world. I admit I am perplexed about this American penchant for hating lawyers; it must be something uniquely cultural. In the majority of American sitcoms I have seen, the lawyer is portrayed as a slimy and greedy weasel free of ethics. I wouldn't say that describes George Andrew who seems to be in control of things down there. I allow the minor distractions beneath me to dissipate from my thoughts.

I continue applying my technique – wedging my bound fingers and the tips of my toes hard into the edges of the window frames and pushing upwards with my feet, pane by pane. Quickening and slowing my pace I try to find the harmonics of the Sears Tower so I may move in tandem with them.

I try to find a wise and steady rhythm, but after half an hour I am still having difficulty finding it. The movement I am using is physically draining and even quite painful. My fingertips are bruising as I ram them into the slender gaps, but still I am progressing well and the pavement has already sunk away from me. In the periphery of my vision I notice the subdued flicker of the flashing lights of emergency vehicles reflecting off the glass. A look down reveals an ambulance, a fire engine and a couple of cop cars plus a bunch of people gathering. All seem to be pointing or looking upwards. Some of them look like commuters on their way to work who have stopped to catch the Alain Robert breakfast show. I can only assume that my lawyer is in there handling the cops.

After a dozen more floors I pause for rest and observe that I am now slightly higher than the Citicorp Citibank building that I climbed five years ago. This means I must be approaching the midway point. Encouraged, I feel glad to have made this benchmark, but a glance upwards reminds me that the distance above me is still absolutely huge. The set-back sections jut inwards on either side above me and the lines of the centre of my path converge on a distant point. It is an awesome and breathtaking sight. My next target is to match the height of the next tallest building not far from the Sears, 311 South Wacker Drive. Once I draw level with that I will have climbed 293 metres. That milestone will give me a boost but it will still mean I have another 150 metres to go...

I push on to my next target, sweating and grunting. I am fighting very hard to keep my rhythm and once in a while I am forced to stop to rest. I grip the window groove in one hand by the tips of my fingers, then shake my free forearm to banish the accumulated lactic acid. I peer around to survey the skyline and I am quite happy with my progress, but when I behold the task ahead of me it is still overbearing. Very few of my escalations have ever got this high and virtually none have been so technically demanding. If I complete this challenge this will be the highest building I have ever climbed. The Petronas Towers were recently completed and took the title the year before, but of course I was intercepted at the terrace 80 metres shy of the top and never made it to the summit. Technically this building, with its sheer glass and lack of texture, is immeasurably more difficult. The Petronas Towers have struts and ledges to grasp onto, with ample opportunities to rest. The towers also curve gently inwards toward the spires at the summit, providing support for the climber underfoot. In contrast the Sears is a mirror of featureless black glass, with only narrow grooves around the window panes for grip. The unyielding structure is bolt upright all the way to the top. It is completely flat! Naturally that makes it a lot more tiring.

I flick off the lactic acid in my other arm and resume the climb. But now I have moderated my technique a little and I do not squeeze my fingers into the groove with too much strength, as this is both tiring and taxing on the flesh of my fingers. By now I have settled into my stride and have finally found my rhythm. I am totally focussed on my target. I neither think nor feel. I am like a climbing machine. The building and I are one. Steel and glass, skin and muscle, both fuse into one entity, one being. It is as if we were both created for this moment, this intense present tense. I barely notice the presence of helicopters for the live TV news channels buzzing around the Sears Tower, nor the sirens of the fire trucks and cop cars 200 metres below. I sense the rotating blades of the choppers as they hover nearby but they do not perturb me. It is something akin to the background conversation in a restaurant.

One hand up, fingers wedged, the other hand up, fingers wedged, foot up, toes wedged, push through the foot... metre by metre... floor by floor... total concentration. I am completely alone up here and this is terrific! As I climb ever upwards I am really enjoying the ascent, especially now I have perfected my technique. I know exactly how to jam my fingers and feet in the narrow grooves so I do not tire or hurt myself with each move as I did for the first half of the escalation. I can use precisely the right pressure for a firm but gentle grip.

As I ascend I have to solve various problems as the structure is not regular or uniform all the way up. Sometimes my fingers are not well accommodated by the grooves around the panes or else I encounter difficulties getting my toes into the gaps and need to improvise.

Another positional check and I realise I have exceeded 311 South Wacker Drive and must be a shade above 300 metres! Less than 150 metres remain between me and the top. With two thirds of the escalation behind me, my confidence rallies. I know the home straight will be arduous but I still feel in decent shape and know that despite my mounting fatigue I have a very decent chance of making it to the top.

I climb another two floors, taking care with my feet at this irregular juncture. I am now entering the more dangerous section of the climb. After a while, a climber can't help but tire physically and mentally, and this is when he starts to make mistakes. I have toiled long and hard but still I am nowhere near the summit. Only now do I really appreciate the enormity of this climb. I try to maintain precision in my technique and concentration but it is getting harder. As each floor passes my strength is sapped a little more, but I remain positive and determined.

I am not sure how high I am but I know by now I have climbed higher than I ever have on a building. I am entering new waters. Maybe another 20 storeys or so remain? As I grab the structure, suddenly one of my feet betrays me and slips a little! For a chilling split second I have the heart-stopping sensation that I am falling. But at the crucial moment I am able to react. In a flash I tighten all my muscles simultaneously, arresting the slip before my foot leaves the pane and the rest of me with it. In the blink of an eye I somehow avoid utter catastrophe. Shock sweeps through me. *Fuck!* What was that?

I check out the glass panes and see that the building is dusted in a fine layer of damp... Almost invisible, this condensed layer of vapour took me totally by surprise. When rock climbing, a climber receives advance warning signals from his cliff. Limestone for example is quite white and when it gets wet it darkens significantly to a muddy brown, giving the climber ample notice to take extra care. In such circumstances you are not surprised by the dampness – you can see it. But glass and steel are impervious to moisture and do not react to it, giving no clues as to its presence. You just can't see it until the later stages when it is sodden and pools into droplets on the surface.

I check my airborne surroundings and notice mists. No, not mists. Clouds! Around me float the gentle swirls of stratus fractus clouds which are subtly encircling the peak of the building. As I watch, a grey layer of stratus nebulosis seems to drop, to leave ghostly mists smothering the summit.

There is no doubt that this is a very, very serious development. The clouds pose a considerable dilemma. A wet building is difficult if not impossible to climb. Glass is one of the worst surfaces imaginable when in contact with even the slightest moisture. Unlike rock, water just sits on top of it, lubricating the surface like oil – and I am hanging onto a 442-metre wall of glass.

The grey sky exhales its damp breath like a curse all over the upper floors of the Sears Tower. Climbing further would be unwise in the extreme. I should reverse out of this deadly zone but it is far too late to climb down, there's no way I would make it. Cold fear wells up within me. There is no escape. But I have to avoid panic, and instead concentrate acutely on the side of this building and think fast. I rack my brains to think of another strategy, but can find none. It's a long way up… and an even longer way down. Clouds above, tarmac below. That's my choice. I peer up once more and note with an awful empty feeling that the clouds now obscure the summit of the Sears Tower. The building must be drenched. My chalk will be useless. My feet will be skating around on a vertical ice rink. A second pulse of fear swells through me, shooting out of my kidneys and surging through my veins. I freeze.

I am petrified and at a loss for what to do. If I move, I could slip and fall. But I can't stay here! If I let it, fear will consume me and I shall probably be dead within the hour. I hang onto the building for an eternity, paralysed with fear. I am hoping for a miracle, a blaze of sunlight and a drying wind, but I know it will not come. I am trapped in a diabolical spot.

But my resolve has not totally deserted me and neither has my rationale. It feels like suicide to attempt climbing into the clouds but I know I have enough stamina to put up a fight and I will fight to the end, whether that means reaching the top or, more likely, falling to my death. If the Sears Tower is destined to become my glossy ebony tombstone then so be it. But not yet. I am still very much alive. As I accept my fate, my fear mutates and distorts into something more useful. I draw a deep breath and climb upwards.

Slowly… painstakingly slowly… my focus is absolute. With utmost delicacy I see if I can make the next floor. Right now that is all I can realistically aim for, all I can hope to achieve, but I'll settle for that.

I barely dare to push against the building and try to ascend a little. The effort is momentous, both mentally and physically, and it takes me several minutes to dare to complete this move – but finally I make it up one slippery storey. In all honesty the situation has not improved much, but shit, I am grateful to still be here! If I can pull this off 20 more times then I can make it.

The task ahead of me is overwhelming, and fatigue will most likely claim me before I reach the top – if I don't slip off. Or else fatigue will compel me to hurry and make a fatal mistake. But I am still alive to fight on to the next floor. And I am determined to live.

Time moves very slowly when you teeter between life and death. Seconds, minutes or hours, they are all the same. The world becomes spectacularly vivid and moves in slow motion. The escalation is strenuous and stressful. My fingers jam firmly and painfully into the narrow grooves like they did on the earlier floors, as I try to count less on my unreliable feet. I expect them to go at any moment. More than once, my foot slips a centimetre or so as I gingerly push upwards. My arms are beginning to suffer. This day without doubt has dished up the most challenging climbing conditions I have ever known, far worse than freezing, windswept Paris. Climbing in the clouds is totally uncharted territory for me.

It has taken me well over half an hour to complete just a handful of floors. Despite my exhaustion I remain determined to give it my absolute best. Every now and then I am blanketed by clouds and lose myself in eerie mists. I begin to wonder if this is what heaven will be like. I realise that at any moment I may find out. Climbing an eternal skyscraper through the clouds? Sounds like my idea of a nice afterlife. In one way or another I will be in heaven today: either the spiritual one due to my demise or a very earthly elation due to my improbable success.

The city below and around me becomes lost. I try to remain positive and manage to put another floor beneath me, torturously slowly. I have to hang on a while to recover. Minutes later, with much anxiety and difficulty, I pass another. It seems to go on forever and it feels hopeless but I keep going. Sound distorts in the mist and I can hear my breathing in my own ears. For a moment the clouds break above me and I see the summit within reach, only seven or eight floors above! I get a real boost from seeing the progress I have made. Almost immobilised through exertion, the sight fires me up. The clouds pour over the top like steam from a kettle, obscuring the summit once again, but I have seen how far I have to go. It would ordinarily be impossible in such circumstances, but realising what I have already put behind me, there is a chance I might survive this!

I squash my fingers into the crack and with great effort, blended with the subtlest poise, pull myself another storey closer. Condensation is dripping down the panes. They are sodden. It is insanity to try to climb them. Sweat mixed with dew trickles down my face. My breathing is laboured, my arms feel leaden and my hands are numb with the punishment. Despite my eternal optimism I know I can't hold on much longer. If I don't get out of this soon, that will be it. I really don't know if I can make it but I know I still have a few dregs of fuel sloshing around in the pit of the tank. Gently I wring the lactic acid out of each arm again and press fastidiously upwards.

The clouds break once more and I can now see hazy outlines of people leaning over the edge. Quite a few people by the looks of things – cops, firemen and security personnel – but that is the least of my worries. I dream for a sadistic beating at the top right now! A screaming policeman? A baton charge? I can only dream of such sweet agony.

With the immense mental effort I have put in, I realise my mind is drifting. I refocus on the Sears Tower. I have to be extremely careful, maintain full concentration and not get distracted. Most mountaineers die on their way down, as their concentration lapses and they make fatal errors. I calm myself before I attempt moving upwards again.

My foot judders a little and I lock my muscles in agony. The slip is halted. I am perilously close to tumbling away and I really don't know if I can stop the next time. But soon I make yet another of these cloud-soaked floors, getting to within ten metres of my goal. With the utmost commitment of my life I close, inch by inch, to within touching distance of the summit.

I am forced to stop. My muscles are screaming at me and I am growing a little giddy. I feel the grip of my foot creep a centimetre downwards again, and I haven't the strength to stop it. I'm going to fall. No… my foot holds. It's anyone's guess how much more grip my soaked slippers can provide but I can hear voices very close by. The summit is just beyond my grasp!

With an agonisingly slow yet fully committed push I pause a foot below the top. With all the strength I can muster I stretch out in one final move…

and grab the lip of the wall! I am at the summit and I can barely believe it. My feet are still placed on wet, slippery glass but with a superhuman surge I throw my other hand over the top and finally, *finally* make it to the roof of the Sears Tower. Alive!

I mount the wall surrounded by cops and clouds. My body wants to collapse but instead I stand proud and let rip the biggest roar of victory and passion that ever sprang from my lips. I stand right on the edge of the narrow wall with my arms aloft and bellow from the pit of my soul the cry of a man whose life was taken from him and was then returned. It is the yell of pure life. This ten-second roar must fill the whole of Chicago!

From my surreal pedestal I observe the two dozen cops around me as I continue to explode like a beast then, when my lungs are at last empty, I drop my arms. There is a moment of silence. Mists sweep among us in the still air. Nobody dares touch me or even move. Everybody just stares, many with dropped jaws. Then, after around 30 seconds of this unworldly face-off, I drop down from the wall to the floor of the rooftop to surrender to the authorities. My legs buckle and I sink to my knees and collapse face-first onto the cool, damp concrete.

I feel the sweet sensation of cold handcuffs snapping around my wrists. The muscles at the corners of my grit-speckled mouth are the only ones functioning. Even though I am cuffed and arrested, by definition restrained and captured, I feel the power of freedom deep within me. I know that I am free. I am thousands of times freer than these cops and security people in their rigid uniforms, with their narrow minds and their regulations and their orders. The world is mine! And it is a truly wonderful world and I am alive, truly alive, to enjoy it.

The Sears Tower was without doubt the most challenging urban climb of my career. Ghostly spirits came for me but I broke through them to reach my goal and reclaim my life. I nearly fell to my death but fortunately, of course, I did not! It is a new day, a new life, and everything is utterly beautiful.

Well, nearly everything is beautiful – these guys certainly aren't. As the police and security lift me to my feet I produce my passport and they inspect my ID as usual.

The number of cops and guards sent to arrest me is way over the top. It is certainly overkill and all a bit daft. I have difficulty even communicating, as total exhaustion and several hours of adrenaline have reduced me to jelly. Physically I am bowed but nothing fazes me in the warm afterglow of victory.

After the usual sea of funny looks we head inside for the lift and it doesn't take long to descend to the bottom of the Sears Tower. I watch the numbers passing by on the little display. They pass so effortlessly. Of course I could have made it to the bottom a lot faster if I had given up. But here I am, in the safety of an elevator filled with cops, descending to the ground. We are all making an invisible abseil down a vertical shaft on the end of a secure metal rope... 3... 2... 1... G.

The doors open and the lobby is filled with people applauding and whooping. Cameras and journalists fill the foyer and swarm around me – even I am surprised by the magnitude of the welcome. I am in an electrical storm of photography and microphones are thrust towards me, wavering as close as their bearers' arms can stretch. A barrage of questions comes from all directions.

"Why did you climb the Sears Tower?"

"Is it true you managed to climb all the way to the top without equipment?"

"Were you not afraid of falling? I mean, you could have died, right?"

"You've been arrested! What do you think will happen next?"

I do my best to answer their questions as the cops hustle me out of the building towards the waiting squad car. I can see George Andrew conferring with senior officers on the scene.

Although I have been busted countless times before, I have no idea about the consequences of my latest climb. This is my second escalation in Chicago and after my first here, plus New York, San Francisco, Las Vegas and Philadelphia, my punishment will surely be worse than those that went before. Things definitely took a more unfriendly turn in Philadelphia. But who cares? Not me, that's for sure. I am so exultant I could blissfully spend a year in jail. Whatever you've got, throw it at me – I'll take it with a big smile and be grateful for it!

The car pulls away from the press pack and heads to the police station, sirens wailing and lights flashing. At the station I have my fingerprints taken and pose for the obligatory mug shots. Happiness still radiates from me like I am a blazing torch dipped in paraffin, so I can't help beaming a huge smile on what should be very miserable photos. The cop taking the photo is a bit pissed off and tells me to stop smiling and wear a neutral expression, but I just can't stop grinning like a maniac. I can't help it. The criminal record of Alain Robert is filed away in the Chicago police records with a smile that would have got wedged in the revolving doors of the Sears Tower.

Less than two hours later I am exiting the police station with George Andrew. George has paid for my bail. He tells me straight away that loads of journalists want to interview me and that he has offered to defend me *pro bono*, that is, free of charge and for the public good, as for once he feels he is defending a humorous lawbreaker.

Since there is nothing stopping me leaving American soil I take the return leg of my ticket and depart Chicago, but I return to the city to see George for my lawsuit. On my first court appearance George tells me that if I plead not guilty it may be possible to request a trial by jury. Now this would likely last quite a while, but George reckons I have a good chance of winning it. He thinks that few juries would send me down for what I did.

The bad news is that if I should lose, then I really would get a year in jail. A guilty plea would be much easier to wrap up but of course it would guarantee me a fine and perhaps a brief custodial sentence. How much the fine would amount to or how long the sentence might be, he cannot say, as there is no case he can refer to as a guideline. Well, apart from mine, but that was years ago and things have changed. It largely depends on the judge and his mood.

I head back home to weigh it all up. Back in France I learn that George has negotiated with the prosecutor and in a plea bargain he suggests I should plead guilty to the charge of trespassing on private property, an offence that should result in a minor sentence. I return to the Chicago court once more and make my solemn plea before the judge.

"Guilty, your honour," I declare in answer to the charge of criminal trespass. As defence and prosecution slug it out I sit back and watch the show. It's good entertainment and George seems to enjoy the trial as much as me.

The charge of trespass, as it turns out, is a bit of a masquerade. Since the revolving doors of the Sears Tower start spinning at 6:00am, I committed trespass by climbing the building at 5:45! Strangely enough it is just those 15 minutes that are illegal in the eyes of the law. The rest of the climb is not an issue.

The case quickly wraps up and the judge rules that I am forbidden to climb the Sears Tower before 6:00am for a year! And that's it. No fine, no jail, nothing!

Well done, George. I shake hands with him and thank him for his assistance. George is gracious and tells me he has relished every moment of it, though he too is surprised by the ruling. We hit the bars and celebrate this slapstick conclusion to my incredible adventure in Chicago.

11

ASIA RISING

It seems an easy enough request. Could I climb that traffic light for a photo to go with the story? I am sitting in a little café near my home in France, nearing the end of an interview with a journalist. We have spent two hours talking about my life and as we wrap it up she asks me if I might stand upon the traffic light for a nice and wacky accompanying photo for the article. It is such a ridiculous idea that of course I cannot say no. No problem. So I sprint across the road as she pulls out her camera and I choose a decent-looking traffic light.

The road is a little wet after the morning rain. Not knowing I was to perform a mini climb, I turned up to my interview in my trademark leather trousers and my pointy cowboy boots. But a piffling traffic light hardly warrants climbing slippers or magnesia chalk so I leap up it without a care. We chat casually as I adjust my feet to stand upon the top for an artistic snap, much to the bewilderment of passing vehicles. And then, as I position myself for the photograph, I trip...

I plunge sideways about three metres and find myself sprawled on the ground, half on the road and half on the traffic island. I feel a bit idiotic to have befallen the sort of juvenile accident that would occur to an 11-year-old, but I am more concerned about my left elbow. It has taken the full brunt of my fall and a quick checking over tells me it is quite badly hurt.

The journalist rushes over to see if I am okay, and I tell her that I am basically fine. Blood is dripping off my fingers, making the fall look dramatic, though at least I managed not to land on my face this time and bust my nose again. Still I know I have hurt myself quite badly – my forearm is totally numb. The area from the tip of my fingers to my elbow is completely anaesthetised. Immediately I worry about the nerve I damaged in my second fall of 1982. That time, I severed the nerve which controls the two smallest fingers of my left hand. I was left with restricted mobility.

After numerous operations they did save my hand but since then I have been unable to fully close my fingers – making a fist is impossible for me. Also I suffered quite a bit of muscle wastage in my forearm due to certain nerves and motions being lost. But I learnt to live with it and adjusted my climbing techniques accordingly.

At the foot of this traffic light I can feel that I have done something to that nerve again. My fingers are dead. They won't budge. I cross the road to sit down for a closer examination and it is not good news. But I am keen to finish off the interview, so ten minutes later I am crossing the road and climbing the traffic light again. My left forearm lacks sensation and my fingers are paralysed but still, I can climb it. I stand atop the traffic light, get photographed and then descend. The journalist leaves with her interview and her snap and I head off to the accident and emergency ward to get my arm sewn up.

As it turns out, I need 16 stitches. My fingers are a more serious issue and instead of asking these doctors to look at them I decide to go home and ask my friend Dr Gérard Hoël.

Stitched up, I return home. Since Dr Hoël is not yet available I try some moves on the climbing wall up in my attic. Even basic movements cause me to fall again and again. This is not good at all. I ring my surgeon again and this time I get through. I tell him about my accident and describe how I fell, and report my lack of mobility. Dr Hoël asks a few questions which I answer and after a pause he answers thoughtfully.

"Maybe it will recover in a few days. Leave it and let's see how it gets on. If it continues to cause you problems, Alain, give me a ring and we'll take a look at it."

I take his advice and rest it for a while, but after two or three days it feels even worse. The paralysis has spread and my elbow is swollen like a balloon. So I ring the good doctor up again and report my medical status. On hearing of my lack of progress he suggests I come in.

But there's a problem: in less than two weeks from now I am due to fly halfway across the world to Taiwan, to climb a spectacular new building in the capital Taipei. This structure is the world's newest tallest building, overtaking the Petronas Towers of Malaysia by quite a margin. The building is the much-trumpeted Taipei 101 and for the opening week the government has planned a host of festivities, beginning on Christmas Day and culminating in a gigantic firework display at the official inauguration on New Year's Eve. As part of the celebrations, I have been invited to Taipei to climb it on Christmas Day, for a nice fee. There is obviously no way I can postpone this climb and I will need to be fit on Christmas Day if I am to complete it. The doctor nods and understands my position, but suggests climbing whilst injured is unwise.

"But I can't give up on the assault. I have to climb Taipei 101 and I need my left hand back," I reply. Dr Hoël frowns but responds decisively.

"Okay, in that case we have no time to lose. If you want to make the ascent in Taipei, we will have to operate on you as soon as possible. It will not heal in time, but hopefully at least some functionality should be restored."

I'd happily go under the knife right now, but unfortunately his operating schedule is full and I will have to wait a week before he can fit me in.

It is only six days before my escalation in Taipei, and I have an appointment at Grenoble Hospital. Dr Hoël inspects me once again and admits me for surgery. Within minutes I am wheeled into the theatre. I stare at the operating lights hovering over my head like a UFO as the mask goes over my face. After only a few breaths, the general anaesthetic starts to kick in. The surgeon opens me up and gets to work fixing my paralysed fingers.

Upon folding back the skin and muscle of my elbow, he discovers a lot of blood and fluid around the damaged nerve which needs to be drained off. Dr Hoël next locates the severed nerve and deftly rewires me before stitching me back up again. The operation concludes and I am wheeled out from the theatre unconscious.

Before I went under, I had been worried most immediately about my upcoming escalation in Asia, but more so about my long-term future. Falling time and time again from my climbing wall in my loft gave me a taste of what escalation would be like without these two fingers. I may never be able to climb properly again.

But when I awake, I come round to a success. The surgeon has done a fine job and I can immediately feel the difference. I don't have all the mobility I had before this accident but I have almost all of it, enough to climb, which at the end of the day is all I need. Pleased to have my fingers back I thank the doctor for his handiwork and, a little groggily, I leave Grenoble Hospital. I feel a bit under the weather after the operation but I head to my car. My fingers are able to open the door and grip the steering wheel once more. I put the car in gear and drive back to my place in Valence, something you are not normally supposed to do. I am also supposed to rest, but later the same day I am climbing again in my attic – and this time I don't fall off.

My first impressions of Taipei 101 as I am driven towards it are positive. As I expected, the building is magnificent. Taipei 101 is now officially the world's tallest high rise, smashing the record held by the Petronas Towers. It measures in at a cool 509 metres. That's over half a kilometre high! The centrepiece of the capital's new business district has 101 floors, hence the name. And I will be on hand as it opens to the public next week. Being sponsored by the Taiwanese government to climb the world's tallest building is not the sort of invitation I am going to turn down, even if I am still carrying an injury. The stitches have been removed from my arm but my fingers are still not back to normal. They work, but I am far off 100%, and my elbow and fingers are bound to slow me down.

Assisted by engineers I have inspected the building thoroughly inside and out, and feel amply prepared for the escalation. Taipei 101 is an innovative piece of architecture. I am struck by the originality and intelligence of the structure. Just as the Malaysian Petronas Towers are unmistakably Islamic, Taipei 101 immediately strikes you as Chinese. Robust and block-like, it features a stacked profile which reflects Chinese architecture through the ages. The architects apparently drew upon the pagoda as their inspiration. And also, I am told, they invoked another very Chinese influence in their blueprints – bamboo. The resemblance is more than passing, as eight sections – each tapering inwards towards its base – are inserted into one another in a similar way to the conjoined segments of a stem of bamboo. The design is filled with symbolism, the eight segments representing good fortune as the number eight brings prosperity to the Chinese. Other oriental touches are more obvious, but only a trained eye would note all the abundant *fung shui* references sprinkled throughout the building to bolster fortune and wealth.

Before I know it, the day of the climb is upon me, and I am hanging around at the base of the building. Naturally there's a big press presence for what is a national event and I pose for the cameras with various smiling dignitaries. The building, though unusual, should be relatively straightforward to climb. The first third or so of the tower is effectively a giant base tilting in towards the waist of the structure in a steep incline, roughly ten degrees off the vertical. This part does not bother me too much, although it is primarily a wall of glass. The eight sections above, however, jut outwards with a slight overhang, again around ten degrees off the vertical. At the top of each overhang is a lip upon which I may be able to stand and rest. These overhanging sections are each approximately 50 metres high. Eight sections of glass overhangs on the tallest building in the world! It is quite a challenge even if I were fully fit, not necessarily in terms of technicality, but more in the endurance I will need to display. With the skies clouding over and rain a real possibility I do my best to hurry proceedings a little but of course this is not my show.

And then I feel it... a speck, a tiny drop against my cheek. I glance around and check Taipei's ubiquitous grey horizons. Is it raining? I feel another tiny droplet on my knuckle and then another on the bridge of my rugged nose. There is no escaping it – there is a light drizzle and the wind is also picking up. The media are all assembled and awaiting my escalation but the skies are grey and if it rains heavily the organisers tell me the event will be called off.

In fact they are not happy about me going up there at all even in these conditions. The last thing they want is a dead climber to usher in the opening of their glittering project, a project which cost the best part of two billion US dollars. That sort of opening would not only be a public relations disaster, it would be seen as an omen of bad fortune, something that could affect the desirability of rental space and have financial repercussions, not to mention severely denting the image of success this new building is meant to impart.

So they insist that I use a safety device to scale the tower. I have mixed feelings and try to talk them out of it, but in truth I expect this stance from these guys. There were mentions of such safety devices before I came. I ask if they don't mind dropping the idea but they are adamant they will not risk my life and say the deal is only offered so long as I take these precautions. But they are still keen for me to go ahead if I feel the conditions are not dangerous. A little reluctantly, but philosophically, I agree.

Soon, equipped with a simple belt attached to a cable, I am at the foot of the building gazing up. This cable does not support me in any way; it is only there in case I fall off. It feels a bit of a con to have this thing attached to me, but still it is a ropeless escalation and I am getting paid to climb the world's tallest building.

The summit is very distant and the tower has a weird appearance from this angle, as if it is collapsing or folding in on itself like a house of cards. Someone asks me how long I think the ascent will take. I gaze up at the structure and hazard a guess, responding that I believe I can complete this climb in around two and a quarter hours.

On the carpet in front of the assembled press and audience I focus my mind on the gargantuan structure above. I blot out my surroundings, and once the tower and I connect, I attack. I clasp the edges of the glass panes and step upwards at a similar angle to a ladder. Quickly I note that the fingers on my left hand provide some resilience, but with surgery less than a week behind me, they lack proper strength and grip. The ability of my left hand is significantly reduced but I believe it will be enough. As I test it out I am fully confident that I will complete the climb.

As I ascend I familiarise myself with my physical limitations and the building itself. The tower is fully glazed, with each pane set an inch or two in from steel sills, giving me a narrow ledge to hold onto with my fingers and push against with my toes. There's not an awful amount to play with, but in urban climbing terms it is comparatively generous. It is much more supportive than the Blue Cross-Blue Shield or the Sears, for example, which were bolt upright and offered no protrusions at all. The unfortunate incident with the traffic light means my movements are curtailed a touch and it will take me a little longer to make the summit. But it does not handicap me that much and the base proves easy enough.

Being not quite vertical, the first section is a nice warm-up. I adapt to the dimensions and materials of each floor and start to find a sensible pace. Every eight floors I stop for a breather, which pleases the assembled Taiwanese. The little cable dangling down to my belt makes the authorities feel better but it rather irritates me. I would like to detach it for a little more freedom and a lot more fun but I can't upset my gracious hosts. And besides, I have given my word. I put up with this annoying dangling thing and despite both the cable and the gentle rain I complete the base, the first third of Taipei 101 and the best part of 200 metres, in good time.

I pause a while and give the crowd a little wave to happy cheers, though there seem to be a few less of them now then when I started! It's not that wet but people are always averse to a bit of drizzle. The next part is going to be a little more tricky. I must get past the first of the overhangs. I reattach myself to the cable and attack the first of the eight overhanging sections. Climbing an overhang is of course technically and physically more challenging, as the outwards slant means gravity wants to pull you away from the surface. If you slip there is no recovery. The weight of my body pulls on my fingers but they feel secure. Ordinarily this overhang would be easy, but doing it with only one good hand means I need to take it a little more seriously. But I find it is perfectly manageable and I adjust my movements until I find my rhythm. After a quarter of an hour or so I reach the top of the overhang and make it onto the first ledge. Almost 50 percent of the building is behind me in terms of height, but the overhangs will be much slower than the base.

Still feeling fresh and with no problems so far, I don't pause for rest before taking on the second overhang. I grasp onto the ledges and ascend the first floor of the second section. But by the time I complete this section the drizzle has given way to a proper downpour. Big raindrops tap against me now. Below me is a mosaic of umbrellas but the crowd has shrunk significantly. I survey the structure above me. The building is soaked! This appealing escalation was originally quite straightforward, even if it boasted the grandest dimensions in the world. But now it becomes a lot meaner. With the ledges and frames it is not impossible but it is certainly a lot more difficult. If this had happened on the sheer glass of the Sears Tower or in Philadelphia I would certainly be dead by now, but here the abundant metal features of the building provide a still graspable structure.

The rain belts down more heavily as I make progress. The organisers have rather superfluously stationed nurses and rescue teams at each section, to step in if needed. But even though I am not particularly pleased with the weather, not for a moment do I consider abandoning the ascent.

The wind and rain is really picking up. Coming down in sheets, it forces me to slow down. I am completely drenched! My left hand begins to seize up with the damp and the wind chill, but I overcome the fourth section and take a breather. I don't bother waving this time and just get on with tackling the fifth. I need to stop regularly for rest because of the gusts pushing me sideways. The rain abates a little as I tackle the sixth overhang, but then picks up again on the seventh. Although I am towering above Taipei the truly miserable weather means I can barely see anything of the city. It is lost in an opaque milky blanket. While most of the western world must be waking up to Christmas morning in their cosy homes, unwrapping their presents, I am buffeted by gales and having buckets of cold water thrown over me by the heavens.

Christmas Day is not an especially good day to make an escalation in Taiwan, and certainly not the day I would have chosen. Dripping wet, I reflect that this is not the first time a date imposed by sponsors has caused me big problems due to adverse weather.

Back in 1999 I made an aborted ascent of the Grande Arche in La Défense. For many years I had harboured a desire to go up this modernist cube-like version of the Arc de Triomphe. The arch had caught my eye when I first searched for likely projects in the Parisian business district and had stayed with me ever since. The finale, a huge and only hypothetically climbable overhang, represented an immensely difficult – and irresistible – challenge.

I got the perfect excuse to ascend it when a company stepped forward to sponsor me for this technically demanding 110-metre climb. Everything looked good except for one thing: the date. Unfortunately for me, the date they set for the climb was in September, and September that year was unseasonably hot. If the choice had been mine I would have postponed the climb to a cooler day, but my sponsor had already set wheels in motion and against my better judgement I found myself climbing a hot marble arch in searing sunlight. How did it all end? I became blinded by the dazzling reflection of the sun off the white marble, and ill with heatstroke and dehydration halfway up the arch. I had to be winched down to safety by rescuers on ropes. It was an ignoble conclusion to what should have been a noble climb, and it taught me that I ought to set my own parameters when making escalations. Right now, hanging off the world's tallest building with an injured left hand and going through nature's carwash, I am beginning to wonder if I have made the same error again.

After numerous pauses due to the withering effect of the relentless rain I arrive at the top of the seventh section, where the president of the building leans out of a window to greet me. We enjoy a friendly chat about how each other is getting on, the weather, and the other meaningless small talk you might exchange with your neighbours. After this interlude I make for the final overhang. Continuously drummed by heavy raindrops, the going is slow and laborious and my hand is becoming increasingly bothersome. But I slog it out and eventually close in on the top of the world's tallest tower. It has taken all day but the summit is at last within my reach.

It is a great relief to clamber over the top. I am tired. I am aching. I am bursting for a piss. But it's all smiles up here. Instead of the usual grim gathering of security guards and police, a festive public relations reception welcomes me. I give a big wave to the loyal crowds far below and I am interviewed by the TV crews. Then I follow the organisers' carefully crafted script and fly the flag bearing the building's logo for the cameras.

In the end the escalation of Taipei 101 has taken me almost four hours, nearly double my estimate. My hand feels pretty bad but I am grateful that it held out for the whole ascent. The management have raised international awareness that their building has taken the title of the world's tallest, so they are happy. I have my climb and the reporters have their story. Even the cops and security guards are happy. I tell the organisers that I would like to return one day and climb this building without a rope, and they make positive noises. I would certainly like to come back and do it my way. But overall I must be content, especially bearing in mind the state of affairs I found myself in with my lifeless hand just a week ago. A lot was against me but I have pulled it off and added the world's tallest building to my sticker album. All in all it's been a good day's work and I retire to my hotel room satisfied and relieved. As the raindrops tap on the window I switch off the lights and sink into a blissful and much-needed sleep. And since I have been invited, I stick around to catch the gigantic firework display which bursts from Taipei 101 six days later. Rockets and explosions of every shade of the rainbow flare and light up the night sky, ushering in a quite brilliant new building, a bold new year, and exciting new challenges ahead.

There are a lot of exciting things going on in China at the moment and the statistics coming out of that country are staggering. What we are witnessing is probably the adolescence of a potential superpower. For climbers the country has always been a marvel, with countless mountains and rocky crags spread across its vast territory, not to mention the entire northern side of the Himalayas. The limestone region of the southwest, for example, contains no less than half of the world's caves, many of which are undiscovered by potholers.

From an architectural perspective China's great cities have always been broad and flat with wide boulevards and few high rises. Although the traditional buildings were designed with artistic grace, the architecture of the communist era was decidedly ugly and drab, and sometimes so utterly disgusting that the completed structures may quite seriously be considered masterpieces of grotesqueness. A drive around the suburbs of Beijing reveals some truly revolting buildings, buildings that surely required a concerted effort to be made so hideous. This assertion however is likely to hold less water day by day as China tears itself down and rebuilds, such is the construction whirlwind sweeping the country. There are plenty of monstrosities left today, but who knows what will be left of the suburban belts of old carbuncles tomorrow? What is certain is that as the country booms China will play a leading role in taking construction to new extremes. The Three Gorges Dam, for example, is a mammoth endeavour and formerly flat cities like Beijing and Shanghai are suddenly rocketing skywards with ambitious construction projects. And as Chinese cities transform, a generation of new world-class skyscrapers are sprouting up and attracting the eyes of the world... mine included.

It is a late spring night and the streets of Shanghai are quiet and empty. Four of us are squashed into the back of a stationary taxi in the Lujiazui financial district of Pudong. This neighbourhood on the banks of the Huangpu, which thrives by day, has become the premier business zone of China. Lujiazui sports some attractive new buildings. The Oriental Pearl Tower dominates the skyline with its pink and silver space-age spheres and concrete columns pointing to the stars like a rocket on a launch pad. This impressive television tower however is impossible to climb and is not the reason I am here. Having attacked the three tallest buildings in the world – Taipei 101, the Petronas Towers and the Sears Tower – I am here to conquer number four: Shanghai's Jin Mao Building.

In the car with me is my photographer friend Emmanuel along with John and Pete, two British friends based in Hong Kong. We are sitting across the darkened road from the entrance of the building, plotting. From here we can see the Jin Mao Building clearly and I can plan my assault on it.

The building itself may be very tall but it is also very, very easy to climb. The latticework cladding means it is effectively a giant climbing frame from base to peak. My six-year-old son could climb it. In fact I could quite honestly make the summit with one arm tied behind my back. The management of the Jin Mao Building are well aware of this, and low-key earlier inspections revealed a substantial security presence as well as the installation of anti-climbing spikes around its base. These unfriendly additions are similar to anti-pigeon spikes and are placed on the exposed ledges with the aim of making it impossible for a climber or intruder to scale the exterior of the building. Somehow I must get past these well placed spikes, spikes which the security services have placed at strategic positions after consulting professional climbers. If I manage to breach the protection afforded by the security forces, who in China are usually ex-PLA soldiers, and if I can get around the anti-climbing obstacles, I will be away and no one will be able to stop me.

In the hushed rear of the taxi I describe my plan to my accomplices. The entire base of the Jin Mao Building is ringed with a protective barrier of these spikes, and guards are positioned at regular intervals around the tower. Security here is tight. But for all the precautions taken by the security team I have uncovered the Achilles heel of China's tallest building. Sure, there is no way up any of the flanks of the tower from the ground, and the security team looks quite sharp. But adjacent to the tower is a theatre, and this is attached to the Jin Mao Building by a glazed lobby area which allows passage between the two. The theatre is clad in marble but its walls are not quite vertical, each marble panel very slightly set back from the last. Scaling the theatre will not be too tricky if I can get up it without any interference, but I will be totally exposed for several minutes and highly visible in the heart of a crowded business district. Even more so bearing in mind I intend to do this climb in my Spiderman costume...

From the roof of the theatre I can get across to the tower where, at this elevation, there are no anti-climbing spikes. But it all depends on the security guards. They patrol the building and its entrances in their dark suits and sunglasses and there is not a sufficient gap between them to allow me to run and make my assault. But I find a partial blind spot at the corner of the theatre, a place where I can go up just hidden from their view. John and Pete will need to distract the guards at the entrance to keep their eyes off this corner while Spiderman dashes up and across the theatre and crosses onto the Jin Mao Building. Their distraction may involve the ruse of being lost tourists with a huge map unfolded and flapping in the wind. A documentary film crew will be there tomorrow, once again keeping their distance and acting as if it is all one big coincidence. For this climb, timing and positioning are absolutely crucial.

We go over the plan in the back of the taxi like bank robbers then decide to head up to the 87th floor of the Jin Mao Building to enjoy a drink in Cloud 9, the world's highest bar. From the swanky interior of the darkened bar I survey the night horizon and take a little glance at the latticework cladding. Then quietly I raise a glass and toast the next day's climb.

The next day the documentary crew is ready and we all meet in my hotel lobby. My Chinese fixer Mr Lu is also on hand as the film crew prepare their equipment. I am a little concerned about the weather, as the sky has clouded over. If the marble walls of the theatre get wet I might well struggle to get off the pavement, something I cannot afford to do. But the weather forecast for the coming days is worse, so it is clear that if this is to go ahead, I will need to go up today.

I prepare my Spiderman costume and bandage my fingers in the hotel bar. I have informed a Reuters journalist of my climb but I am a bit concerned when a BBC reporter also turns up. The number of cameras and reporters is growing in the hotel lobby. It seems more and more media know about the climb. This could be problematic if not properly managed, as a sudden press presence at the tower would certainly alert the security services.

After a few coffees I decide it is time to go and immediately everybody splits to take their positions. Emmanuel has managed to negotiate a prime elevated position in a luxury apartment facing the Jin Mao Tower. I jump in a van with some of the crew while the cameras head for a rooftop bar opposite the theatre. John and Pete mill around not far from the Jin Mao, preparing to look lost. As we cruise around the Lujiazui district in the van I don my Spiderman costume. I tell the crew to translate to the driver that it is imperative they drop me off at exactly the right place. It must be inch perfect – I cannot be seen crossing the road dressed like this and I must be dropped in the tiny blind spot between two guard positions. If he gets this wrong we must circle again.

We take a turning and approach the Jin Mao, and I prepare to either run out or tell the driver to make another pass. But he nails it perfectly and I spring out of the van and attack the near-vertical marble of the theatre. There is a security guard only a few metres away from me, just around the corner, and I cross my fingers he is currently occupied. Marble is an unforgiving surface but I grip the inch or so jutting out of each slightly staggered panel and rapidly climb ten metres onto the terrace of the theatre. I am glad I am off the ground but I am still very vulnerable up here on the terrace. It is totally exposed to the street and the entire tower.

Some 50 metres dead ahead of me is a set of double doors leading from the top floor of the theatre onto the terrace. To the right of that, the terrace leads over to the roof of the glass entry lobby between the theatre and the tower. While the theatre is windowless and marble, the region ahead is pure glass. Anyone in that lobby looking up will see Spiderman running across the terrace. My fear is that there will be a guard or two behind the double doors. I worry they may spring open at any moment! Already, as I sprint along the terrace towards the glass lobby, I notice that a pair of businessmen below have stopped dead in their tracks and are looking up at me. There is no guard here but now I am right above a glass lobby full of security guards, concierge staff and passers-by. I must make it to the lobby rooftop and cross onto the tower without delay.

I hop over the banister and drop onto the rooftop, but of course with all this glass I am immediately noticed. Black-suited security guards are scrambling in all directions under my feet. I make it over to the tower just as they pour out into the courtyard and onto the terrace. But it is too late for them! I reach the scaffold-like cladding and grab the bars and vault up the side of the tower. In no time at all I climb the first floor. To my right, the courtyard now holds a small group of people gathering to see what the fuss is about. Security are running around like headless chickens holding their earpieces and barking into their radios. People in the courtyard are pointing at me. Who is that guy scaling the Jin Mao Building? It looks like Spiderman!

The Jin Mao is a piece of cake to climb. A pushover! It really is as easy as climbing a ladder. It slightly resembles Taipei 101 in terms of architectural influence – again the pagoda is the source of inspiration and there is a series of overhangs, but everything about it is much easier. The overhangs bunch together the higher I go, but all are minor and brief. The Jin Mao is a nice leisurely climb offering no real test at all. The only real obstacles, the security measures, are well behind me.

As I climb I remove my face mask for ventilation and to get a better look at my surroundings. I see excited office workers on the inside gleefully photographing me with their mobile phones. As I gain more height I decide to climb around a corner and onto a new face to get a better view of Lujiazui and Pudong. Next to this tower, work is underway on a mighty skyscraper that will surpass the Jin Mao – the Shanghai World Financial Center. It is only half-complete but I can already see how the tower will narrow to a chisel-like blade at the top. What a building that will be… I can see that hundreds of construction workers have downed tools and are watching my ascent. Some construction manager somewhere will wonder why he is behind schedule!

With my vivid red-and-blue costume I can be seen very clearly from the ground, and below me there's quite a commotion. The road has been closed and people are flooding towards the tower. The courtyard has been taped off, cops are everywhere and a fire engine has turned up. Later my friends will tell me that men they guessed were government agents were on the scene, no doubt coming to check that my ascent was not political. Had I climbed with a Taiwanese flag or a portrait of the Dalai Lama on my back I imagine things could have been very different. In fact my legal research into this ascent had not left me particularly confident about what would happen on my arrest. China is obviously one of the world's strictest countries, and falling foul of the authorities here can get ugly. But I am only climbing for fun and I am here purely to enjoy myself. The way I see it, China is joining the world's elite in high rise construction, and I want to embrace their integration with the world in my own special way.

Below me the firemen are going to town. They unravel a giant inflatable mattress directly under me. It always amuses me when I see this pointless fuss and I decide it is time to mess them around a bit. I start climbing diagonally, so that if I fall I will miss their mattress completely. As soon as they realise I am wandering away from them, I see them scampering around and dragging the enormous semi-inflated mattress after me. I let them settle it under me and start inflating it again, then I reverse and move back in the other direction. Again they shuffle this colossal mattress back to its original position. I keep on climbing upwards, negotiating overhangs, but every now and then I shoot off sideways, dragging King Kong's orange lilo with me below.

In only 20 minutes or so I approach the 88th floor, the summit of the building. The firemen have given up. By now I have climbed around the corner of the tower and back over the entry lobby connecting with the theatre. If I were to fall I would smash through the glass lobby in glorious Hollywood fashion.

The number 88 is of course representative of good fortune and it has also turned out to be a lucky number for me today. I make the summit with ease and take in the city, enjoying the moment. I have not climbed right over the top, as up here I see the angry-looking men in black from the security services as well as the Chinese police. I don't fancy getting arrested up here away from the eyes of the media and the crowds. I have no idea what these guys will do to me, and besides, the cheerful crowds below deserve a big finish. So, just as I reach the top, I give the crowds a big wave, to loud cheers. I pop my head over the edge, give the cops a friendly wave, then I reverse down again. More cheers from the ground! I start my descent, hopping rung by rung down the latticework cladding, vaulting in bounds down the overhangs. Every now and then I stop to encourage the crowd. As I near the lower floors I see all sorts of people on the streets: chefs and waiters who have abandoned the little restaurants across the road, taxi drivers, business folk, scores of joyous international school kids, and amongst the flashing lights and throng, badly parked coaches which have pulled up and deposited dozens of tourists who point their camcorders skywards.

I am returning to my starting point, the roof of the entry lobby, and I see that directly below me are the same police and security guards I saw at the summit. Any arrest will be in full view of the crowds and the news cameras, which should help protect me from any aggression. The police at ground level look like they are struggling to contain the crowd, which edges forward as I near the lobby rooftop.

A few floors above the glass lobby I pause. I pull out my mobile phone and make a call to Nicole to let her know everything went well. The impatient police shift uncomfortably as laughs ring out from the masses. After a brief chat with my wife I decide it is time to call it a day. The climb went as well as I could have hoped and was well received – by the crowds anyway. For the grand finale I replace my Spiderman mask, to applause and laughter. Then I descend the final few rungs of the cladding into the hands of the police. The police restrain me in a civilised manner in front of the cameras, and as the crowd pushes forward through the tape they quickly push me through the double doors on the theatre terrace. As I am led inside I see some of the crowd breaking into a run for the rear entrance where, I imagine, rumour has it I will be transferred into a police car. The cops barricade the doors as the Jin Mao Building is besieged by the fervent public and media.

Within hours the story is distributed nationally and throughout the world through the internet and on various international news channels. But what makes this climb a little different is the size of the country. Here in China the story features quite prominently. Television pictures, radio broadcasts and newspaper stories spread out across the world's most populous land. The news that a slightly strange Frenchman climbed the country's tallest building dressed as Spiderman, and was then arrested, is fanned out to more than a billion people.

So what is it like being arrested in China? Well, you are definitely on your own. A word of advice: don't bother hiring a lawyer. It may sound crazy not to acquire legal counsel in a country where you have no understanding of the language, let alone the judicial system, but believe me, it's a pointless exercise. The lawyer I hired in China is a total waste of time. He can't even visit me in jail – not even once – and I hear nothing from him. He did warn me that the legal system in China is different to other countries but I did expect more for the US$1,500 I paid up front. All he did was to tell me a while ago that I could expect a fortnight in jail. This advice, which I could have been given in less than a minute, turns out to be the full extent of his legal services! I never see him again and he leaves me to rot in there. What a crook. One wonders what lawyers actually do in China; they seem more like expensive translators of legal text than people able to represent your interests. I would guess that the Chinese have greater reason to hate their lawyers than the Americans.

The legal system here is a quagmire and being on the wrong side of the law is not pleasant. I have no idea what is going on. My fate lies totally in the lap of the authorities and whatever they decide, and that's all there is to it. The French Embassy is involved in my case but they have no real power or influence.

I am however pleasantly surprised at how well I am treated in prison. I am placed in a cell with five Chinese inmates and our whole day is very well organised. From six in the morning until nine at night there is always something to do, apart from weekends when some sessions do not feature. At 6:00am we listen to the national anthem and then other inmates bring us our toothbrushes. Next, they bring us each a bowl plus a container of hot water so we can freshen up. These are refilled three times a day so we can drink, wash our dishes and take our daily improvised shower. Cameras in the cell keep an eye on us and three times a day we sit for hour-long meditation sessions where we have to remain seated and silent. The cell is clean and the food is okay for a non-Chinese prisoner. While I am there we are never allowed out of the cell, but I have enough space to stretch and exercise and perform some of my climbing techniques, which greatly interest the prison guards who have probably never seen a European inmate. Also I find that I can communicate with my cellmates. Even though their English is basic we still manage to communicate throughout my incarceration. Some prisoners give me milk and pastries, things they are allowed to purchase every two weeks. I learn that some of them have been in this cell for two years, for petty crimes such as stealing a hundred dollars. Besides our chats, every hour or so there is something happening and I am surprised at how quickly the day passes.

Soon I learn my fate. Unlike other countries there is no trial to speak of, and I am told that the cops themselves decide how much time I will get. Cops, judiciary, army – the distinction in China is not all that pronounced. According to my long-departed lawyer, a swindler who ought to be in here for two years instead of my cellmates, I can expect 15 days. Apparently it goes to a vote and they elect how long they think I deserve. A couple of cops might have said ten days, others none, one may have said three, another 20 and so on. They total it up and split the difference and the number of days I end up getting inside turns out to be five. It is good news, not least because I am still wearing the clothes I was arrested in, since they do not issue prison clothing. Five days in a Chinese jail dressed as Spiderman is a bit of a drag. I like the costume, I really do, but enough is enough.

I am told I am being deported and must purchase a ticket to France. I state that I would rather go back to Singapore as I already have a connecting flight to Paris from Changi Airport and I need to collect my luggage there, but I am told that as a deportee I must fly to my country of origin. I speak to the vice-consul but she informs me that they have no power in this matter and if the Chinese authorities say I am being deported to France, then I am being deported to France. It is annoying but I have no choice.

The days pass quickly and before I know it, it's time to go. I leave my cellmates behind with some warm handshakes and wish them all the best, and the cops escort me from the jail to a waiting car. They take me directly to Shanghai Pudong International Airport and march me through immigration without delay. Immigration officials join the party, none of them leaving my side for a moment. They all take me through the gate and onto the plane. Once I am on board they inform me that the People's Republic of China will not permit me to enter the country again for at least five years. From previous experience I know this sort of episode does not bode well for my next visa application.

Once they have served this notice, the cops and officials disembark. The doors shut, the engines whine into life and soon afterwards I am airborne. Within eleven hours I land in Paris and quickly purchase another ticket and then fly to Singapore – to pick up my fucking luggage.

Not long ago the internal magazine of the Quai d'Orsay (or more specifically, the French Ministry of Foreign Affairs, rather than the quay upon which it sits) published an interview with me. The magazine is intended for French diplomats and is distributed to every country where France has diplomatic activity. With the embassies having intervened a number of times in countries like Malaysia, the editor of the magazine felt French diplomats may be interested in my escapades and what could be learnt from my various cases. Many diplomats have heard of my escalations and my arrests in far-flung corners of the world.

The opportunity to feature in such an article attracted me. I felt there was a chance it could be beneficial if these guys knew a little about the problems I encountered and how things unfolded in various countries. I figured that perhaps one day in the not too distant future, having climbed a high rise in some country with a frosty judiciary, that the embassy might be aware of some strategy or approach which might help me out. In numerous countries diplomatic intervention at the right time, before irreversible decisions are taken, could indeed get me out of jail. There have been times when embassy staff have been helpful even if they are actually quite limited in their power. In Shanghai they could do little to assist me other than express an interest in my case. But this in itself is useful as it does at least help ensure humane treatment. Here and there, diplomatic intervention has saved me days or weeks in jail. The French embassy managed to help me out of a real corner in another Asian country where I could have ended up spending months in prison.

Generally speaking, my experience of the authorities – the police, judiciary and jails – in Asian countries has been eventful. With one or two notable exceptions the countries of the Far East tend to take a hard attitude to the apprehension and incarceration of their citizens, or indeed foreign nationals. And it has very little to do with the level of economic development of that country, or its political climate, for you may be surprised to learn of the nation whose police gave me the worst welcome at the top of a building and whose judiciary took the sternest stance. Sure, Malaysia may be the worst once you are arrested, and its jails are hellholes from another century, but the most violent police while making an arrest? Japan. This escalation in Japan took place nine years before my recent ascent in Shanghai.

As expected, I find Tokyo an immensely crowded city with a very vertical skyline. The term 'concrete jungle' is more apt here than just about anywhere else on the planet. The metropolis is a heaving mass of concrete and glass crawling with humanity. After a day or two's location scouting I realise that as modern as Tokyo is, most of its buildings are very similar and functional, and they seem to have gone up in the 1970s and 1980s. For such an advanced people the architecture is actually rather homogeneous, unadventurous and bland, even in their most prestigious buildings. One or two pleasing exceptions to this include the Yokohama Landmark Tower, which looks like a giant cuboid rook in a space-age chess set, but on closer inspection this tower turns out to be impossible to climb. Tokyo's architecture is really quite a reflection of the uniformity of this remarkably harmonious society where individuals also seem to make a concerted effort to blend in. I am a little surprised to learn there are few outstanding pieces of architecture in terms of aesthetics or dimensions, but having said that, Japan is a fun place to be and I am certainly not short of options.

After some touring I settle on the Shinjuku Nomura Building, a satisfying white skyscraper in the Nishi-Shinjuku district standing a few inches shy of 210 metres. The architects have thoughtfully separated the hundreds of windows with little vertical pillars which run top-to-bottom only a metre or so apart, giving the skyscraper a decidedly grille-like appearance. The chief reason I opt for the Shinjuku Nomura, beyond its respectable height, is that these sharp pillars also give me a pair of parallel surfaces to wedge myself between.

The day before I am due to climb, I inform the media about my impending escalation. I call a number of newspapers and television channels to let them know what I intend to do. One of the calls I make is to NHK, the public broadcaster of Japan.

On the day of the climb I approach the Nomura Building with a friend. As the building comes into view I immediately see that it is surrounded by a sea of cops, security guards, curious onlookers and a sizeable contingent of journalists – from Nippon News Network, Fuji News, NHK, All-Nippon News and TV Tokyo, plus all number of newspaper journalists and independent paparazzi – hundreds of people are awaiting my arrival! A police cordon is in place, not that I would be able to get that far, such is the impenetrable wall of bodies before it. I am stunned by the turnout. Yes, I was expecting some sort of reaction, but nothing like this. Even though the scene is a hive of activity, as I exit the car hundreds of eyes turn towards me and fingers point in my direction. I am wearing a bright red leather jacket and yellow pants and of course they all know I must be the guy who is going to climb the building.

Immediately everyone closes in, cameras rolling as a bunch of serious-looking cops approach me and read out a statement. They inform me that I am prohibited from climbing the building, that they are very serious about this, and that the law in Japan is very tough. I am listening to the Japanese police delivering their stern warning and, you know, I am laughing a little bit. This stand-off with the cops, surrounded by microphones and cameras, is a mildly humorous exchange. The cops aren't quite used to all this media attention whereas I am quite relaxed. They try to impress upon me the severity of their warning but as they do so they struggle to communicate, tripping over their words a little. I know my English isn't great but their hapless effort, delivered as if it were a diabolical tongue-twister in front of the nation's press, is pretty hard to take seriously. I shrug and laugh a little more. What they say is not going to have any effect on my actions. I am smiling playfully and thinking to myself, "Yeah, sure, I don't give a shit!"

Of course, cocooned within a cornfield of human bodies, I can't hope to make the ascent right now. But in spite of the enormous scrutiny of security, police and barging press I know I can make an escalation today. Surrounded by this circus, the Shinjuku Nomura Building is conspicuously off-limits, but it is only one of three buildings in the area which is climbable.

I leave the cordon of the Nomura with a smile, trailed by press and police. I guess it is obvious to everyone that I am unperturbed by the warning from the cops. As I walk down the street the police follow several paces behind. If I want to, I could head towards one of the other buildings I have earmarked as backups, though I do have an inconvenient number of journalists and cops in tow. Both buildings are close by. I know that if I get within a few yards of my alternative site and start running the cops won't catch me – I can be off the ground and out of reach within seconds. I walk a few blocks but the cops are still sticking to me like limpets – or perhaps some other local variety of immovable shellfish they like to serve sliced up and raw.

A Tokyo ascent is achievable even with my escorts but I am not sure if it is the best time or the best way to start a climb. Right now I feel a little under pressure. Every time I pause in the street, the cops are radioing in the latest on my movements. I enter a mall and they follow; I pop into a shop here and there and the cops come with me. I go into a space-age public toilet and they come in there as well. While I urinate the cops watch on, crowding the restroom and drawing bewildered and nervous looks from my fellow urinators. What man wouldn't feel uncomfortable in such an exposed position under the watchful gaze of the country's law enforcers?

Maybe like Singapore these strange guys have toilet-flushing laws and the local urinators are afraid they might be caught for some sort of lavatorial offence. I can't help but be amused by this bizarre level of dutiful detail. Who knows, judging by the Japanese obsession with cleanliness and order and the eccentricity of their toilets, there could be such laws. In case you have never sat on one, Japanese toilets are fitted with controls and buttons that would look at home on the Starship Enterprise. Functions include seat warming, air extraction, water-squirting bidet controls for temperature and power (we French appreciate this) and even an air dryer to gently evaporate any moisture left behind by the electronic bidet. Going to the toilet in Japan is certainly quite an experience, and perhaps for many, the highlight of their trip. But I am not here to sit around with a newspaper, I have only popped in to release a little pressure on my bladder.

The omnipresent cops report to base that urination has ceased and that I have washed my hands. Once I am done, we all emerge from the toilet together. And as I emerge from the lavatory with a bunch of cops I find that the press are still waiting expectantly. This whole situation is getting increasingly weird. I am just trying to go to the bathroom. Why should this be of such interest to everyone? News reporters ask me what I am going to do, what my plan is. An escalation is a possibility but I prefer to be better prepared and with a slightly safer distance between myself and the police force. So I keep walking, followed by the police and a few diehard reporters until I take the subway train. Finally, as I pass through the turnstiles, the cops and the last of the press drop off and I board the train with only my friend for company. He shakes his head and smiles at me. I shrug and smile back. Okay, we won't be doing it like that again.

Back in my room I reflect on the day's events. Today's shenanigans did offer some comic relief but it was clearly not the best time to make an ascent. Obviously someone amongst the press must have grassed me up to the cops. As it turns out, NHK were the ones responsible for the phone call to the police informing them of my intentions. NHK is funded by the government and therefore does not operate in the same way as the rest of the nation's press. Usually the press value confidentiality and won't shoot themselves in the foot by sabotaging a developing story. The public broadcaster though is compelled to put the law before protecting its sources. After a period of contemplation back in my room I make another few calls to the news correspondents.

"Okay. I am going to make it tomorrow. But this time, I will not reveal exactly which building I will ascend. This time I will just tell you the time of my climb and that it will be in central Shinjuku – and that's it."

Of course they ask me which building I will climb, or try to narrow it down to a street or a few buildings to make their job easier, but I will not reveal any more than this. Any more information will severely dent my chances of penetrating the already-heightened security. And besides, I reckon it is more fun for everyone this way.

After breakfast the next morning I head discreetly out of my hotel with my friend. Fortunately no media or cops are hanging around, at least visibly, and we jump into a taxi. My new target is the Shinjuku Center Building in Nishi-Shinjuku. Built in 1979, it is a year younger than the Nomura and also a little taller at 223 metres. It is broadly similar to the Nomura in design and dimensions with only the colour, a sandstone and red-brick hue, plus the angles of the ridges between the windows being significantly different. It isn't quite as good-looking as the Nomura, nor as easy to scale, but it will still be a reasonably straightforward climb posing no major problems.

The car cruises towards the Shinjuku Center Building and as we pass through Shinjuku we notice a strong police presence. Remaining as inconspicuous as we can, our eyes flicker around to assess the opposition. The Nomura Building is cloaked in cops though not as heavily protected as it was the day before. There are gaps I could run through if I wanted to make a break for it. Other tall buildings, most of which I wouldn't have climbed due to their being technically impossible to surmount, are also bestowed with a stiff police presence. It is quite surprising they have gone to all this trouble.

As the car nears the Shinjuku Center Building I note that there is indeed a police presence here too, though there is no cordon. Ten or so cops are deployed in little clusters here and there. It seems they have more of a deterrent mindset than the defensive back line you might see on a rugby pitch. They obviously think that a verbal warning will deter me as it did yesterday – at least in their eyes! Of course they have no way of knowing that for me, the stiffer the challenge, the more I want to overcome it. I haven't come here just to visit the shrines and parks or sit on their toilets. I flew to Japan to climb, and naturally I prefer to go up the exterior of buildings when the police are off guard, to even the odds a little. One against ten is hardly a fair game. It must be a boring job hanging around outside a building all day, only half-expecting some law-breaking gaijin to try and run past you. But this aids me as they do not have the focus that I do. Everything looks good and I am pumped up, primed. The cops stand there chatting idly and a nice gap between them leads right to the springboard.

Just as the car reaches the ideal location on the pavement I give the signal to the driver to stop. I burst out of the back of the car and break straight through the police line, and streak towards the building with the speed and stealth of a ninja. Immediately the cops turn and start bellowing at me in rage, but amazingly they don't run, as if an angry shout in Japanese will stop me as effectively as a samurai sword. They briskly walk after me, obviously resenting the indignity of running, but when they see me grab the side of the building and lift my foot off the ground they simultaneously explode into sprints and fury. But it's too late, guys! What kind of tactics were those?

I am already two storeys high by the time they reach the wall below me, absolutely berserk. Almost as fast, a journalist materialises with his camera and I can see a few more darting across the road and running with video cameras to capture the action. The police are still shouting, waving their arms around, no doubt calling for reinforcements on their radios. But it's too late. I'll see you at the summit! We can discuss Japanese law in jail.

The Shinjuku Center offers reasonable comfort and allows me to move at a relaxed pace. Several hundred people are already in place behind the police cordon and a huddle of police cars and vans is parked at the bottom. The floors pass swiftly by while the number of people peering upwards starts to swell. Before long I reach the halfway point. A news helicopter suddenly rears above a nearby building and hovers not far away. The chopper stays in place for the rest of my ascent, moving here and there for different camera angles for the evening news. I keep moving up the gap between the windows, very much enjoying my start to the day. The escalation of the Shinjuku Center Building turns out to be fairly standard and I make the summit comfortably. Happily I throw a leg over the railing, jump down to the rooftop and bring my head up to greet the assembled welcoming party. The very first thing I encounter is a punch in my face.

I crash back into the wall as the cops – not the security guards – all wade in to bash the crap out of me. I cover my head as blows pummel me into the ground. Knees and feet go in and I am flung to the ground by my hair. Half the Tokyo police force sits on my back. Angrily they chop at my wrists with the metal handcuffs while another cop delivers a few hearty slaps to my face for good measure. For such a civilised people I am surprised at the behaviour of the Japanese police officers. Several kicks and punches later I am dragged to my feet and propelled through the access doors away from the top of the building. My feet barely touch the ground.

In the descending elevator I can taste blood in my mouth and I wonder if I have collected yet another nose fracture. It doesn't feel too good. The police van is right by the entrance, within the cordon, and the press cannot see me. I am shoved into the van and sprawl across the seat, dazed and sore. The van roars off to the police station where again, despite my lack of resistance, I am roughed up. These guys mean business! The cops in this country have no qualms about meting out liberal doses of brute force with a trademark guttural growl. It's all par for the course. And another thing, they don't have much of a sense of humour, especially when I try to joke about the whole affair! Unlike everywhere else I have been, where despite the audacity of my actions at least some of the cops grudgingly respect the feat I accomplished, joke with me, or even openly applaud it, no one here seems to appreciate my climb in the slightest. If anything they seem to resent it personally. It doesn't seem like I am connecting with these guys on a human level, though I imagine that quite a lot of what I am trying to communicate may be getting lost in translation.

My lawyer arrives on the scene, and ignoring the grazes, cuts and swellings on various parts, my face soon spells out my current circumstances. Impassively he states that I am to be remanded in custody for 23 days before trial and then I should expect two months, maybe three months in jail, he doesn't really know. I listen as my lawyer reinforces comments made by the police on several occasions – that the law here is strict and severe – and his deadpan expression tells me there is no way out of this scenario. Various ploys that have helped in other countries are futile here: the law is the law. The news is not good. As he leaves, I face the prospect of spending almost four months in detention in a Tokyo jail before my expulsion from the country, a rather downbeat conclusion to an otherwise stimulating day. Several months in a prison where no one speaks French or English doesn't sound too great.

I am thrown back in my cell and the door slams, leaving me to chew over my situation. I check my nose which seems to be in one piece. I am okay, although a bit pissed off to have been beaten up like that. But in spite of the news from my lawyer I do not worry too much. It is all out of my hands now. Here I am. C'est la vie. I am in the system and whatever will happen from now on will just happen.

But while I am languishing in my Tokyo cell something unexpected occurs, something I know nothing of for several days. And it has a dramatic bearing upon my situation. Unbeknown to me, the news channel helicopter that had been following my progress up the building was still filming me when I made the summit. As luck would have it, the cameraman caught images of the beating I took from the nation's finest at the top of the Shinjuku Center Building... and they showed it on TV!

As the story was beamed across the whole of Japan my friend saw the footage on television, and he had the good foresight to record the entire bulletin from beginning to end. His action was especially fortunate because although they continued to run the story, they transmitted the incriminating footage of the police attacking me only once, censoring the rooftop drama in following broadcasts. It was a fluke he had recorded that particular bulletin as he knew nothing about the pummelling I had taken on the rooftop. Having seen the assault he swiftly submitted the tape to the French embassy.

Soon afterwards I meet a representative from the embassy who enlightens me as to the developments on the outside. The news that the rooftop incident had been recorded and the evidence is in the hands of the embassy is a big boost for me. For the Japanese cops the footage is acutely embarrassing and with the intervention of the French embassy the case is not something they can ignore. The embassy now has some leverage to help free me, and for me it suddenly means I have a case to file a complaint. Of course I am not interested in complaining, I only want to get out of here and climb more buildings. However the embassy encourages me to raise a complaint and to follow procedures. An unprovoked assault of a French citizen by the Japanese police when he was not resisting arrest is a matter that they believe they should pursue.

I do as they suggest and in the end the embassy and the cops strike a deal. I spend only five days in jail before being released without trial. My complaint will be dropped and no police officers will be disciplined.

I am delighted with the outcome – a couple of punches in the face and ribs are fine if it saves me a few months in jail. I also learn from this case. In countries where the police may be violent, I might choose to descend after climbing the entire building and surrender amid all the cameras and commotion at the bottom. Cops by nature tend to be power-mad control freaks. Let's face it, these types of people feel the need to dominate those around them. None of them would be in the job unless they enjoyed the authority the state allows them to exert over other human beings. In the heat of the moment some of them can go berserk at the thought that a mere civilian might not feel like bowing down to them. And of course we know that there is a small but significant proportion of cops who are attracted to the job only because it allows you to smack the shit out of other people. Give them the seclusion of a rooftop with no witnesses, and any cop who wants to dish out his own justice can do so with impunity.

Staging my arrest before the cameras will help secure my safety as the cops, as desperate as they might be to put a sneaky punch in, won't dare do so on national television. This ought to ensure I am arrested calmly and don't get beaten up. Well, not until I get to the police station!

After being thrown out of China and having to make a 19,000-kilometre round trip from Paris to Singapore to pick up my bags, I return to France to consider new projects and challenges. A number of ideas and proposals are on the table but before long one in particular stands out as especially intriguing.

Despite the displeasure of the Shanghai authorities in May 2007, it soon appears that my five-year deportation is forgotten. Only six months have passed since my expulsion from the country but guess what? I am climbing in China again, and this time at their invitation. After my escalation of the Jin Mao Tower was beamed across the land by the national media, a number of people have expressed interest in this crazy Spiderman guy.

South of China's heart sits Hunan province, a green and mountainous region comparable to France in terms of size and population. Officials here wanting to promote the romantic natural beauty of Zhangjiajie National Forest Park in the northern reaches of the province decide that I may be just what they need to help garner publicity, interest and ultimately tourist revenue.

Naturally the fact that I was jailed and deported for my last ascent, and also banned from returning to the country for five years, is a bit of a sticking point. But my manager in China, Mr Lu, somehow convinces officials in seven government departments that I could help boost tourism to the region and help showcase some of the motherland's interior abroad. To do so, of course, I will need to be allowed back in.

I hadn't been expecting much luck until at least halfway through 2012 but within a short period of time I receive a rubber-stamped invitation from the Hunan provincial authorities to feature in a nationally televised climbing event! I am not sure how all this happened. The inscrutable Mr Lu has somehow pulled a rabbit out of his hat. But perhaps my medal from the IOC has been useful, since Beijing is hosting the Olympic Games in the coming months.

The reception I receive at the airport is a pleasant contrast to my send-off in May and soon I find myself in a very scenic part of the country performing an energising free solo up a crumbly 200-metre section of one of China's most famous mountains. A good local crowd, media and government officials warmly applaud me as I reach the top section of the charcoal-coloured Tianmen Mountain. And to top it all off, the trip comes with a very respectable sponsorship fee.

Bearing in mind events only a few months back, it's quite a turnaround and a startlingly open-minded move by the Chinese authorities. And who knows what wonderful opportunities this mountain ascent might spawn? A flick of this domino may well result in new adventures in China or somewhere else, somewhere totally unexpected. It never ceases to amaze me how quickly things can change. You can never tell what waits around the corner.

12

THE SANDS OF TIME

Since you have been with me this far, I can let you into a little secret. You may not notice it but when I walk down the street you may detect a little rattling noise coming from my rucksack. It is not the sort of thing which draws attention, not when a guy is bejewelled and wearing a sky-blue leather jacket and trousers, but for the last few years I have been carrying a little plastic container with me at all times. In this translucent cylinder are a bunch of white tablets clattering around. And once or twice a day I need to pop a pill or two to keep my body in check, since I may or may not have a certain condition. The name of this medication? It has a rather appropriate label for an urban climber. Urbanyl.

On the 27th of December 2003, a few days after we had spent Christmas together, Nicole saved my life. During winter I am often unable to train on the cliffs so I work out regularly on the climbing wall that I have installed in my attic. It is only two and a half metres high, but by organising the holds it is perfectly sufficient for me to work on the majority of the moves I need to test my coordination and keep my muscles trained.

Part of the wall is a large overhang onto which I cling for no more than half an hour at a time, often with my feet at the same level as my head. I have attached a number of holds to the ceiling and the ground below me is concrete. I have never bothered to carpet the floor, nor place a protective mat on it, since I have rarely fallen from this position. But when that does happen, I release my feet and regain my equilibrium with a swing of my arms before I hit the ground. I never fall from very high and with a swing or two I usually land on my feet, and if not it's only a minor stumble. I train two or three times a day for only up to half an hour because these workouts are intense and my muscles need to rest in between sessions. This time limit is often frustrating when I am perfecting a particularly difficult move. I know that given enough practice I will master the move I select, but if I fail more than three times I have to rest before trying again. Not being particularly patient, I tend to get frustrated. This is exactly the situation I find myself in on this December day.

Gradually I warm up my muscles and after a few minutes I make an attempt at a tricky move. I need to insert my feet into two small holds and then throw my body towards the ceiling to be able to catch an edge. At this particular moment my feet are higher than my head. I contemplate the move and prepare to hoist my torso upwards, but after this point I have no idea what happens. It's a total blank...

The rest of the story is told to me by Nicole when I recover consciousness a few hours later. Nicole had been chopping and dicing in the kitchen, two floors below the attic. The house was quiet and the children were not at home. Suddenly she heard a thump from above. She knew I was practising on my climbing wall and immediately imagined the worst when I didn't respond to her calls. Quickly she ran up the stairs, and when she opened the attic door she found me lying in a pool of blood on the concrete floor, having a seizure. Amongst all that blood and frothing saliva was the form of her shaking, contorted husband. Freaked out, she had no idea what to do to help me but fortunately had the presence of mind to call for an ambulance. Ten minutes later I was surrounded by medics. I don't remember anything but apparently I came round and started mumbling unintelligibly. My words were muddled, my sentences incoherent, but I seemed to be asking the same thing over and over again.

"What happened?"

The medics secured my body into a scoop stretcher, a type of protective case that avoids disturbing the position of an incapacitated casualty. Lowering me down the narrow spiral staircase was not easy but the scoop stretcher was necessary to keep me immobilised and prevent further injury.

Three hours later I am awake but have still to recover complete consciousness. I am still woolly and mentally docile. At Beziers Hospital the doctors slide me into a scanner to check what state my head is in. Blearily I learn that instead of two turtle doves, the second day of Christmas has brought me a double cranial fracture. For safety reasons I am kept overnight in the hospital in case I develop complications such as a cerebral oedema. After an uneventful night in the ward they discharge me and I can go home. The fracture is not too serious, my head has seen worse. But what does bother me are the convulsions I suffered. According to the doctors, I have had an epileptic fit… a fit!

The big question is this: did the epilepsy appear as a result of the fall, or did I fall because I had a fit? It's the most important chicken-and-egg question I have yet faced. There is a cavernous difference between the two. Questions race through my throbbing, fractured head. This fall changes everything. If I have become epileptic then a fit could come anywhere, at any time. The prospect greatly disturbs me.

To settle the issue I schedule an appointment in January to see a neurologist. I arrive outside his office two hours before our meeting and wait outside in my car. It's fairly typical of me to turn up like this since I dislike being late and I have a habit of listening to CDs in my parked car. Time passes by with the music. But, ten minutes before the appointment, I am struck by a panic attack. Instinctively I turn the key in the ignition and head back home. I don't want to go through this rigmarole all over again: the tests, the results, the doctors' prognoses, the medication… And I will not take an electroencephalogram either, nor will I learn whether I have become epileptic. I have made my decision. This will not stop me from climbing. Instead I decide that from now on I will have to concentrate even more acutely before each climb so as not to ponder this question while gripping onto a wall of glass 150 metres from the ground.

This accident has brought Nicole and I much closer. It is the first time she has seen me unconscious at the foot of a fall and in a bad state. When I try to imagine how I might have reacted if I were in her shoes, I have to say I find her very courageous. I now realise how much I need my family. To be in Pézenas, my home for the last few years, and to be surrounded by my family also helps me to prepare mentally. I draw energy from it. The walls of my old house are as twisted as I am. It must also be why this ancient house has acquired a warm aura of peacefulness. Our house has managed to survive the ages by bending, distorting, but never breaking. I feel it is more solid than any building I have climbed! No steel girder, no pile nor concrete slab has survived the passage of time my house has. They built things to last in the old days.

Athletes have teammates, trainers and coaches on whom they can count to help them train and instil motivation. I don't. My team consists of my family and friends. Like anyone else I need a rock to hold onto without fear of falling; an anchor point, a reference, a base to withdraw to in difficult

times, a solid wall to shield me. This rock is the people around me, those
who will not lie to me, and those who know how to reassure me. These
are the people who respect me not for what I do but for who I am. To be
under the spotlight, to be complimented, to be the centre of attention, is
of course very agreeable. But crashing back to earth amongst my family is
fantastic. It is here I can let myself go. I am not afraid that I will be seen as
I am, vulnerable, sometimes worried, with hidden pain, regrets, remorse,
uncontrollable feelings... in short like everyone else.

Just before my climbing wall accident in December, I had received an
interesting proposal. The University of Abu Dhabi in the United Arab
Emirates was organising an international conference with the title of
'e-education without borders', a large event held once every couple of years.
Sixty-six international delegations were expected to attend the conference.
Among the numerous academics and speakers they also wanted to invite
an adventurer. After the Swiss traveller Bertrand Piccard, who went around
the world in a balloon, and Bernard Harris the American astronaut, they
thought of me! It was very flattering. This year the conference theme was
focussing on the 'without borders' aspect more than in previous years.
They felt that with my global approach to my sport, I fitted the concept
perfectly. But to go this far to a foreign country that I didn't know only
for a conference seemed to be a real shame. Therefore I had countered by
offering to climb a building in the city in order to participate more actively
in their event.

As I am unfamiliar with the Middle East I immediately start digging
around on the internet for more information. On *www.skyscrapers.com*,
my reference website for first impressions, there are dozens of gleaming
buildings in Abu Dhabi. And for good reason. It is one of the newest
cities in the world. Thirty years ago there was nothing here but a small
town marooned in the desert. An entire city was planned from scratch.
Sheik Zayed helped form the UAE after the British withdrew in 1971
and after becoming its first president he forged forward with a vision to
build this city in the middle of a sea of sand. A city originally planned for
600,000 inhabitants sprung up, but today the population has blossomed
like a desert flower into almost two million. Every month new buildings
are going up, always more handsome, always higher.

Surfing the website and leafing through my climbing bible I spot a few
good-looking skyscrapers. But the latest building techniques have been

used and this is not particularly good news for me. The installation of windows and glass has changed quite a lot over the past decade. Right now there aren't even metal joints to keep the windows together – simple rubber suffices. Unfortunately for me, rubber does not allow for climbing. It is soft, irregular, springy and giving, an unkind surface for any climber, and to make matters worse my feet can never stick to this gelatinous material. In the modern boomtowns of the Middle East, where the heat is oppressive and structures expand and contract, this may be popular. The trend there does seem to be towards these annoying new fittings. I'm crossing my fingers that there will be a few decent towers in Abu Dhabi available for me to climb, some without these rubber window joints.

Days later the event organiser calls me back. Dr Kamali, director of the university, approves of my proposal. He finds the idea terrific. We discuss the general outline of what I will contribute to the conference. Without any fuss the building is chosen, the authorisation obtained and the climb set for the opening day to help launch the conference. Mission well and truly accomplished. I only have one small worry – that the building joints are made of rubber… The prospect of attempting an escalation and then discovering it is loaded with rubber joints is a dire one and would definitely torpedo the ascent. I won't know until I get there, and I toss and turn at night wondering how they will turn out. I must be the only person in the world who frets restlessly at night over whether the window joints of a building in the United Arab Emirates are made of rubber or metal. Thankfully Dr Kamali sends me a ticket to see the building as a matter of course, and I jet out to the desert city for a quick two-day trip to the site for the usual ground checks.

The building I will attempt to climb is the city's tallest building, the new headquarters of the National Bank of Abu Dhabi. The skyscraper is a fine-looking building, abstract at the summit and base with sharp triangulation but utterly sensible in the middle. The National Bank is not yet occupied nor is it open to the public. The interior decorations and fittings are not finished but the structure and façade certainly is. Despite the irregular base of the building an escalation is indeed possible. The base is a surrealist jumble of concrete blocks and table legs that appears to support the central, more orthodox body. But this chaos is only true from certain angles. One face of the building is certainly climbable as it soon gives way to a glazed stretch. Much to my approval, the window joints are metal, and every 70 centimetres the architect has felt the need to decorate the building with horizontal metal bars of a healthy depth. In short this will be one of the easiest climbs of my career. The bank is inadvertently tailor-made for urban climbing. For me it looks like a ladder – a ladder 180 metres in height.

The 17th of February is set as the departure date for the Emirates, and I will climb a few days later. I fly out for the conference accompanied by my friend Marie-Ange who will be filming the trip and the climb. But I feel a bit apprehensive. First of all, I am uneasy because I still have the nagging thought floating around my head: am I epileptic? This thought is not obsessive but it is still there. This strikes me as a normal reaction to events over the New Year since epilepsy could prove fatal to me.

However, my main worry is my left thumb. During my brief stay in hospital the doctors were principally concerned with my twin cranial fracture. I complained about pains in my thumb, but they had found nothing wrong with it. Two days later, when I returned home, I felt sharp shooting pains that prevented me from properly holding onto my wall grips. Something was up so I made an appointment to see Dr Hoël.

On the X-ray he spotted a fracture in my thumb and, on top of the fracture, a torn ligament. I asked if it could be fixed and he told me yes, it could. But he gave me some bleak news too. There was only one way to achieve full recovery – operating to reattach the ligament and immobilising the thumb for two entire months. With my upcoming climb in Abu Dhabi, it was of course impossible for me to undergo such a procedure. It was less than ideal but I decided I could climb the National Bank more easily with a painful thumb than with a thumb in a plaster cast. So I refused the operation, at least for the time being, and started my training again with my broken thumb.

Climbing is not easy without a thumb, but it is nevertheless possible. However, when I had inspected the National Bank building a few weeks before, I had assumed my bothersome thumb was a minor injury and that I would be fully fit. I hadn't taken into account the fact it might be broken. It is with this small worry that I shoot down the runway and head into the French clouds. I confidentially share this little problem with Marie-Ange on the flight over.

The plane touches down with a screech of rubber as we arrive at the international airport in Abu Dhabi, creatively named 'Abu Dhabi International Airport'. The interior though is quite original with a curved tiled ceiling drawing upon elements of the internal design of a mosque. As we pass through immigration and proceed to our hotel we note the buzz about town. The arid city is effervescent. More and more delegates stream through the airport and the hotels are fully booked by the conference participants. Everything is well organised and we have to adhere to the demands of the organisers, to attend pre-arranged meetings and hang around in between.

I cannot go by myself to the skyscraper to try it out as this may be misunderstood and would risk the cancellation of our authorisation. It is only the day after our arrival that we can get out to Al Khalifa Street to a scheduled meeting at the National Bank. There I am required to meet the chief of police, shake hands, smile and answer the habitual questions. Pleasantries are exchanged but we have been at the foot of the building for more than an hour and I still haven't had a chance to try it out. I cannot wait any longer! I make my excuses, put on my slippers and start climbing a few metres.

The most dangerous part of the climb is situated less than 20 metres from the ground where there is a small roof to climb through. There's no major problem here since I can bypass it to one side, but I still want to check that the move is achievable without using my thumb. I go up and down the first few metres a few times. My thumb does interfere with my movements quite a lot but I can still ascend and descend okay. The climb will be possible but it will effectively mean going up with one hand! The ascent is scheduled for Friday the 21st. Fridays in the Emirates are equivalent to Sundays in the West, a holy day and a day of rest.

Relieved and mentally invigorated I go back to my hotel to take advantage of the dazzling sun and the fine swimming pool. My worries have largely dissipated as I now know what is in store for me. I relax by the pool like everyone else, using the time to focus and collect my mind. But sadly I can't do this for very long since the next two days involve intensive public relations and promotion. These two days are anything but relaxing! From morning till night I meet literally hundreds of people, without really knowing who they are. I confess that when I am introduced to these people I have difficulty remembering their Arabic names as they are often very long. What is more, the men all wear traditional Arabic dress consisting of broadly identical djellaba and keffieh. And the bountiful profusion of moustaches in this part of the world makes it even more difficult to remember and recognise everyone. I do my best but I am introduced to someone new almost every minute of the day. I end up trying to memorise these wonderful moustaches and spend quite a bit of time staring at the bristles below these guys' noses, trying to put names to them. Without a moustache I am beginning to feel somewhat underdressed.

As I am expected and the news of my climb has spread, everyone seems to know me and they all greet me warmly. And what a hospitable people they are. After Wednesday's meetings and greetings, in the evening I am invited to the palace. Whose palace? I don't know. Down here, a lot of people have palaces since they are all part of the extended family of the president.

Tonight Marie-Ange cannot come with me as the ceremony is restricted to men. It's a shame she can't be there as she is often much more attentive than I am and helps me later on by summarising the people we've met. Personal meetings are the only way to conduct business out here. In this country everything is done by meetings and handshakes, it's all face-to-face. I understand that being invited to the palace is very important so I had better find out whose palace this is. It's a bit embarrassing to ask, but we manage to weasel out the information. We discover that tonight I am heading to Sheik Nahyan's palace. Sheik Nahyan is the Education Minister, the man who has authorised my visit and the climb.

I arrive at the minister's wondrous palace in the hot evening. I was expecting a meeting in an office for a few minutes, a handshake or two and a bit of a chat in order to get to know each other. Was I wrong! More than 300 men are here. We all line up, one by one, to greet our host and his associates. A welcoming word, a smile, a handshake, a photo… and my turn is done. After that, mint tea in hand in the middle of a crowd, I chat with people I don't know. We sip tea, of course, since alcoholic cocktails are strictly forbidden in this part of the world. From time to time, Dr Kamali introduces me to someone and I chat some more. Then our host leaves and, within seconds, everyone disappears as if whisked away on magic carpets. I take my cue and likewise make for the exit. The following day I learn that Sheik Nahyan was delighted to have met me. I too enjoyed his company – though I hope to have a bit more time to talk to him next time.

On the morning of the climb, I have breakfast with Marie-Ange in the hotel. With few worries ahead of me I slept well. The event is scheduled for the late afternoon to avoid the scorching midday sun, giving me the whole morning to rest and prepare.

As I nibble on a croissant I pick up a newspaper. My eyes widen. To my surprise, on the front page of the national newspaper, I see my picture and an announcement that I am to take on the National Bank of Abu Dhabi later today. A quarter of a page is dedicated to the story. A quick glance at the other papers reveals the same. What a superb way to publicise this! Usually the people who witness my climbs are just curious passers-by in the right place at the right time. This public announcement will enable those people of the Emirates interested in watching the ascent to come down and enjoy my escalation first-hand instead of hearing about it afterwards. Without a doubt there will be more people at the foot of the tower than usual.

The police have decided to close off the entire road to provide access to the public. There is plenty of space since Al Khalifa Street, like most of the city's main arteries, is nearly as wide as a 12-lane motorway. Marie-Ange is as pleased as I am about the coverage. And the two of us are now placing our bets. Usually when I go up a building spontaneously I get a few hundred up to maybe a few thousand people, depending on where and when I do it. In Borneo, my climb was publicised and 15,000 spectators turned up. In Poland, when I took on the Marriott Hotel, a crowd of more than 10,000 watched on. Both were very good crowds and ringing successes for the organisers. Here in Abu Dhabi the organisers say they are expecting 5,000 people. Okay, we're betting there will be double that.

An hour before the start of the climb, a long limo with dark windows pulls up by the lobby to collect us. Marie-Ange packs her camera equipment in the boot. I leave the hotel wearing a big smile and with the encouragement of the hotel employees, disappointed at having to work and miss the show. The chauffeur and I chat on the way, telling each other daft stories and generally having a good laugh. I am glad this guy is a bit of a joker as I typically need a release valve before I climb.

But I can't help noticing that we seem to be going very slowly and the trip is taking us a lot longer than I expected. As we make our way to the bank the streets are all packed. I ask the chauffeur if it is always like this on Friday, and he says that it is not. All around, crowds are heading in the same direction as us. They are all walking towards the National Bank. Cars have stopped in the middle of the road and people are just leaving their vehicles where they are. From time to time I flick open my window to say hello. I don't like to be remote from people, to be imprisoned in this mean-looking limo. We continue inching through and the crowds thankfully part when we tell them that I am the one who is climbing the building.

After a while we arrive at the cordon and the cops wave us through to the parking lot just behind the building. The chauffeur kills the engine and Marie-Ange takes her equipment and makes her way to her position near the foot of the tower. I now need to gather myself, to calm down, and to enter my zone. I drop my gear and attentively clean my slippers. Once I am happy they are immaculate I put them on and prepare my pack of chalk and drinking fluids. My thumb is then immobilised and I bind and protect my fingers. As my preparations end, I settle in the back of the limo and enter a semi-meditative state. The climb has no exact scheduled time and I don't expect it to start quite yet. Time passes.

We've now been waiting behind the building for more than half an hour. Marie-Ange is in place and she is filming the scene already, which I understand is packed. Attached to my clothing is a button-sized microphone that will enable me to contact her. She will be able to hear me all throughout the climb and will be able to act should any unforeseen hiccups occur. I am ready and waiting for the green light. But we have to wait. And wait…

We wait more than an hour. After a while I get fed up with all this waiting. On days like this I miss the climbs where I break the law, when I alone choose my target, when I choose the day and the time that I go up. We are told we have to wait a while longer. Sheik Nahyan is caught up in the crowds and has not yet arrived, and it is obviously impossible to start the escalation without him. And more news – it seems that Sheik Zayed, the President of the United Arab Emirates, has also decided to come and watch the climb! But his car is also stuck in traffic. Although I can't see what is going on, the vibes I am getting are telling me that this thing is certainly turning out to be big. A certain electricity is in the air and I am growing increasingly excited. I feel like a rock star waiting to burst onto stage. The major difference is that a rock star does not risk his life by singing to people. There is a palpable buzz in the air and tension is rising. Finally I get a call and the green light from Marie-Ange.

"They're ready, Alain. You can go!"

"How about our little bet?"

"There are a lot of people here, Alain, a lot."

"More than in Malaysia?"

"I really don't know, but it looks like a rock concert out here. You really just have to see it."

"I'm not Mick Jagger! I can't play to a hundred thousand people!"

But it's on, and it's time to face the music. I open the car door and step out. As soon as I'm out of the limo I am surrounded by bodyguards. We make our way to the edge of the parking lot which is already filling with spectators who ought to be around the front. The bodyguards manage, with difficulty, to find a route for us through the crowd towards the entrance of the bank. I am swamped! Arms are extended. I instinctively shake and tap as many hands as I can in this dizzying throng. My spirit is not on earth any more but way up there in the air. There are definitely thousands of enthusiastic and jubilant people here.

The bodyguards get me through to the foot of the tower where I need to pose for some photos, shake hands with a few dignitaries and climb onto a table for some unknown reason. The usual pre-climbing media routine is in full swing. It seems to make everyone happy but I am keen to get out of all this. Finally I break free of this madness and touch the face of the building. I gently brush my fingertips over the structure. I feel it. I absorb it. And now I can do what I came here to do – put on a show. For some nervous wrecks this would be the beginning of hell but for me it is deliverance. Deliverance from the overwhelming crowds and attention, the bodyguards and the press, the weeks of anticipation. At last – at long last – I can start the climb.

I pull myself up from the ground metre by metre and those at the front start applauding. The cheers grow the higher I go, as more and more people see me. As I imagined, the climb is not particularly difficult. The early stages pose the technical challenges but I pass the lower roof structure without any problems. As I had discovered a while back, the window joints are indeed metal rather than the dreaded rubber, and the horizontal bars stretch out before me like rungs on a gigantic ladder. My rigid thumb makes things awkward but such is the nature of the exterior of the National Bank that it is not a significant handicap. My thumb does get in the way, aching and generally irritating me, but I have enough grip in my four remaining digits to climb. I need to stay focused but with such an audience it is not at all easy.

As I come into view to those further back, the cheers of the crowd are increasingly impressive. I make my way up another floor of the bank to huge stadium-like roars. It feels like I might be blown off the side of the building, such is the volume of the support behind me. The crowd are with me all the way, clapping and roaring me on, but I keep my eyes and my mind on the task in hand. I put another floor behind me. The noise is awesome. This crowd is huge! It's like I have scored a goal at the Stade de France.

At the tenth floor, the temptation is too strong. Holding on with only my good hand, I turn around and face the streets behind me. And I cannot believe my eyes… it is impossible to see the smallest bit of tarmac or earth. People are absolutely everywhere, everywhere, packed into the streets further than the eye can see. The buildings opposite are swarming like beehives. All the windows on every floor of every building, the balconies, the terraces, the rooftops, all are crammed with people! It is a truly astounding sight. All these people… and they are here to see me. Little Alain Robert, a mere rock climber from the south of France. It is humbling.

With my free hand I wave to the crowd. Before I left the ground I was comparing this climb to a show. If that's the case then let this be a great show! I have a duty to all of these people, the thousands and thousands who have decided to spend their free day watching me. This is their day off, their Friday. It is a time to be with their families, a day of relaxation, fun and smiles. I must make sure that they are pleased with my performance, that I do my utmost to bring a little something to their day. The building permits it. The people demand it.

So I play to the crowd. After each of my moves, the crowd screams. I continue my climb slowly and methodically to heighten the experience – for me as well as for them. To be honest I am still blown away by the atmosphere here, and despite the wild reactions below surely no one is as excited or as amazed as me.

Through the windows of the National Bank I can see film and television crews with cameras and video cameras. With the crowd-control measures in place, only journalists have been admitted inside the building so it is not as crowded as the towers opposite. Nearby a helicopter is holding a stationary position, with a harnessed cameraman seated at the open door. From where I am the view is mind-blowing but from his perspective the view must be even more fantastic.

I can't help but get lost in the view below. The roads look like Venetian waterways flooded with humanity. The crowds seem to wrap around buildings so there must be many more people out of sight. Several times I turn around to wave at this blanket of spectators and they go bananas. At these times the cheering is so loud that I literally can't hear the helicopter blades.

No one likes to go to a boxing match and see a fighter knocked out in the first round, so instead of climbing at a logical pace and finishing this escalation off within minutes I continue to take my time and please this awesome crowd. I feel an overwhelming joy at pleasing the spectators so much. To be doing what I love, to be sharing this consuming joy with others, and to be bringing a smile to the faces of all these magnificent people is the best thing in the world. How could I ask for more out of life? It really does not get much better than this.

When I get to the summit, 40 minutes after my feet first left *terra firma*, I raise my arms in victory to an explosive cheer. What a noise! What a sight! Then, as a little flourish, I brandish a flag of the United Arab Emirates, dramatically flying it from the rooftop of the building in triumph. Everyone is ecstatic. And how many people are there? How many people turned up today? More than 100,000 people are applauding for me at the foot of the tower and across the surrounding streets! Over a hundred thousand! It's an astounding figure! That's as many as a Rolling Stones concert! Our bets were indeed very low. No one imagined such a mind-boggling turnout, least of all me.

The security and police are all smiles as they guide me graciously off the rooftop. Whilst descending via the elevator I am told that the President himself wants to congratulate me. As always, I vaguely hear the usual recommendations as to what I should do and say… The thing is, now is not the time to try to tell me anything as my brain has been shot to pieces by sweet and intense emotion. I am running on pure adrenaline and instinct.

In the lobby of the building, TV stations have set up mini-studios, each erected like little booths at a trade fair. Interviews, congratulations, camera flashes, questions, all are in my face and my head is spinning. I am tossed around from pillar to post like a baseball. But I am on cloud nine, so I am perfectly happy to comply. After an hour I am told that the president's car was not able to force its way through to us and that for security reasons, he won't be able to commend me in person. It would have been great but it doesn't matter. Right now I am living an intense moment that I am not going to forget in a hurry.

I pose for a few more photographs and then the police shepherd me to a car with an open sunroof. The cops tell me to stand through it, apparently as a way of letting people know that the event is over, and to help disperse the crowds. Instead I hop up and sit on the roof, face to the wind as we drive through thousands of smiles. They seem to scroll by forever, becoming one big intoxicating blur. All this warmth and joy... It is a glorious and magical moment. You can read it on my face. I am radiating elation, happiness and serenity.

Thanks to this experience, I now understand that transmitting my passion to others is my duty. This will be a big part of my future. I have already started by participating in conferences and forums where I express my heartfelt belief that we should never renounce our dreams. Man creates his own limits, but we all have in us the power to overcome them and to reach our goals. We just need to find this power within ourselves and harness it, for it is there within all of us, within you. We have the ability to soar to great heights if we direct our energies away from doing other people's work, fulfilling other people's dreams. That may be easier said than done but the good fight must be fought. Each man or woman must stay master of their own destiny. Of course some things are out of our hands. It is impossible to foresee a plane crash or a serious illness and one can't build a rocket and fly to Saturn. But a man must make his own decisions in life, and be true to himself. And he must define his own vision. You may suffer quite a lot for your dreams – I certainly have – but the fulfilment gained from pursuing them is second to none.

I am going to spread my passion for climbing with children and the young, those who have always held the brightest dreams. I will be doing this by creating a school and I have obtained the agreement of the Education Ministry of the United Arab Emirates. The Alain Robert Climbing School will see light very soon. The idea came to me after my climb of the National Bank, when I saw the fire lit in the eyes of the kids at the bottom. The looks on their faces reminded me why I climb. It is children who inspire me the most and it is an honour and a joy to be able to share my desire with them. To be able to perhaps help a youngster discover this miraculous activity and excel in it would enable me to pass on this magnificent torch, a fire which turns any mountain or tower into a fiery volcano or brilliant lighthouse.

The young climbers of tomorrow will have a very different vision of climbing to the one that me or my peers have held throughout our lives. For the generation before us it was all about conquering new peaks. For many of my peers it was a matter of climbing solo. A lot of my old climbing partners strove to conquer mountain tops and take more audacious routes to their icy summits.

It must not be forgotten that most of my serious climbing companions have died in climbing accidents over the years. Of course losing them is sad but it is vital to remember that these men were fulfilled and were following their dreams. And by reinventing climbing they hopefully helped open up a brave new world for the young. Today, you need not climb the same peaks that have challenged men and women before you. You can find and create your own mountains, define your own world. And you need not be French, Swiss or from any other nation living in the shadow of a craggy escarpment or peak. You can come from anywhere. Who knows, one day there might even be climbing champions from the flat arid plains of the Emirates.

One thing I hope to impart is a sense of urgency, a desire to break free of the apathy which so easily invades our lives, a need to fend off our cancerous comfort zones. You must strike out and seize your goals while you can, because you don't know what tomorrow holds. Sometimes something totally unexpected or unthinkable happens and a dream which was eminently achievable can go up in smoke.

I remember back in 2000 I was in New York preparing for an inspirational climb, a climb I had been eyeing up for a number of years. I spent ten days checking out the World Trade Center, planning my ascent in the sub-zero winter. But that year the Big Apple's weather was oppressive, and the cold meant that I couldn't feel my fingers. I wanted to go up but eventually I had to turn back. I left the twin towers and went home to France. I hadn't given up on the assault and I rescheduled the climb for a year later. But of course disaster struck, destroying the beautiful towers and thousands of innocent lives. Who could have foreseen such a terrible event? Things we may take for granted can be snatched from us at any time and it is imperative to remember the transitory nature of our world and indeed our lives.

My ambition is not just to climb for myself but to achieve some good through my escalations. I have been involved in charity climbs for a while now, but over the last few years I have decided to chalk up the odd ascent in the name of things I believe in. I climbed the 180 metres of TotalFinaElf in Paris to protest about the war in Iraq. In London I climbed the 27 storeys of Portland House to support a campaign against climate change. I find the prospect of our world being ruined by global warming much more frightening than falling off a building. It is probably the most important issue humanity has ever faced, but the world is ordered now in such a way that progress is almost defined by consumption of the world's resources. With Russia and China abandoning communism, the capitalist system is now rampant worldwide and virtually guarantees exploitation, pollution and environmental catastrophe at some point in this century. We will need a lot more maturity and a lot less greed from our leaders, but to be honest I doubt that we can expect much when our political systems select people whose lives are centred on the generation of money and the creation of laws to ensure society is geared towards it.

Any solution will have to come from the populace and that can only happen when we all wake up to the fact that our world is choking and growing seriously ill. I know that a mad Frenchman climbing up the side of Portland House isn't going to solve the problem but hopefully I can do my bit to support the movement.

Of course I want to keep climbing as long as I can. And not only that, I have to keep climbing! What job could I possibly get at this stage of my life that would pay the bills? What are my skills? Well, actually I am highly skilled, but only in an area outside the system. Put me in an office and I wouldn't last a day. But hang me outside it by my fingertips and I am in my element. How many CEOs could do that?

It is obvious that the only way I can earn a living is to carry on making ascents. And as I grow older I need to get one or two big ones under my belt. I have tens of thousands of Euros in unpaid fines and a 218% surcharge on my car insurance. I finally splashed out on a driving licence and decided this year to get my car taxed, something I do once every four years on average. My police record will soon be thicker than the Paris phone book. But I don't care. I shall pursue my solitary road and keep following it for as long as I physically can. I am not bothered by those who chastise me for not knowing when to stop, for pushing the envelope too far, or for wanting to perpetually warm the same soup.

Fortunately I am well known now and the climbing requests keep on coming. On average I receive one every week. Many of these are just speculative, submitted by people who haven't thought the proposal through. Due to legality and logistics only a handful actually end up taking place, which is just as well because physically and psychologically I wouldn't be able to climb a building every week. Right now, although a seasoned veteran, I am far from retirement. I have more projects in mind than there are days in a year.

And I am also getting more and more requests to climb buildings which are utterly impossible. Saudi Arabia, for example, offered me a lucrative contract to climb one of their grandest buildings. But this building is sheer, with nothing at all to hold on to. It would be impossible to scale unless I used suction cups. Climbing with suction cups is not really my forte. But when the equivalent of several years' pay is waved in front of your deformed nose for just one climb, it is hard to say no.

I used suction cups once before, when I made an ascent in Doha, the capital of Qatar. To be honest I didn't like them very much. They are a little scary. When I climbed in Doha I used two suction units, one for my hands and the other for my feet. I successfully reached the summit of the Qatar Gas Tower but I never felt especially safe. A suction cup is designed to repeatedly stick and unstick, in contrast to a permanent architectural feature like a window ledge or grille. For me the seal, a rubber-ringed vacuum, can never match the solidity of set concrete or reinforced steel. Additionally the suction cups I purchased for my climb were not particularly good ones. There are three suction pads per grip, each holding about 30 kilograms. A better model was available on which each pad held 60 kilos and I should have bought those ones. That way, if the surface of the building is dusty and one or two pads don't stick, then just the one pad would be enough to support my body weight. In the Gulf it does get a bit dusty and mine tended to slip a little.

Using cups also means radically altering your climbing technique. When climbing with suction cups you quickly find it is much easier to shuffle upwards in baby steps. If you try to vault upwards in big strides then you find it difficult to get the cups to stick. Although I much prefer climbing unaided, without ropes or suction cups, I plan to buy some new cups soon as there is a chance I might be needing them in the future. Personally I feel they are a little bit of a cheat, but if a proposal like the Saudi one materialises then I would have to seriously consider it.

Will I ever be able to stop climbing? I don't know. To end my escalations would be a kind of death for me. What will become of me when I can no longer climb? I have no idea.

As I cross into my fifties, if my physical condition no longer allows me to take on any more extreme ascents, perhaps I shall engage only the less sheer and more textured façades, with the odd useful grip, buildings that lend a little helping hand to the ageing rock climber. Or perhaps I'll do battle with buildings of a hundred metres or so rather than the giants of 400 metres plus. I may decide to go solo up the easier routes of Verdon, looking not for extremity but more for leisure.

The prospect of taking my foot off the pedal is a big deal for me. It's excruciatingly difficult to stop the activity which has guided your entire life. But today I am not the young man I once was. My greatest successes are behind me. It's difficult to accept but I know it, I can feel it. I can no longer pull off the outrageous moves I once managed on the Night of the Lizard, for example.

Muscularly I am now weaker so I compensate with my experience. Despite the inherent risk of losing my life I think I make good decisions when climbing. My crippling falls all occurred on cliff faces when I was young and careless. I have never fallen from a building, even if I have had a few close shaves. But what am I going to do when my body starts to give out on me? What will I do in 20 years' time? I feel it is impossible for me to voluntarily stop climbing. I cannot imagine life without a passion. Could I find another one? I'm thinking about it.

But right now I am still in good shape and I can't help dreaming about new challenges and adventures. What buildings would I like to climb?

Well, I have unfinished business with the Petronas Towers, having been stopped twice at the same point. I was arrested on the terrace again in 2007 on the tenth anniversary of my previous escalation and, despite the serious legal ramifications of a third attempt, the towers do still tempt me. I like iconic structures, having taken on the likes of the Sydney Harbour Bridge. Big Ben in London would be great though I can imagine the fuss after climbing that would be quite serious since it forms part of the Houses of Parliament.

Other buildings? Quite literally, where on Earth do I start? The possibilities are almost limitless. There are thousands of skyscrapers, towers and monuments around the world. Of course everyone can appreciate scale, but visionary architecture has always drawn me first. I have gained great satisfaction from climbing charismatic buildings like the Torre Vasco da Gama in Portugal even if they aren't the tallest.

Those buildings which are cocooned behind layers of security or iron national laws are also magnetic. I recently ascended the Western Federation Tower in Moscow just to see what would happen to me. I have no doubt that over the next few years I will gain more experience of the world's judiciary, diplomacy and policing. Much of it will be an interesting cultural exchange; some of it, I fear, might be less than enjoyable. In an ideal world I could go on climbing forever. I still have half of the planet yet to visit before restarting it all again.

As I write these passages, there are wonderful new buildings going up around the globe. There is a colossus going up in the UAE, a needle-like spire which will smash all the records and put any controversy to rest. The models of the building are incredible. It rises from the city like a spike on a graph. Right now the final height of the Burj Dubai is a closely guarded secret, but it has been guaranteed to be over 700 metres tall – and reliable sources put its height at a staggering 818 metres! That's enormous... almost like stacking the Petronas on top of the Sears. I can't wait to go to Dubai and see it for myself.

The Middle East is taking the lead with other dreamlike projects on the drawing board. The Murjan Tower in Bahrain, Burj Mubarak Al-Kabir in Kuwait and Al Burj, again in Dubai, are staggering proposals which will all measure over a kilometre in height. Of course I don't know if such buildings will structurally accommodate urban climbing, or even if it would be physically possible to maintain such an effort, but if so, how can one resist? If they are built while I am still fit enough to climb them, then I would love to take a closer look.

So what will tomorrow bring? Who knows? Resuscitated once, I am not going to linger in a grey land of paperwork or tedium. All I know is that I must keep following my dreams and remain true to myself. When I look in the mirror, I still see a decent guy, a fellow with whom I could be friends. And this is maybe my biggest satisfaction of all. For a lack of wealth, I have gained that which is most important and elusive – happiness and a full heart. And I have acquired it with my bare hands.

I am the owner of nothing, but I possess everything: a woman, three children, and a passion. Escalation is my life – and maybe also my death. So what? We have been warned more than enough that domestic boredom and apathy breaks up couples. This at least is a risk we do not take. We have no time for that, nor any opportunity.

Nicole and I married for better or for worse. Till death do us part. If my fate is to die at the foot of a building, then it is one that I seek. I know that one day I may fall. Maybe it is my inevitable end. Who knows, perhaps I have already gone by the time you read these lines. But today I am alive. And at the end of the day, today is all any of us have.

I am craving new adventure even if, one day, it proves to be fatal. And by sharing my experiences and my philosophy of life, and by following my dreams, I shall continue to live the way I have for as long as I can remember – with passion.